Poetry and the
Sociological Idea

HARVESTER STUDIES IN CONTEMPORARY LITERATURE AND CULTURE

General Editor: Patrick Parrinder, Department of English, University of Reading

This is a new series of original, full-length studies of modern literature and its cultural context. Although a variety of historical, theoretical and critical orientations will be encouraged, each title will aim to illuminate the common themes and conditions of twentieth-century writing, rather than to explicate the work of an individual author. Taking 'literature and culture' to indicate the whole of organized verbal expression, the series will extend to include studies of modern criticism, the press and the communications media, as well as offering new and stimulating approaches to the fields of English and comparative literature.

1. LANGUAGE IN MODERN LITERATURE: INNOVATION AND EXPERIMENT Jacob Korg
2. MODES OF POLITICAL DRAMA Darko Suvin
3. LITERATURE AND SOCIETY IN GERMANY 1918–1945 Ronald Taylor
4. WRITERS IN EXILE: THE IDENTITY OF HOME IN MODERN LITERATURE Andrew Gurr
5. THE LOST TRADITION OF THE BRITISH LEFT: POLITICS AND LITERATURE IN BRITAIN 1926–1951 Alan Munton
6. POETRY AND THE SOCIOLOGICAL IDEA J.P. Ward

POETRY AND THE SOCIOLOGICAL IDEA

J.P. WARD

Lecturer in Education,
University College of Swansea

THE HARVESTER PRESS · SUSSEX
HUMANITIES PRESS INC · NEW JERSEY

First published in Great Britain in 1981 by
THE HARVESTER PRESS LIMITED
Publisher: John Spiers
16 Ship Street, Brighton, Sussex

and in the USA by
Humanities Press Inc
Atlantic Highlands, New Jersey 07716

© J.P. Ward, 1981

British Library Cataloguing in Publication Data

Ward, John Powell
   Poetry and the sociological idea.
    1. Literature and society
    I. Title
808.1 PN1081

ISBN 0-85527-363-1

Humanities Press
ISBN 0-391-02321-7

Typeset by Inforum Ltd, Portsmouth
in 11pt Bembo
and printed in Great Britain by
St Edmundsbury Press, Bury St Edmunds, Sufolk

All rights reserved

To my wife, children, parents and brothers

We will fall down and worship him as a sweet and holy and wonderful being; but we must also inform him that in our State such as he are not permitted to exist; the law will not allow them. And so when we have anointed him with myrrh, and set a garland of wool upon his head, we shall send him away to another city.

– Plato, *Republic*

Poetry matters little to the modern world.

– F.R. Leavis

Yes, from up here the idea of society is just about tenable.
– Tom Stoppard, *Albert's Bridge*

I might be expected to speak of the social, that is to say sociological or political, obligation of the poet. He has none.
– Wallace Stevens

If poetry is a form of 'communication', yet that which is to be communicated is the poem itself, and only incidentally the experience and the thought which have gone into it.

– T.S. Eliot

The prevailing attitude of most communities toward love is curiously twofold: on the one hand, it is the chief theme of poetry, novels and plays, on the other it is completely ignored by most serious sociologists and is not considered one of the desiderata in schemes of economic or political reform.

– Bertrand Russell

And it was at that age . . . Poetry arrived
In search of me. I don't know, I don't know where it came from.

– Pablo Neruda

Contents

Preface ix

PART ONE
INTRODUCTION

1. Introduction 3
2. The Five Types of Sociology 30

PART TWO
POETRY BEFORE THE SOCIOLOGICAL IDEA

3. Spenser and Social Phenomenology 61
4. Donne and Social Interactionism 76
5. Milton and Marxist Sociology 90
6. Pope and Social Functionalism 103
7. Wordsworth and Social Anthropology 115

PART THREE
POETRY CONTEMPORARY WITH THE SOCIOLOGICAL IDEA

8. Introduction and Baudelaire 129
9. The Poem Itself – Mallarmé, Stevens, Williams, Yeats 144
10. The Poem and Society – Eliot, Pound, the Communist Poets 164
11. The Poet in the Sociological World – Hardy, Berryman 181

PART FOUR
CONCLUSION

12. Traditional Views of the Poem 201
    Contemporary Language
    The Influence on Criticism
    Defence

Notes 225
Acknowledgements 236
Index 239

Preface

This book is not a sociology of poetry. Rather it implies that no such thing could usefully exist. When the sociology of literature appeared in the late sixties and early seventies in Britain, it became increasingly clear that no sociology of poetry was going to appear with it. I for one then found myself admitting more and more that I had been suppressing an instinct about the matter; namely, that sociology could not account for poetry, and that it was in sociology's nature that this was so. It is not that my attitude is one that dismisses or despises sociology; rather it is perhaps 'Render unto Caesar the things that are Caesar's'.

The inability of these two things greatly to concern each other raised a wider question about how far any book can be about two things at once. I think it can, so long as one thing is central and the other orbits it. My method is to give a summary of the central strands of the sociological tradition in order to have these to hand when engaged on the discussion of poets, which is confessedly the main part of the book. This doubtless betrays a traditionally Saxon interest in close reading of the text, but I have tried to locate this in the context of wider critical theories in the first and last chapters. I came later than some to the recent French school (Lacan and Derrida), although they are mentioned; their views, particularly Lacan's on the 'Word' and Derrida's on writing, seem to me immensely fertile, yet they necessarily do not engage with the unique experience offered by each poet, and I remain convinced that only there does the ultimate means of arbitrement lie, as to the arguments here put forward. Consequently theories of criticism, or allied theory, are referred to largely in so far as they do or do not seem to support the sociologies also put forward.

An important matter has been that of the distinction between poetry on the one hand and other imaginative forms, particularly the novel and drama, on the other. (There has of course been a quantity of work in the sociology of the novel and drama.) To deal with this properly would take a whole separate study, but I feel it should be mentioned here. At many points in the book the reader might feel that even if a point about poetry's distinctiveness from sociology has been made adequately enough, nevertheless it has not been shown why this was not true of other literary forms as well. But it would delay discussion impossibly if I made the necessary qualifications at every point, and so I have had to hope that the general tenor of my argument covers that issue, at least for the purposes of this book. I have discussed this in the Introduction to some extent, but after that only where some special emphasis seemed necessary. The essential if oversimplified distinction, which I believed to be valid, is that poetry uses language for itself, whereas other literary forms (which may include 'poetry' in a somewhat different sense) use language for some outside purpose.

Certain parts of the book draw extended, though rephrased, passages from previously published papers of mine, and these are cited in the footnotes.

I would like to express my special gratitude to C.C. Harris, who laid the original foundations for such sociology as I can claim to know; and to Janet Wolff, Professor Brian Morris and Patrick Parrinder, all of whom read the manuscript and whose detailed comments have been extremely helpful. Only one suggestion of any size has not been taken up, and that was Brian Morris' idea that I should widen the poetic analysis to include such matters as oral poetry and the poetry of war, as well as some other things. I had to decide that this would have made the book rather too bulky and unwieldy, but his suggestions are obviously of considerable interest, and I hope that later work may return to them. I have, I think, incorporated the great majority of suggestions made by these colleagues, but they are clearly not responsible in any way for my use of them; and I only want to record with gratitude their help and enthusiasm. The encouragement and critical perception of Sarah Ward (who also twice read the manuscript) have been with me throughout the writing of this book. I should also like to thank Patricia Alsalihi for typing the manuscript so beautifully.

J.P. Ward
January 1980

PART I

INTRODUCTION

CHAPTER 1

INTRODUCTION

In the summer of 1978, only a few weeks before writing these lines at the start of this book, I received through the mail notice of the latest Sociological Review Monographs (published from Keele University); namely, numbers 25 and 26, both on the sociology of literature. Number 26, edited by Diana Laurenson, is called confidently enough *The Sociology of Literature: Applied Studies*.[1] Apart from the introduction it contains thirteen papers. Ten of these are on individual novels or novelists, one is on 'the literature of alienation' and the two others are on film.

To receive this when I did, right at the end of writing the book (for one often writes the beginning at the end) was useful confirmation of what was already long clear, that despite the growth of the sociology of literature in the last decade there has been no sociological attention to poetry and there still is none. The Penguin *Sociology of Literature and Drama* edited by Tom and Elizabeth Burns,[2] which appeared five years before, anticipates this absence perhaps even more emphatically, for the failure of Laurenson's book to refer to drama either might have been taken to imply an emphasis on narrative (whether on paper or celluloid) rather than a hiatus as far as poetry is concerned. In the Burns' book there are thirty-three selections and nine of them are on drama, a fact doubtless mirroring the importance given to that topic by Elizabeth Burns, who had already produced her own sociological study *Theatricality*[3] the year before. The Burns' book contains six papers directly on the novel, but treats poetry only by means of one piece by Northrop Frye and one paper dealing with Dante, who is a rather exceptional case. Duvignaud equally deals mainly with theatre, and there have been many studies of the novel from a sociological point of view.[4] Raymond Williams, not strictly a sociologist but a writer of considerable influence and perspicacity on the relations between formal literature, culture and society, has written very little on poetry in his enormous body of work.[5] Other sociological studies exemplify the same tendency: attention to the novel, to drama, and to literature as a generic cultural phenomenon, but if you look for a sociology of poetry, or any sociological attention to poetry, you will find a yawning absence, a void.

Perhaps we should say straight away what we mean by 'poetry'. I use the word in a simple and straightforward sense. I recognize what is meant by 'poetic' passages in novels and essays, but in this book we shall think of the word in its overwhelmingly accepted use to describe what is found in formal poems.

It is of course true also that most work in the sociology of literature, whether on poetry or anything else, has not been cast in the mould of mainstream academic-liberal sociology as that is understood by most university departments of sociology; that is to say the sociology of Durkheim, Parsons, Weber, Mead, Merton, Cooley, Goffman, Garfinkel, Schutz, or the 'community studies' movement of social anthropology. This fact has emerged clearly enough at the various British conferences on literature and sociology in the last decade, and the absence of reference to poets (for it is Brecht as dramatist and the Brontes as novelists who regularly hold the stage) has been accompanied, bewilderingly to me, by an equal absence of allusion to any of the names mentioned in the list above. I do not recall one of that representative list even being named in the half-dozen or so conferences I have attended, nor are they referred to commonly in the literature. There are reasons for this, not least of which may be that many patrons of this general area of intellectual activity have been literary rather than sociological people by training, commonly sharing a growing feeling that literature should be related to 'society' rather than kept autonomously sealed as a set of objects available to meet the desires and principles implicit in Practical Criticism. That at least has been the argument. But even so, the very fact of the growth of such interest in the social connections and bases of literature, and the appropriation of the word 'sociology' to describe this activity, showed at first an obvious common area of concern, one brought out by the

Burns in the introduction to their collection. The interesting thing is that as the evolution of the sociology of literature has proceded, by whatever means (for example Marxism, straight sociology, or sociolinguistics), so has the pre-eminence of the lyric poem as the prototype of the literary object declined. No matter what form of sociological approach has been used, insofar as it has been indeed sociological, poetry has been ignored.

This general observation was one of the two that led me into the enquiry which results in this book. The other observation was of the traditional, centuries-old views about, and apparent tendencies of, poetry itself. For in virtually every aspect of its tradition poetry seems *prima facie* to be oddly separated from what the twentieth century has demarcated as the 'social'. Rather poetry tends, in matter and mode, in the opposite direction. The mode of poetry, in general, is self-referring; a poem is not a piece of discourse or one piece of an interaction, it is itself sealed and encased as separate from any such interaction.[6] It furthermore results commonly from deliberate attempts to reinforce that characteristic by formal means, such as rhyme, regular metre and so on, such that its lines and phrases could not conceivably be part of ordinary discourse. At other times deliberately elevated language (as it was called by Dr Johnson) or 'poetic diction' have been regarded as essential to poetry. Our century has seen deliberate attempts to free poetry from such regularity, but the innovators of free verse, such as Pound, never tired of stressing that this did not mean linguistic licence to say or write anything at all, but was a setting-free (*vers liberé* rather than *vers libre*) which thereby enjoined the poet to an even more difficult discipline, that of finding the unique form that each poetic idea needed for its expression — 'the exact curve of the thing', as it was put by T.E. Hulme. And equally, for as many poets as have responded to the communication-saturated modern world by the mimesis of colloquial language or language something like discourse, so have others resorted to the sculpted, unspeakable, imagist or symbolic or iconic mode of poetry whereby an image or idea is rendered or represented, with little or no echo of the human, articulated, felt voice. More generally, the mode of poetry has entailed an aspiration to the condition of music, object, or silence.

These suggestions are supported by a consideration of what have normally been seen as the themes of poetry. Poetry has commonly concerned itself with anything but 'society' and 'social action' as those are now conceived. Some characteristic preoccupations have been: nature and identity with nature (both enchanted and existential); the solitary and the egotistical; God, and dead people — both of these commonly entailing, very revealingly, the apostrophic mode, by which poetry can seem an address precisely where there is no interaction and it cannot be answered; time, roots and the mythic past; Eros (that is, the desired consummation of sexual love, rather than the 'social interactions' leading up to it); the transfigured or literally divine epic hero; and finally, and importantly in terms of poetry's self-referring quality, poetry itself. As Wallace Stevens put it: 'Poetry is the subject of the poem,/From this the poem issues and/To this returns.' This projecting of the poetic text as its own reference, and the way that, in Jakobson's terms, the poetic function of language is predominant when the message itself is the object of that same message's attention, results in the equally important fact about poetry, that its form and content seem to become one and the same. And the fact that they thus cannot be separated or paraphrased itself seems to argue that any content cannot be abstracted for its social message, its statement as by one person to another. (It is this feature of poetry that has most led recent criticism to cease to ask 'the meaning behind the meaning', or the question 'What is being said by what is being said?' The attempt to 'understand' the poem is now not at all the same order of understanding as the ordinary interpretation of discourse, or indeed any spoken or written communication from one person to another, where what is intended by the hidden mind or feeling is what is sought by the reader or listener. The poem intends only itself.)

Most revealing of all, we observe that when poetry undeniably does deal with clearly social matters, it is commonly the constraint on the social, not the social itself, that is the burdening and inescapable presence with which we are left. This is most obvious with satire, the mode that suggests humans are blind to this constraint; but it occurs also in the more laconic tone of such poets as Larkin, the fatigue of Eliot, and the *angst* of the suicidal, suicide being society's clearest and blackest boundary. And those responses have markedly increased during the secularization of the modern world.

Summarized thus briefly, that set of views about poetry may not convince everyone. But at present I am only reporting an observation which seemed to me not to square with the ideas of those who think all language is necessarily communication in the ordinary sense, and who think also that any language-act — as indeed any act — is necessarily located in a social context which is largely sufficient to explain it, and without which context the language-act cannot possibly be understood. Such have been characteristically the views of academic sociologists about language. But such views, even if true, leave the central question unanswered. For if all language is communication, and is also context-embedded, why does poetry apparently strive to leave behind those conditions and constraints? If those language-characteristics do exist, it would seem that the very attempt to overcome them is itself in some way constitutive of what we find we call 'poetry'. The tensions which are set up when language, and what it expresses, most strives to be exactly what it is normally not, perhaps are close to the nature of poetry itself.

From these two general observations — that there is no sociological interest in poetry, and that poetry itself seems to strain away from the social dimension of reality — the preliminary conclusion would be that, far from being remiss in not attending to poetry, sociologists have acted on healthy instinct in staying away from the subject. Perhaps they are simply not interested, an idea that itself would presumably need explanation in terms of sociology's interests. But the conventional formulae, for example that language is simply communication, have had to live with a deeper sense that poetry is not for the sociologist's attention. The aim of this book is to explore this seemingly fundamental incompatibility between poetry and the sociological idea.

The question must surely be a profoundly disturbing one both for poets and for those who, as Peter Levi once put it, draw their sustenance from poetry, for it would appear that the sociological idea (a phrase we shall need often in what follows) has established an apparently unshakable grip on the consciousness of modern man, the way we organize ourselves, see ourselves, and in fact manage to exist at all in the secular world. By 'the sociological idea' I mean a set of beliefs and notions now deeply ingrained in most people at some level of consciousness. These are, that there is 'society'; and that this abstract thing exists over and above its members, by virtue of processes which we inescapably inherit, so that much of what we do is functional to such overall processes. Second, that we 'relate' to one another at microcosmic level through daily interactions; also that we live in classes, work-groups and communities subject to and only understandable by such equally significant processes; also that we ourselves are bound into such procedures by the ways we collectively think of them and interpret them; and finally that there is social change, even revolution, but that such revolution is itself the projection of fixed laws, whether social or historical. Even if they are historical, that historical stage we are now in is one that has precipitated us into the modern, sociological world. If this is true and if this idea and its manifestations is in some way inimical to poetry, then it gives sobering and ominous significance to the words with which Leavis started his first major work in 1932: 'Poetry matters little to the modern world.'[7]

Perhaps we can first support the view that the sociological idea is as strong a force as I have suggested. It may seem a strange contention, at a time when sociologists are themselves bewailing the complete lack of success of their subject in its hundred-year history, so that the Cambridge sociologist Giddens[8] can say that, on the positivist front at least, the social sciences *'must surely be reckoned a failure'* (his italics), and so that the 'despair' in Geoffrey Hawthorn's recent book can be taken by his *Times Literary Supplement* reviewer to indicate Hawthorn's sense that 'the whole enterprise has been a failure and that no new beginnings are evident'.[9] But these views, and others like them, normally suggest that sociology has failed to establish itself as an academic discipline capable of providing reliable, explicit and testable laws about human social behaviour, whether that discipline is conceived of as an interpretative one or on the model of the natural sciences. But the way the general sociological idea, as I am calling it, has permeated our collective perspective on the world and each other seems to be undeniable.

The general, familiar point to be made is that the sociological mode of thought comes into the world as a result of the materializing or secularizing of the descriptions of all other phenomena. If the palpable world, the planet and universe, are seen as more than mere matter, mere resource for human use, then the sociological idea cannot develop, because that 'more' might have some autonomy or mystery of its own and not be so respectful of any merely sociological orientation to reality as we might think it should be. But when the scientific and technological enterprises of the modern world appear and, apparently successfully, treat the material world as just that — simply material — then the hold of theological and mythological world-views declines and, in effect, we are left with only ourselves as the seat of meaningfulness and consciousness, and of any understanding of those things. It may well be argued that recently – even in the last decade — this process has itself been reversed, so that we cannot take so materialistic a view of reality, even under the ideology of historical materialism, as the last hundred years has experienced. But even if that is so, that new stage is still very new, is far from certain to survive or take any predictable form, and has surely not superseded our sociological era sufficiently to make us think the effects of the sociological idea have yet left us, or that idea has evolved a wholly new, perhaps metaphysical, meaning. In short, that materialistic period occurred; it has developed, and we have long been in the period in which the nodal concepts of sociology and social science have themselves seeped down into the words and minds of ordinary people, so that we do actually see ourselves through the terms of the social sciences. This is not because they are accurate in their description of us (which they may or may not be); rather it occurs through an enormous tacit agreement between everyone to speak as though such descriptions are valid and true. Thus it is wholly normal now to hear people talking about their 'social relationships', interactions and roles, norm, function, conflict, class, institutions, social organization, group pressures, group structure and cultural patterns, as though the examples they cite of such phenomena are merely earthly occasions of some ideal version of these things: as though for example a 'social relationship' between two people is an example of, a shot at, some Platonic pure form of that, the existence of which it never occurs to the social scientist, or layman influenced by social science, to doubt.

The broad result of this enterprise for human consciousness and indeed our very idea of meaning at all may be that we enslave ourselves, narcissistically perhaps, to the social-scientific, or at least rigidly orderly, pattern of conceptions we have about our collective and plural existence. The universe — our entire conception of all reality — can easily be reduced to two sets of phenomena only; the material, and the social, or self-consciously experienced. And the material, although we concede we by no means know all about it, at least 'stays put'; it does not jump about of its own volition, and even if in some senses it does seem to, our vast collective act of scientific faith assures us there is nothing to fear in terms of a world disordered intellectually, for known laws or future ones rather like them will take care of all. Of course we are in enormous danger (through pollution for example) from our own activities, but the remedy is in our hands, and for most laymen the laws of science itself do not thereby seem threatened. The only other level of reality is the social. At that level we reconstitute ourselves (as the new sociologists now say) socially every time we reproduce our social orderings; we reconstitute not only our society but our description of it and our names for it, as a pattern of abstractions in which we then place our trust.

Given the scope of this book I can do no more now than suggest some aspects of the levels at which the sociological idea has hold on us. There is first the level of everyday discourse, and the way that educated, or partly educated, people actually cognize and make explicit these things. I am not denying the force of theories of language, as diverse as those of Whorf and Lacan, that see an autonomy in language itself, but we have to consider the nature of language in the sociological world, and the way that the profound presence of the sociological idea itself may be seen as altering our use of language in that all language to some extent is drawn toward an expression of our sociological condition, our idea of ourselves as, not 'sons of God' or 'four buckets of water and a bag of salts' but '*homo sociologicus*', social things, devoid of existence (bar a certain biological base) outside our social relations. The argument here is that the very presence of the sociological idea in our midst itself draws language, including everyday language, toward what is expressed in that idea and subject, however tenuous the connection may seem between that mode of thought and the ordinary man, woman or child in their various daily activities. (Needless to say I am myself drawn to such a use, as will doubtless be clear in what follows.) The process is furthermore compounded by the emergence of language-study and linguistics, so that deep at the heart of the social consciousness there appears 'language' itself, rather than this or that language; and thus any use of language is deeply felt as not just itself, but an example of the workings of that fundamentally social thing, language, more generally. But I suggest that the deep presence of 'society', the social idea, is itself felt to be the context of context-embedded language. New theoretical ideas about language and its legitimate uses are themselves premised to some extent on our ideas of society — and vice-versa. As a result the very terms of self-knowingly social discourse pass into ordinary linguistic interchange. People talk generally of their relationships and their place in the group; more specifically they speak of 'work situations', 'modern marriage', 'race relations', 'a tourist area' (even the terrain is subjected to sociological movements), or 'participation in the democratic process'. We also work out these relationships with each other verbally, saying 'I'm sorry, I over-reacted there' or 'he doesn't fit in' or 'you're just expressing middle-class values'; or more neurotically, as in R.D. Laing's book *Knots*.[10] Of course it may be held that this is an educated or middle-class phenomenon only, but, even leaving aside the question of how far the middle classes (for better or worse) do control a modern society's modes of communication, there is the deeper question of how not merely the reference but the grammar and structure of language has been altered and in particular stripped down and elided by the presence of the all-embracing sociological context. This seems to go well beyond the normal amount of shorthand speaking we might expect in any earlier, shared people or culture. A sequence like 'Going home?/What's the time?/Four/I'm not then/But what about John/Ask the manager' etc. etc., is characterized by the quantity of reference not mentioned explicitly because already known, shared, and seen as social; and the fact that more and more of modern life is shared at its deepest expressive level by virtue of the sociological idea; the idea that every human phenomenon is an example of some central social reality which explains it. This has transmuted itself through to the ordinary person at the level of the mass media, which is always more and more able to elide language,[11] by centrally controlling the Lowest Common Factor expression of language, and by being able to rely always on the hearer's or reader's previous experience, on television or in tabloids, of just such language. But it also occurs in widespread education, where, most crucially, the very notion of what constitutes 'good English' as a value or skill, has itself been modified by the structural demands of the expression of the sociological idea, an idea which suggests that any language is good if it expresses our relationships or cements our institutional ties; for that idea is increasingly what seems the uniting bond of our existence. This process is continuous and circular. The actual language by which we repeatedly reconstitute the social reality itself results from the internalizing of that reality's centre. It is not that there are no dialects, or surviving regional or racial linguistic differences or that they will disappear. They may be growing again now as a re-attachment to our physical and natural world as something sacramental perhaps re-emerges, in a new form. If so, the sociological idea is threatened. But that has not happened yet, and what is clear at present is the structural similarity underlying such lexically different things, and the access all have to the central, context-embedded and increasingly abstract language which is circulated by the media and supported by education.

These modes of deep social connection also tie in with the large-scale obdurate parts of the social order. The conceptions of institution, organization, bureaucracy, the economy, the family, education and so forth are equally felt as parts of what make that general entity, the social order seen as the central reality, perhaps the main reality, we have. Conceptions as diverse as 'the divine right of Kings' and 'the British way of life' disappear since they are particularistic, and the universal quality of all sociality itself displaces them. Most importantly, though in a way impossible to develop here, it is the political embodiment of these notions in the general idea of social democracy (perhaps particularly the growth of the Social-Democrat parties of Western Europe, North America and elsewhere, and even the more diluted communism of some Iron Curtain countries) that illustrate this. Such parties, the Labour party of Britain included, stem directly from the hold of the sociological idea in the late nineteenth and twentieth centuries. At the heart of such political activity is the general formula of 'creating a better society', and the cognition that 'society' does so exist and can also be created is now irreducible in its significance perhaps even, if it does not sound too extravagant, for the structure of our minds. The solid parts of the social democracy — planning, social welfare, comprehensive education, regions and local communities, 'public life', local authority, management, organized labour — are all general abstractions for which in any one nation particular embodiments are required so that that central thing, a 'society', may exist and render us secure and able to recognize our place in the world. This is to hold good even in an otherwise undirected world where more metaphysical or natural (physical) forms of supreme existential appeal decline in force. For those things, even if they exist, cannot be used as implicit directives as to how we see the human condition. Most revealingly from an etymological point of view, nature is now 'environment', that which is around us, the suggestion being that man-centredness does not need a Cartesian (individual) view of reality, for 'man' is now a collectivity which still embodies consciousness even though the individual man's perspective may not be held to be ultimately valuable. Religion too, even if not demolished by the sociological idea (a point people disagree about) is rendered different — a shadowy thing, disturbing but not to be formulated; mysterious, and in the realm of death, death being something we do not deliberately and teleologically work toward, but simply negatively know to be there, and which the society will survive. But again, this sociological idea in its political guise is not in some alarming way merely a denial of human freedom and individuality. Rather such freedom and individuality may well now only be expected to occur as a result of the acceptance of the sociological idea. Far from itself being merely tyrannous, the sociological idea asks to be accepted so that individual tyranny can never hope for success again. Unfortunately, technology may always be brutally appropriated by individuals, but, at best, the sociological idea of ourselves as both necessarily and beneficially working together for order, and in order, would be so deep in people's consciousnesses as itself a social perspective that ideally it would prevent any power-grabber having any long sway which could be legitimized. This somewhat Platonic view is not merely utilitarian (like the 'checks and balances' of James Mill): it is an appeal to a central reality in which we believe. Of course the sociological idea itself may become tyrannous in certain circumstances, but that is precisely when human sociality becomes simply aggregation (as Raymond Williams puts it, the social becomes deformed to the collective)[12] and intersubjectivity, itself a crucial sociological concept, ends up counting for nothing.

Finally our cognitive disciplines, our attempt to understand reality itself, have become drastically influenced by the sociological idea. We must necessarily be content with a few references only. In economics it was Alfred Marshall who first introduced the idea of the importance of sociality itself in economic understanding. T.S. Kuhn has introduced the idea in the field of natural science. Psychology and human genetics are curious cases in the sense that any reliable statement they make about even individual constitution must necessarily have a collective implication if such statements are universally true. The really important change is in philosophy. Through a new understanding of language, developed in philosophy from Wittgenstein onward, philosophers have found it necessary to examine the relations between the idea of pure thought itself and the possibility of a true sociological knowledge. As Gellner has put it, 'It hardly matters whether such an enquiry is called philosophy or sociology.'[13] Theology has had to come to terms with — among other things — the knowledge that much of what was traditionally regarded as the organizational embodiment of God's power and grace on earth is explicable by sociological theory of organization.[14] As a result religion, which has by no means disappeared nor looks likely to do so, has become an existential matter of ultimate reality unknowable by definition.

But as well as these various epistemological areas which have felt the influence of the sociological idea, there is another more immediate to our interest; namely, criticism itself. If we are going to argue, as most of this book will try to argue, an incompatibility between poetry and the sociological idea of reality, then the inference is that a criticism equally affected by the sociological idea will itself look somewhat askance at what has usually been called poetry. We have already observed that the sociology of literature has devoted no attention to poetry, and if that branch of sociology can be regarded as a branch of criticism too, then we there have one apparent effect on criticism straight away. However it seems better to leave any comments on criticism to the end of the book, and concentrate now on merely illustrating the point that criticism too, as suggested, seems to follow the lead of the sociological idea. I will therefore here offer only the suggestion that if the narrowly sociological approach to literature ignores poetry, other branches of recent criticism influenced by the sociological perspective, although they do not go so far as that, do still find themselves in some difficulty in dealing with poetry. For the moment I want to support the view that these new branches of criticism are influenced by the sociological idea.

Prima facie, it is scarcely difficult to argue. The very first sentence of Donald Davie's influential book *Thomas Hardy and British Poetry* reads thus; 'In this book I have taken it for granted that works are conditioned by economic and political forces active in the society from which these works spring and to which they are directed. . . .' Not spiritual or biological forces, one notices, but still 'forces', which 'condition' works in 'society'. The remark would have been impossible in the Renaissance or ancient Greece. (It is fair to add that Professor Davie has more recently referred to matters 'that shall be truly "human", not merely "social" '.)[15] John Weightman writes, 'An important, and relatively simple, sense of literary modernism would be, then, this feeling that literature should always consciously keep abreast of the social and cultural situation, and should even, in its more prophetic manifestations, anticipate developments'.[16] The use of that now near-universal cliché the 'situation' is only less impressive than the notion of what literature 'should' do, at the behest, obviously, of the 'social and cultural situation' itself. Both these remarks are characteristic expressions of what in the last decade has commonly been called the 'crisis in English', the view suggesting, in numerous journals and magazine articles,[17] that the study of English at universities is lost unless such studies accommodate the change of perspective criticism itself is undergoing. This change of perspective can be summarized as a decline of interest in the question 'What does this text mean'? in favour of the question 'How is literature possible; what are the conditions and processes by which any work of literature is able to mean anything'?[18] And the approach to answering those new questions is a matter now of adopting some outside discipline, other than an autonomous practical criticism itself, from which to proceed. Thus, instead of examining the text as a matter of direct, personal and unsullied engagement, the critic comes equipped with the knowledge and principles of Marxism, structural linguistics, psychoanalysis, or whatever it may be, and in the light of that cognitive specialism considers literature in its general terms.

My argument, naturally, is that these disciplines are themselves a product of the evolution of the sociological idea, and the movement in their direction is an attempt, in part, to meet the instinct to incorporate that idea in criticism. Yet the earlier twentieth-century views of criticism's nature were not devoid of that influence either. Most well-known is Leavis' own view of the collaborative nature of criticism as public discussion,[19] although that view emphasizes criticism, not poetry itself, as communal and social. Eliot and Frye, like Leavis, see literature as a totality, so that any single work of literature exemplifies 'Literature' generally. All three of these views have gradually encouraged the interpretation, in the era of the sociological idea, that literature is itself an institution in the full sociological sense; that is to say, according to sociological theories of institutions. I mean that the literary canon, the great works of a country's heritage, whether those of Montaigne, Racine and Moliére or Homer, Aeschylus and Sophocles, are seen by a pre-sociological culture as a matter of nobility, reverence and treasure, in the latter case perhaps even semi-sanctity (in the literal sense of works of some religious significance); and that views such as those of Leavis, Eliot and Frye are a secularizing and modification of that earlier attitude in the light of the sociological idea. That is to say, while Eliot and Leavis in particular (Frye less so) preserve a tinge of elevation for the literary canon they speak of, they all also introduce embryonically analytical and structural notions into their understanding of the nature of that canon as a whole. The pronouncement of T.S. Eliot was that every new work of literature modifies those that have gone before, rather than being merely modified by them; and that is a profoundly process-orientated remark. With Frye the deep attachment to catholicity, rather than preference of one author to another, is the basis which enables him to work toward his very formal account of the pattern of literary categories. Notably he calls this account an anatomy of criticism, not of literature itself, suggesting thus that literary works fit into it, so that it is that pattern which provides the structure of contexts for works considered individually. But in all these cases the treating of literary works collectively, whether as amounting to a tradition or responding to an overall set of principles without which they would have no meaning, implies an approach to meeting halfway the demands of an age which sees human beings publicly and collectively.

Doubtless this trio would themselves deny what I have just said. The idea of literature as autonomous is strong in their work; Frye himself compared his scheme not with anything sociological or psychological but biological, on the Aristotelian model, and his model of myths is seasonal.[20] But I am suggesting only a tendency, a movement partly to accommodate literature, and especially poetry, to deeper themes present in the thought of the modern world. The conscious designation of literature as an institution comes far more recently. It is referred to — a little — by the earlier steam-age sociologists of literature, but has fuller expression in Jonathan Culler's *Structuralist Poetics*.[21] Culler suggests that our understanding of literature works entirely through a pattern of conventions or, as sociologists would put it, norms. I want to comment on this view in the last chapter; but for now there is the even more striking emphasis, almost compulsion indeed, in Culler to defend the tangible 'institution' of literature— though he does not call it that — which comprises the schools, university departments of literature and the whole enterprise of the teaching and learning of literature as itself a public phenomenon without which, one gathers, literature could not proceed and without which past literature would be lost. This view seems necessary to Culler's belief in 'literary competence', something which must be carefully trained and nurtured so that the reader may then 'perform operations' (sic) on the texts he encounters. The competence-performance dichotomy is of course reminiscent of Chomsky, and also of Habermas who uses it in his discussion of our procedure in wielding any language or speech much more widely.[22] Surely these views fail to square with the value Culler places on the 'native reader'. The 'native reader' is one whose view of a text must be respected as evidence in the same way as — so sociology increasingly puts it — an ordinary inhabitant of the social world is someone not to be improved by sociological knowledge but listened to for such knowledge. Again I will draw out one or two references in the last chapter, but, as before, the point for the present is to illustrate how criticism is itself under the sway of the sociological idea. In Culler's case it arguably shows itself in a failure to resolve the contradiction between his institutional notions and the reality of poetry itself. The undoubtedly pioneering nature of Culler's work has perhaps itself put him in the position of suggesting these tendencies.

As for mainstream linguistics, the sociological emphasis is paramount. It would surely be interesting to study poetry in the light of certain linguistic findings about language's internal, physical structure; for instance that words are multitudinous short expenditures of breath and energy because of our physiological constitution.[23] But linguists generally are simply not interested in that now. Such undeniably stimulating distinctions as metaphor and metonymy, and what those reveal about psychological and sociological processes, are what attracts most linguistic attention at present. In a recent *Times Literary Supplement* Bob Hodge wrote that linguistic departments in Britain fail to get students precisely because students want the sociological emphasis. ' [The Chomskyian emphasis on the connection of language and mind] is what students object to, and rightly. The courses they ask for are socio-lingustic, concerned with language and society'.[24] The huge influence of Bernstein's sociolinguistics in educational studies suggests that linguists, of the Anglo-Saxon variety at least, were already responding.

Structuralism itself, in its linguistic aspect, descends very much from the work of Saussure, and particularly his *langue/parole* and signifier/signified distinctions, both of which can be tied to a sociological perspective. The question of how far Saussure was influenced by Durkheim seems to intrigue every commentator on Saussure,[25] and the *langue/parole* distinction is especially interesting in the light of Saussure's statement that it is language that is social while speech is individual. This might seem the reverse of the obvious inference, since speech acts are clearly public and visible (and oral) whereas language is an abstract term and hidden thing. But Saussure is consistent in the terms he uses, in that language is common to all its users whereas speech acts strictly are individual, physical performances. And poetry is at least as much language as it is speech. Therefore to approach poetry by means of a discipline (structuralism) which emphasizes the sociality of language above all else would appear to argue strongly for the influence of the governing social dimension in such work. This is particularly true if the pattern of thought employed comes at only one remove from the ideas of the founding father of sociology, Durkheim himself. It reaches its logical culmination in Barthes' idea of the 'death of the author'; the author is no longer a genius, or even inspired or talented, except quite incidentally, and in fact is scarcely in any important sense an individual at all. He is the catalyst by means of which the text comes into existence: the text is then taken over entirely by its readers. Connected with structuralism and Saussurian linguistics is the psycho-analytical view of Lacan. In his view discourse itself is structured in the subconscious, and language, or the 'Word' in our traditional and biblical sense, is something autonomous of its own. For Lacan, symbols 'envelop the life of a man in a network so total that . . . they bring to his birth the shape of his destiny . . . they give him the words that will make him faithful or renegade . . . [they bring him to] the last judgement, where the Word absolves his being or condemns it. . . . .' 'The law of language is the law of man'. This Calvinistic belief is saved by one phrase: *unless* he attains the subjective bringing to realization of being-for-death' (my italics).[26] I mean here, and again must put it briefly at this stage of the argument, that Lacan's view of the autonomy of language is itself collective, but is also itself in danger of being drawn into a sociological, public domain (rather than a mechanical, predestined enslavement of humans to the rigid laws of language) by our idea of consciousness, for that idea is itself a social production insofar as there are features of it other than the biological, genetic ('rigid laws of language') and so on.

This brings us to the final member of this cluster of disciplines which surround literature today, namely Marxism, since Marxism claims for itself an explanation of consciousness. In this book I shall regard Marxism as a type within sociology and therefore expand on it further in the chapter on sociology, although Marxism is, of course, much more than sociological. Marxism's difference from sociology lies not so much in the historicism which emphasizes the unique and the particular event against the abstract generality of most sociology; it is in the materiality of Marxism that the difference lies. It is for this reason I suggest that Marxist critics seem, even more than linguists, able to give place to poetry among the literary arts. And since Marxism is indeed itself a champion of the material and the unique historical event, it seems able profoundly to respect the poem's quiddity aside from any notion of the work's status as social comment or product of its time's general qualities. The text may necessarily answer back to an ideological position, but that position is at any time a unique historical occasion in the dialectic. Therefore the Marxist critic can allow himself, as Jameson superbly does, the luxury of writing imaginatively about literature, for there is not the constraint always to be consigning the text to its place as a mere illustrator of abstract laws.[27] As Jameson says, Marxism is itself a form moving through history. The dynamic of dialectic, whatever one may think of it, allows what Eagleton and Macherey both call the derangement or disturbance of the ideology as itself a response to the ideology. But I myself see no need to take Eagleton's position that criticism's role is to 'show the text as it cannot know itself', in the sense of acquainting the text with its own ideological origin, stimulating though the idea certainly is.[28] It is this aspect of Marxist criticism that makes it, too, vulnerable to the suggestion that it wears an overlay of the sociological idea. Marxism, by *being* an idea, by 'thinking itself', goes away from precisely its own emphasis on the unique, for in that event all actions do become examples of the general mode of the historical after all. As Eagleton says, the aim of criticism is to find why the work *had* to be so; and the very possibility of that notion, I want to argue, derives from the inexorable movement in us of the general principle of our social ordering; although, as always with Marxism, one has to state that it is other things as well.

My general argument then is that we are subject, in this era, to the sociological idea perhaps above all other modes of cognition (in that even the findings of natural science have become technologized to our service rather than revered for themselves); and that criticism has moved massively across into accepting that dominance. The broad critical mode, allowing for its undenied differences in Marxism, structuralism, linguistics and so on, is to see the sociological dimension as the context of meaning within which literary works are structured. While the novel and drama are to some extent legitimately treated in this way (in that in those cases the sociological reality is itself part of the writer's raw material), poetry is not. Poetry is incompatible with that sociological idea. And the immediate inference is this: that in the dominance of the sociological idea, and the resultant absence of real, absorbed, strong comment on poetry by any branch of criticism influenced by that tendency, we are witnessing a parallel to Plato's banishment of the poets.

This banishment is not a matter of imprisonment or fine, of course, or even great social stigma (though there has been some of all three in our time). On the contrary, there is lip-service to the poet's magic, mystery, creativity and cultural virtue, and if he is banished, it is 'anointed with myrrh, and with a garland of wool about his head' — a Creative Writing Fellowship, or an Arts Council Grant. But the banishment still occurs, if in a different form. The form it takes now often seems to be that of enervating and sterilizing poetry's power. Either by being silent on the subject of poetry, or by 'placing' it as a mere linguistic phenomenon in a wider, but still bounded, description of society and language, or by rendering it as (in hindsight) a predictable event accounted for by the economic base and the ideology of the class from which it is believed to come, criticism aids and abets the process by which poetry is already organized into an impotent position the moment it leaves the press. Both poetry and criticism of poetry — as indeed much other criticism — is 'placed' thus; a work is praised not simply as good or perceptive, but as important, significant or indispensable. Important to what? we may ask. To an invisible but real process of absorption already deeply and entrenchedly in existence.

The novel and drama, insofar as they too are not examples of the 'poetic' side of their genres (poetic drama, the poetic or existentialist novel) are not so likely to encourage this banishment. Although they make new things by the imaginative use of language, the material they use is already overtly drawn from the social, public order, the *res publica*, the public thing, itself. The realistic novel accepts the outward frame of society's wholesale description of itself as material from which to make a new perception; a different, disturbing one on many occasions, certainly, but working from the basis of the public description in the outset. Since the whole community, its people, lands, houses, customs, beliefs and practices are themselves the raw material, the language that renders that is to some extent subordinate to it. The language is subject to the demands placed on the author by outside things accepted as already related to one another in a tight network of objects, people and values. The language is the medium but not the raw material. In the realistic drama language is also the raw material, but this time it is the special language of the actual speech that already exists between people. The realistic drama accepts the reality of actual human interaction whether in work, family or conflict, such that the whole text is only comprehensible if its speeches are thought of as spoken by individuals already placed within the same public, social order. The imaginative act of creation in language comes from the way the dramatist uses language conceived of as already spoken, already heard, so that we can recognize its origins in the social contexts in which we ourselves have heard them, or heard about them. Thus, even when they challenge society, both novel and drama can take on society on its own terms, and they thus demand an answer by the critic in the joint terms used by both the society and the fictional work (novel or drama) which looks at society even if askance. The general notion of sociality is not obscured.

But the poet does not do this. The poet uses language itself, the very idea or possibility of language, to achieve his or her creations. Poetry is 'self-referring'. For this reason the poet threatens the very heart of communication itself, or so it may seem to the unversed, the conventional or the easily bewildered. Not the beliefs about the result of communication (society) but the very bond of communication itself, is exploded, or set alight. This is exhilarating or profoundly supporting to a culture that sees its unity not in the abstractions of structure or communication but in a unique myth-of-origin, a sacred text or 'Word' unreservedly believed, for it is poetic use of language that has first constituted that 'Word'; and other subsequent examples of it, even when they allude to different matters, are a source of succour. In the secular world poetry has no such role.

Finally for this reason — and it will be important to what follows — the poet cannot, within the poem, be his own apologist. Again the novelist and dramatist can to some extent do this, for, as we have said, their message about society is explicit (if fictional and indirect), and therefore their justification of that message is clear when it succeeds in having it heard and put across. The poet writes occasional apologies in poetry itself, like MacDiarmid's 'The Kind Of Poetry I Want', but this naturally cannot be done for more than a fraction of the time. The poet has to trust that the audience, however small, is there, an audience that already accepts that, in the terms I am using here, the sociological idea can tell us only about the social dimension of reality, not all reality, and can only do even that when there is (as sociologists themselves have lately put it) a reflexive agreement to use the sociological idea as a heart reference point by which other things are to be measured. This small audience will find it hard to resist that agreement, for it occurs not as a result of objective research but as a shared and agreed method of obtaining meaning. By it, the actual and the obligatory, the 'is' and the 'ought', become one. The deepest pressures exist to accept, for working purposes and certainly normally for benevolently intended ends, as Plato's were benevolently intended, the sociological idea and its implications for our behaviour. I am in no way disputing the value of this, but it is a question of where the final authority for that view lies. If we find the authority just cited (that we are because we ought to be, and we ought to be because we are) inadequate because circular and thus tautologous, we may look elsewhere out of the circle for an expression of the raw form of our deepest convictions. This might be to religion, nature, the physical, Eros, ideas, or other non-social parts of reality. It is to those things that poetry leads; but the poet, by definition, cannot say so in ordinary language, in discourse or 'communication' or prose. Unlike the case for the drama or novel, the apology for the poem and the answers to Plato by Aristotle, Sidney and Shelley come from outside the poem itself. The reader must come to the poem, and the poem cannot be summarized.

In this book I propose then not to attempt a sociology of poetry but to explore precisely the incompatibility between poetry and sociology which would, among other things, render such a sociology impossible. Perhaps I can now say exactly how it is proposed to proceed in this. The next chapter will lay out in as much detail as space allows the features of the main kinds and traditions of sociological thought. I suggest there are five of these, and while no one need accept the picture quite as exactly as that, I do not think any sociologist would dispute the general existence of these five fairly separable traditions. In the following chapters I will then take five poets: Spenser, Donne, Milton, Pope and Wordsworth. Now I suggest that each of these poets can be seen to use a symbolic or intellectual universe parallelling, in each case, one of the five main kinds of sociology. This in fact could be traced as an exercise in the history of ideas. I do not do that, because it is not the book's subject, but for convenience I will suggest the very briefest one-line summaries of those trends now, and they will be briefly expanded at the start of the next chapter. Thus the faery world of Spenser, it seems, derives from the same phenomenological-aesthetic perspective which later through

The Tempest and the hazier parts of Keats and other nineteenth-century writers comes out in phenomenology itself, and so leads to that recent branch of sociology known as social phenomenology, and its progeny ethnomethodology. The classical rationalism which is behind Pope is also the source for the functionalist or organic sociology of Durkheim, Weber and Parsons. The universe of intellectual passion and erotic love which led to Donne leads on also eventually to Freud and then to the synthesis, by G.H. Mead, of Freud with Durkheimian sociology which brings microscopic social interactionism. With Milton it is the uncompromising position of extreme Protestantism that brings the Civil War in Britain, the particular poem of will and struggle for power which is *Paradise Lost*, and the tradition of evangelical (Calvin, Bunyan) and then revolutionary thought which appears later as Marxism and the belief in the central inevitability of social change. With Wordsworth it is the nineteenth-century world of both natural science and industry which is the base both for the realist-romantic attitude to nature and also, eventually, the positivist, down-to-earth branch of sociology sometimes called social anthropology, but also, if rather tamely, 'community studies'. I hope to show from close reading of the poems that in each case the reality of the poetry is incompatible with the sociological idea, incompatible even with the sociological idea to which it might seem closest and with which it might seem to have had most affinity.

But there is something further. I want to suggest that the poetry not only is not, but could not possibly have been, compatible with the sociological idea. That is to say, the very nature of the poetry in each case, what constitutes it as poetry and makes us want to call it that, is precisely that in it which strains away from the sociological idea and the sociality of language; so that what we call 'poetry' precisely *is* the tension between language as it is socially conceived to be, and the poem that results. This point is clearly crucial, for otherwise the short answer to the claim that Spenser, for instance, eschews the sociological idea would be that that idea did not exist in the English Renaissance. We would then have to answer that that very absence enables the poetry that Spenser produced.

In the second half of the book, we come to the modern

period. If poetry is in some timeless sense incompatible with the sociological ideal of human existence, it is clearly in a special and embattled position in the era in which that idea dominates. Poetry was confident, expansive and epic, one might say, prior to the secularization of the modern world, and sociology's appearance. We can expect poetry, from this perspective, not merely to go on taking its outward-yearning aspiration, which it has always had, in the modern age, but to show some strain and self-consciousness when our social orientation in the modern world is a constant pressure. In the second half of the book I consider a number of modern poets, not any longer by the schematic method of seeing them in contrast to separate strands in the sociological tradition, but in terms of the various ways in which they combat that pressure explicitly.

Before starting on this argument it is necessary to make one very important stipulation, without which the whole enterprise might be misunderstood. In attempting to refute the easily-assumed relationship between poetry and 'society', the question is not one of whether poets do or do not embody the materials of the actual worlds or eras or cultures from which they stem. I am not at all saying that *The Faerie Queene* has *no* relation to the reality of Elizabethan England, or the *Iliad* to the Greece of three thousand years ago; in fact, we shall not really consider the point. Of course Spenser refers to actual people of his time, politically and otherwise; Herbert refers to the British Church and works within it; Horace and Juvenal draw material from the Roman *urbs*, as does Wang Wei from Chinese country and civil life; and Wilfred Owen the actual dreadful war of his age; and Arnold and Tennyson Victorian disbelief. But the question is that of whether the 'society' conception, the sociological idea, can possibly deal with those poetic usages. The poet, I suggest, does not write poetry to comment on 'society', rather he takes 'society' and uses it (among many other things) to make poetry, including poetry which may, along with several other things it does give the impression of commenting on human life and existence. Thus I would argue from a wholly different first position. I suggest that the very term, 'society', with which we so often describe these things, is now saturated sociologically, and it is therefore dangerous to talk, not of the Elizabethan Age or village life in the eighteenth century, but of 'the society of the poet's time'. I mean that I can agree that the poet in some sense reflects the society of his time so long as 'society' there retains a very commonsense, neutral, non-technical meaning. When the word means (as increasingly it does) society as sociologists understand that, then there is danger of begging the questions.

Perhaps we can briefly expand this argument. I have often found, in recent months and years, when talking about this subject, that there is what I see as a curious response to the matter. When I say to a friend or colleague that I think poetry and sociological thought are incompatible, the answer is often a thoughtful look and the remark, 'Surely a poet is necessarily related to the society of his time'. My objection is that that phrase itself is a diluted product of the sociological idea. What is 'the society of his time'? Where, for example, does it begin and end? In the context of the remark from my friend and colleague just quoted, it usually means something like, 'Everything people were doing and thinking and saying at the time; how politics affected them, how culture and customs did, and food, dress, and music; how people in families or at the monarch's court or in trades got on with each other'. But if this is so, then either 'the society of his time' simply and uselessly means 'everything', and is not specifically sociological at all, (rather it is anthropological, or socio-historical), or the speaker is seeing all those things (food, friendship, absolutely everything) through the eyes of the sociological idea, an idea which did not exist in the eras named.

Does the user of the phrase include the 'society's' religious beliefs, and their actual content? Does he reject them if he disbelieves them himself, and count them less important than the 'society' did? How far do non-social things — food, minerals, hallucinations, clouds, ideas, mathematical relations, postulated divine entities — affect the social dimension? Or is the whole question begged and the assumption made that all those things are primarily social anyway? When Spenser writes about mediaeval dragons and knights, and about the 'vertues' suggested by the ancient Greek Aristotle well over a thousand years earlier, how do we distinguish the parts of Spenser that are from the society of his time from those that are not? Could it not be that Aristotle and the dragons are actually more fundamental to Spenser's poetry than are the sociological features of his time, whatever those may be? And finally, most important for poetry, perhaps more important than an understanding of poetry than is anything else; what is to prevent the poet arranging words in any way whatsoever that yields pleasure, deep peace, disturbance, rhythmic order, physical and sensuous experience, or anything else? Why do we think the poet gets samples of those notions only from the society of his time, and not from the world of his time, let alone other parts of the world? Why is the poet to be constrained by the narrow and arguably over-rational conceptions of the function of language that have been put forward by adherents of the sociological idea? Of course in some sense the poet is related to the society of his time; but that is merely to say that he lived, wrote and died in our world. Whether he was related to the society of his time in a meaning acceptable to the sociological idea, is a quite different matter.

A poet looks at a river: Spenser, for example, looks at the Thames, as later does Eliot. Is the river itself part of the 'society of the time'? In several ways at least, manifestly not; it preceded the society and will survive it, and is is any case entirely physical, at least part of which physicality is not man-made. So then is it the poet's conceptions of the river that are merely assumptions of the society of his time? Does he perceive solely what convention tells him to perceive? It is precisely the defining characteristic of poetry — making — that the poet takes the perceptions that he has and the associative, material and other qualities of words to capture anything *but* the conventions of the society of his time, and to put them into language that will surprise by not using those conventions. This does not mean that the poet will simply combat those conventions (as the 'derangement' theory of Macherey and others suggests) for that, if universal, would mean that the poem was defined by the society of its origin though simply in exact reverse. My argument is that to a considerable extent the poet is neutral toward these conventions. They are part of his material; they may be useful material for him to deploy or they may not. And this is a matter of fundamental importance for human experience and for knowledge. The sociological idea of the modern world attempts to describe what gives us the widespread phenomenon of human coherence. It is natural that the sociological idea will see human language as one central mechanism by which that coherence is achieved, and will assume that language is always used, consciously or otherwise, toward people's ideas of that end. But there are surely other ideas of language than simply that of the sociological. For the poet, language has its own being; it is physical, psychological, social, and more than all three; each word has a unique history; language is to be savoured, loved, mulled over and newly arranged; and those are not interactive or discursive uses, nor are they necessarily concerned to attack or defend social institutions. If we find that language in poems simply does not conform to what contemporary sociology conceives language to be, then I think we must give credence to the experience the poem, not its sociology, gives us.

Language itself is thrust into existence by modes of cognition other than the sociological, and this renders language itself qualitatively different from what sociology, it sometimes seems, would have it. Epics, sacred books, history, philosophy, fiction, all in their different ways attempt to subsume the experience both of what we, now, call society, and of other things. All do this through language, and make language available for poetic use. The sociological concept of 'society' has no claim to offer a more fundamental explanation of the origin of poetic language than any other. Rather, I suggest it has the least claim. For it abstracts both language and social category (such as 'interaction', 'relationship', and 'institution') from the actual occasions of their occurrence. Sociology thus analyses — legitimately — exactly those aspects of language which poetry primarily does not demonstrate. We must decide on one or the other, or we must, in our always imperfect human situation, allow the two to exist at odds in our minds, unreconciled.

CHAPTER 2

THE FIVE TYPES OF SOCIOLOGY

In this chapter I undertake the first task, that of trying to summarize the intellectual features of the main types of sociology, in order to show how all contribute to, and underpin, the general conception which is the 'sociological idea'. We will not describe how they came into existence, for it is enough to recall as background simply that sociology is a product of certain events and intellectual trends in the last two centuries: these were the age of enlightenment and the scientific method and attitude; the secularization of the world; and the age of revolutions both political and industrial, which freed people to consider what sort of state they wanted rather than accepting that as God-given or sanctioned by original myth. It also gave them the technological means to bring about such bodies politic as far as human error, frailty and malevolence did not prevent it. It seemed to Comte and Durkheim that the range of human sciences revealed a gap in their number, and that a study of societies would reveal reliable social laws which themselves could provide guides to future social organization. At this point the aim is not to make any comment about poetry except incidentally and conveniently, but simply to lay out in organized fashion the areas of sociology we shall need to bear in mind later.

We can begin by naming sociology's main traditions. It is usual to see five, although there are some overlaps between them. First there is what is commonly called 'grand theory', or macrosociology, which is characterized by a positivistic concern to see theoretically how whole societies are constituted and thereby maintain coherence. (By 'positivist' I mean concerned to postulate an objective entity which the observer can study detachedly.) Secondly, at the other end of the scale, there is social interactionism, which focuses on not the largest but the smallest possible unit which is nonetheless social; actual interactions between individual people. These sociologists are as it were the atomic physicists of society; they are still positivistic. Thirdly there is social anthropology, whose main characteristic is its wholesale empiricism. While still using such abstractions as 'society', 'class', 'relationship', and the whole sociological gamut, social anthropology nonetheless begins and ends with the study of actual communities, neighbourhoods, industries and other palpable social groupings and settlements that do exist, and describes them to some extent in tangible terms. Fourthly there is the recent and quite different approach of reflexive sociology. That term embraces social phenomenology, ethnomethodology, cognitive sociology and some other aspects. Its chief characteristic lies in its interest in how society is itself constituted by our consciousnesses, and it is reflexive in that it tends to see society as the sum total of what all (social) members think it is. Finally there is Marxism, and here we are talking of a mode of thought not wholly sociological, and which is conceived of as a unique event in history itself. Marxism implies a certain kind of revolutionary sociology, however (that is, a sociology taking revolution as axiomatic) and implies that this is necessarily sociological. I will summarize these areas in that order, attempting to show how each contributes to and supports the 'sociological idea'.

The first and essential component of sociology as the study of society is the projection of that entity, 'society', as an autonomous thing separate from both nature and individuals, and amenable to objective study in some ways analogous to that of the natural sciences. The most explicit statement of this is found in Durkheim. After the French Revolution, and during the industrial revolution more widely, the question of how human collectivity is to be able to attain and keep an order and coherence when the traditional world has necessarily disappeared, becomes paramount. But those revolutions are themselves illustrative embodiments of the changing of that world from one which has had, as it were, profound respect for and adherence to age-old particularities — actual mythic explanations of our origin; churches; actual aristocracies. When the opportunity and necessity appear for man to decide what sort of society he wants — as though there are 'sorts of society' from which one or more may be chosen — the central question arises for philosophy: what is 'society' anyway? What is it for man, apparently so individual and wilful, to cohere? What sort of morality enables this? Such questions are at the heart of Durkheim's work. In his *Rules Of Sociological Method* Durkheim gives us his famous injunction to 'consider social facts as things (*choses*)', and this comes as near as any sociologist does in any school to imputing a metaphysical reality or quasi-substance to society. Durkheim disclaims such an intention, yet undoubtedly imputes to society an objective quality which is retained by all positivist sociologists to greater or less extent thereafter. For Durkheim society is prior to the individual, it is greater and more than the total of individual consciousness or wills, it does not answer to the individual's needs nor is it the object of his will itself.[1] Thus — and this is crucial for my argument — all nations and communities that have existed exemplify not merely their unique myth-of-origin, their particular monarchy or oligarchy, their own customs and tangible procedures and activities. They also exemplify 'society', they are societies and are characterized, as it were under the surface, by discoverable laws or facts about the irreducible realities of social organization, and social behaviour.

In *The Division of Labour in Society* these ideas, though made less explicit than in his other writings, are essential to Durkheim's description of the way that older (mechanically solid) and modern (organically solid) societies maintain that characteristic which confirms the obduracy of society as a reality: social coherence itself. In *Suicide* Durkheim uses a statistical approach to the study of that phenomenon to illustrate not only certain realities, but also the very existence of the fact of such realities, by measuring the rate of occurrence of what is, presumably, the most uncompromising departure from such realities as one could imagine. We shall refer to *Suicide* in Part III when dealing with certain poets of our time such as Hardy, Berryman and Sylvia Plath. Durkheim's position is diametrically opposed to theirs. These 'realities' to which I vaguely refer — meaning of course the objective components of societies — are far from vague for Durkheim, who saw them as:

... real, living, active forces which, because of the way they determine the individual, prove their independence of him. . . . Thus it will appear more clearly why sociology can and must be objective, since it deals with realities as definite and substantial as those of the psychologist or biologist.[2]

In the Elementary Forms of the Religious Life Durkheim finds an even more striking suggestion of society's huge reality, overhanging the individual much like Wordsworth's 'huge peak, black and huge . . .' which the rower of the stolen boat felt 'striding after me'. For Durkheim society, unwittingly to man, has been the object of man's religious worship in past ages. Durkheim cannot allow the supernatural to be the object of religious worship, yet equally he cannot, as he himself says, dismiss this central phenomenon of centuries as merely a delusion, an approach by man to a phantom or dream. Thus for Durkheim, unlike for Arnold or Baudelaire, it is not poetry but the sociological idea that replaces the religious one.

Solidarity, moral unity, social coherence, collective consciousness; these are Durkheim's concerns, and in his work they inescapably imply the sociological idea itself. Weber's concerns were in many ways different from Durkheim's, but the resulting need to produce sociological generalizations helped to enrol Weber as a contributor to the evolution of that idea as much as Durkheim, if in a different way. Weber wanted to analyse the political structure of nineteenth-century Germany and particularly the decline of the ability of the Junkers landowners to provide political leadership; and this led him to consider the development of Western 'rational capitalism' more generally, finally elaborating a theoretical method that is fully sociological. Thus his theoretical work can be seen as stemming from a historical context, as did Durkheim's. It is true that in Weber's case the resulting central sociological category is, not Durkheim's objective 'society' so confidently asserted, but the concept of 'meaningful social action' as a general process the aspects of which the sociologist is to look for. But when it is regarded as a permanent thing this constitutes a social reality, in the sense this book is deducing from sociology, no less than does Durkheim's 'society'; and this is even though Weber imputes no quasi-metaphysical existence to it, nor the power more or less of taking initiative. What I want to emphasize — not that this is very original — is that what has often been seen as an ambivalence and even a conflict in Weber's thought, can be seen as the gradual but relentless change, by a late nineteenth-century thinker, from the position of a historian to that of a sociologist. This becomes extremely important later in our argument, for it can be directly contrasted to the responses of Eliot and Pound to more or less the same thing. Weber's wish to analyse the overwhelming changes of his time led him to elaborate a method of analysis by which generalizations could be made from historical evidence. This method is the now classic idea of the 'ideal-type' by which, as a device only, a generalized model of a social phenomenon (such as rational authority, charismatic leadership, etc.) is built up from many historical examples none of which fits exactly in the unique case.[3] 'As a device only' is an admittedly repeated emphasis of Weber himself; he did not believe in any objective existence of these types. On the other hand he did believe in the validity of generalization about human behaviour, holding that the vast majority of occasions of human behaviour are predictable, and that the continuation of human societies depended on that fact. And furthermore, although Weber believed that social investigation could never demonstrate what one *ought* to do (which ruled out any possibility of a scientific study of values), this very conclusion meant, naturally, that such investigation was objective and at least analogous to science, even if Weber saw far less analogy with the natural sciences than Durkheim did. The central question about Weber therefore is, from the point of view of this chapter: what status do we give to his categories, both those functioning as analytical tools — social action, social relationships, and types of action (rational, affectual, traditional, and so on)— and those resulting as generalizations from his studies of history — rational, traditional and charismatic authority, bureaucratization, routinization, and all of that kind? Do these 'exist', or are they, as he insisted, analytical devices? I want to argue that they exist in the sense that they, or concepts which function in the same way, have passed into contemporary life and thought, and on which we now rely. Even so, that oversimplifies Weber even more than my necessarily cursory remarks warrant. The further point is that Weber saw his 'meaningful social action' as analysable rationally, in a society which was itself increasingly rational (in the sense of susceptible to the influence of bureaucratization and science) in organization at all levels. He therefore laid the way open for us to say what he himself did not, that the bureaucratization and rationalization of life itself enabled precisely the intellectual attitude and approach which he himself then developed in his methodology. Thus in saying that all sociological investigation is interpretative, Weber means that it is rationally so, and also that social behaviour itself is broadly to be regarded as, if not always rational, a matter nevertheless of interpretative understanding. At some level the socially acting individual must 'understand' the circumstances of his action, and the people toward whom he acts, for it to be meaningful. Now if this is true then there are regularities derivable from the 'understanding' we always employ, particularly in that such understanding is by no means always simply traditional; and these regularities will increasingly have some dependable status. The aspiration to that sort of sociological understanding from history is exactly opposite to that attempted by Eliot and Pound. (This will be discussed in Part III.)

Durkheim and Weber thus began to establish sets of categories by which to analyse social reality. Insofar as we instinctively use them we believe in the existence of the social as understood by the sociological idea. Both Durkheim and Weber, however, still referred *passim* to the actual world; its details and tangible face. *The Elementary Forms*, and at least such work as *The Protestant Ethic and The Spirit of Capitalism*, are both rooted in things; the animals and birds used in the taboo system of primitive tribal existence; actual examples of the effects of Scripture and the components of ascetic life and the influence of European industry and invention on individual Calvinists and Lutherans. With Talcott Parsons the formal elaboration of a wholly abstract social system, devoid of any historical or illustrative material whatsoever, reaches a development beyond which it cannot go. The social and sociological idea touch saturation point.

One might begin by saying, a little wryly, that a summary of Parsons' two main works, the eight-hundred-page *The Structure of Social Action*[4] and the more abrupt (five-hundred and fifty-page) but even more abstract *The Social System* is not possible here. Parsons began his work at Harvard in the 1930s and massively dominated both American sociology and, ever increasingly, the more pragmatic and empirical British version for nearly three decades until the 'reflexive revolution' (and the resurgence of Marxism) in the sixties. He began during the Depression and, it is said, thereby felt the motivation to achieve a vast, convincing description, through a conceptual scheme, of the stable features and equilibrium of the social order. Again therefore he began, like Durkheim and Weber, in response to a historical predicament, although with Parsons the significance of that actual historical period seems less important than the wider and underpinning values of Protestant capitalism in America; that at least has often been imputed. The view also that Parsons' use of language is compulsively complex in its pursuance of the logical details of every possible component of his abstract scheme — put more bluntly, that he is pretentious and unreadable — is understandable but misleading. His work can only be taken as an aspiration to a *Summa Totius Sociologiae*, and indeed a secular Word. The view that our profane and self-examining world is susceptible to an adequate description, in language, of its underlying structure which constrains the social consciousness of every person, has drastic implications for every other sort of Word and every other truth-aspiring use of language.

This is essentially so in that Parsons is huge and unified. Even 'social change' in Parsons seems a static, Platonic conception. The claim of his first major book, *The Structure of Social Action*, is that his theory of social action derives from Durkheim and Weber and indeed Marshall and Pareto as well, and that these are in no way incompatible with one another. The theory, reduced to three lines, is that social action is rational; voluntaristic; utilitarian in that it adopts means to get to ends; and is based on norms derived from values. These last are mediated through ritual, religion, 'moral reality' or some other configuration. Parsons' repeated insistence that the founding fathers are in essential agreement is supportive to his claims to the possibility of, and perhaps his own success in, writing a total sociological theory. Again he is tentative, like Weber, in calling this a 'conceptual scheme' — he is not Durkheimian in this respect — but again the status of his statements has to be considered. If those who did appear at the time of the nineteenth-century sociological enlightenment— man's new sociological awareness; a 'momentous reorientation of European thought'; as Nisbet calls it[5] — were in agreement despite total independence (for Durkheim and Weber did not even know of each other's work), then, if society accepts that it is social, we have in Parsons a statement which to all intents and purposes *is the case*; a true description of social reality; and one which permeates, as it did until more recent developments, the thinking and social conception of the ordinary individual.

Parsons' work was elaborated in a series of later books prior to *The Social System*. I summarize it here particularly to illustrate the *binary* quality of Parsons' thought, which we will later compare with the same tendency in Pope's poetry. In Parsons the 'action' emphasis declines and the 'system' emphasis ascends as the *oeuvre* proceeds. The social system's first subdivision is that of the four functional requisites by which such a system is maintained: *pattern-maintenance*, such that central features do remain in equilibrium over time and thus stay recognizable (kinship and certain organizational features are conducive to this): *integration-expression,* such that the system expresses its integration back to itself through the culture, law, religion and other symbolic features: *goal-direction*, in that the system has a teleological orientation to its activities, responsibility for which is held by government: and *resource-adaptation*, by which physical, utilitarian and other resources are rendered applicable in goal-directed activity, and this is the role of the economy. Overriding values monitor all this and are not 'situation-specific'; they therefore require more particular norms for their interpretation in smaller and more local incidents. The formal organizations which carry out these separate functions themselves depend for success on the presence of all four functions, in each subsidiary institution, working on a smaller scale. The sub-dividing and 'binary' tendency in Parsons' thought is clear enough. The system of interactions between individuals is maintained in an equilibrium functional to the overall system's integration. Within the overall system there is an elaborate differentiation of roles so that the necessary plurality of functions is in fact carried out; furthermore the differentiation of roles individuals are required to play is achieved by a contrasting sharing of values. It is a characteristic of Parsons' position also that he asserts that what an individual has functionally to do he does in fact normally desire to do. The Socratic rather than Pauline or Ovidian quality of that scarcely needs remarking.

But if the social system can be characterized, and in huge if abstract detail, how is it voluntaristic? Parsons' answer to this, the last part of this theory I will attempt to summarize, again takes up much of *The Social System*, and again it is binary. This is the 'pattern-variable' system of fulfilling role-expectations. In describing it I will try to avoid blinding the layman with sociological science as far as possible. In any dealings with other people the individual is a free man, yet the system's consistency must also be maintained. This is crucial, for Parsons (a good American Protestant) wants to reassure us that we are all free while still retaining the sociological idea. The contradiction can be reconciled if we say that the individual has a *dual* choice in any circumstance, yet that it is still a choice: he can only do either A or B, but he *can* do either. Now according to Parsons any situation he may meet confronts the actor with five simultaneous choices of this kind; no more, no less, and on these depend the 'pattern-variables'. Does the individual approach the action as his unique self or as an example of the group to which he belongs (teachers, farmers, parents, etc?) Does he do it to help himself or to help that group (or any group)? Does he treat the situation and role as finite (ending when the immediate task is over, like someone making a purchase) or extending indefinitely, like for example a priest, who might be expected to renew comfort and guidance endlessly? And there are two more choices. Parsons' point is that the individual freely decides which of the two mutually exclusive alternatives to take in any immediate context, but that the entire structure of those five dual choices comes from outside, so that the overall system can tolerate any combination of the five choices made. Those who disagree with Parsons say that, in reality, there is no choice, and that social constraints are 'internalized' simply by voluntary submission. But what cannot be over-emphasized is that we see here the sociological idea reaching its consummation — the very constraint of the social dimension itself.

We will later compare Parsons' cast of thought with that of Pope, and it is precisely the non-poeticality of Parsons' language that most symptomizes this sociological domination. Even the reader unfamiliar with sociological thought will, presumably, see easily enough what the conception 'society', as an object of study, implies in contrast to real, living persons and embodied individuals. The paradox is that 'society' on the large-scale and positivist arguments of Durkheim, Weber and Parsons seems not to consist of people at all, but to exist over and against people and constraining them. The constraints are not those of force but of structure and logic. 'Society', analysed, is an abstraction. We can at no point see it or touch it, or say 'There! *That* is society! Yet this huge abstraction apparently constrains us. It is not surprising that some sociologists began to baulk at this quite early. However, in going on now to discuss these others, my aim is to show that they too remain, willingly indeed, sociologists, devotees of the social and the sociological idea, and that this idea in them too congeals into a reification, a 'thing' of its own.

In contrast to this huge abstract thing hanging over us, the branch of sociology known conveniently as social interactionism gives its attention to not the very largest, but the very smallest, unit of behaviour which can properly be called 'social', the interaction between two people. The seminal influence in this approach was the work of G.H. Mead done in Chicago in the 1930s. He wanted to discover how the whole huge entity of society was constituted in the light of our knowledge of the psychological characteristics of the individual as described by, in the main, Freud. The question was how in small-scale processes the individual could articulate with society by relating to other individuals. Mead probed this question with great feeling and sensitivity; his writing seems totally absorbed in the subject.[6] Mead believed that the mind and self are social products. In this he wholly accepted Durkheim's view of the autonomy of society. But the production of self and mind occurred by, as Mead called it, 'taking the role of the other'; that is to say, the individual came to see and grasp his own self by perceiving the understanding others had of that self. As a result the 'I' and the 'me' became separated in the individual's perceptions, and the individual, as Mead put it, 'came across' his self, as it were stumbled across it. Mead's view was his answer to the contemporary vogue of psychological behaviourism; and he saw a parallelling between the individual's consciousness and his organism (thus for example in sleep the consciousness stops but the organism goes on. Thus they are parallel but not interpenetrative.) Mead also had important insights into the actual processes of this generation of the self, as for example through the nature of language, gesture and symbol. As Mead saw, language does not merely symbolize the object to which it refers. It makes possible that object's emergence. We shall consider this point more closely in talking later of poetry, but the important thing here, too, is that Mead clearly gives dominance to the 'social', this time in the sense that it is our socially originated language that calls objects out from their undifferentiated background into perceived existence. However, Mead did not pin-point these microscopic categories as quasi-objects specifically. That was left to theorists of the fundamental concepts of this school as it later emerged: role, group and interaction.

'Interaction' as itself a near-autonomous entity is proposed by Howard Blumer,[7] and his description of this is uncompromising. According to Blumer, humans act toward things according to the meanings those things yield for us, and such meanings derive from (sic) interactions with other people. Meanings are neither physical accretions, nor are they inherent in the things themselves. They derive from a social origin. (If a poem is a 'thing', a point not yet established, Blumer's view is exactly opposed to that of T.S. Eliot in the quotation at the start of this book.) According to Blumer, both the wider sociological ideas of institution, status and so on, and the psychological schema of motivation, attitude and the rest, fail insofar as they turn interaction into a mere forum through which these things pass. To use another image: interaction is the bar of a dumb-bell or pair of weights the bar holding the weights both together and apart. Interaction simply is the central social reality.

'Role' is in a sense a static parallel to the dynamic of interaction. Role theory has, perhaps, been considerably superseded in sociological theory now, because the derivations of the interaction school in social phenomenology and ethnomethodology (see below) focus so greatly on the subjective interpretations of the individual, and the social origins of such interpretation by a different route. Yet the role concept, as used by Linton, Sarbin, Levinson and indeed Parsons and Merton,[8] gained a quasi-substantial connotation even greater than that of interaction. Roles existed: you could take them, play them, enumerate them, put them on and put them off. A role is a piece of expected behaviour or set of expected behaviours, over and above any actual occasion of its playing. Most role theory in the writers named was largely classificatory. In a sense the very projection of the notion of role as an entity, a *'chose'* in Durkheim's term, left nothing further to analyse, for that would have entailed analysing something the theorist had himself dreamt up. Ideally the concept was used as an analytical tool; again, however, its ready use in sociology and its importance in ordinary life became an actual burden-carrying constraint on those who felt its pressure. ('I'm not sure what my role is on the Parish Council. Some people seem to think it is adviser, some just treat me as a stranger', etc.) The furthest-out use of the concept comes in Merton's highly intriguing notion of the 'role-set', those several persons to whom *one* role is severally played, not to be confused with 'multiple roles', the many roles one person is called upon to play in his round of life. With role theory, 'small group' theory postulated the small face-to-face group of seven or so members as an objective entity over and above those members.

Again then, and just like the conceptions whose centrality these so hotly contest, these microscopic conceptions have an obdurate quality when that is imputed to them. The battle, in fact, is for the same desired prize, the centrality of the sociological idea itself. Interactions become 'real'; and as such, although it may sound paradoxical, they are by that very fact differentiated from the materially real world of people, living bodies, clothes, shops, food, languages and books. Our later remarks about language in poetry will bear in mind Mead's remarks on language, and also the impossibility of a poem constituting an interaction except in the sense of mediating one like any object, a car-key, or cabbage, can. I have doubtless done little justice here to Mead's concerns, nor to social interactionism's overlap with social psychology, the importance of 'reciprocity', Goffman's 'presentation of self',[9] and some other well-known conceptions. But the power of the sociological concept to take on a reality which is all the more demarcated from material reality, is made very apparent by social interactionism. That very point is of course taken up by Reflexive Sociology, which will be discussed in due course. To suggest how poetry seems at odds with social interactionism we shall consider Donne. (The next branch to discuss, social anthropology, will bring in Wordsworth.)

The remaining branch of sociology with a clear positivist attachment, social anthropology, is the only one of that kind which does saturate itself with material and with down-to-earth reference as a matter of central method. Social anthropology, which in Britain has been roughly synonymous with the 'community studies' movement, descends from the peculiar British traditions of early twentieth-century highly empirical sociology with largely practical motives, and from British anthropology. The close association of this early sociology with motives of amelioration ('relief of the poor') and more specifically with, for example, the Town Planning movement, is coupled with its empirical, often statistical methods. Early studies are the large-scale statistical investigations of Booth, Rowntree and Hobhouse. Insofar as it is theoretical it is based on social evolutionism, a branch of sociology clearly amenable to a close identity with practical social betterment.

One intellectual feature is the key to this kind of sociology. If one takes a *wholly* empirical attitude, then by that very fact one cannot allow *a priori* theoretical assumptions behind one's investigations. Two things follow from this. The first and most important is that the information gathered will not itself be couched in, nor necessarily even be appropriately arranged for, sociological theorizing in the narrow sense. Put more practically: if you ask people direct questions about their lives, they will probably not answer in sociological abstractions, or indeed in social terms, simply on their own; they may also talk of money, sport, bread and birthdays, for that is what may be important to them. The second implication assists this, and it is that the absence of pre-judgements about what is important prevents also the placing of a conceptual boundary on the object of one's attention. The result is that what is studied is the *whole* community. There is no reason for omitting any area or aspect of, for example, Banbury, Westrigg, Ashton, Swansea, Africa or the American suburb. Thus the characteristic and central 'community studies' that have appeared in Britain are based not on conceptual divisions, or the wish to examine a theory, but on entire actual places; as Frankenberg in particular showed in his early work.[10] The characteristic opening chapter of such studies is far removed from, for example, Parsons' theoretical concerns. It is invariably a discursive and impressionistic description of the layout of the town itself, its factories, recreation-grounds and housing estates, natural features like hills and rivers, and something of the colour of local life: mums pushing prams in the park, smoke blowing across from the chemical plant and crowds in the busy shopping arcade. This fact is clearly connected to the great emphasis always placed in such studies on family and kinship, for the family is the social group which is most fundamentally defined by physical, that is biological, facts, and for whom at least some degree of continuous residence over time in the same place has usually been regarded as important, if not essential, in community maintenance. As it has been put, the subject of community studies is not that of their approximation to an ideal but the structure of relationships between institutions in a locality; that is, a physical area.[11]

This kind of sociology therefore might seem most to challenge the view of the dominance of the central abstraction: the sociological idea. But it is precisely the dalliance with the physical realities of life that most perversely, in the end, confirms the sociological idea, for the fact remains that, insofar as social anthropology stays recognizable as sociology at all, it is still *social* anthropology. Unlike anthropology proper, the study of man and culture, social anthropology always returns to the matter of how the physical constraints do nonetheless help generate life according to the sociological, theoretical categories of class, conflict, group existence, roles and relationships, socialization, and the generalized features of even more specific phenomena such as religion, the economy and cultural activities. The answer becomes a question: what is the difference between 'anthropology' and 'social anthropology' but the sociological idea? In short, the comparative approach of social anthropology turns out to be premised on the expectation of the emergence of evidence relevant to the general characteristics of sociological theory. It turns out that the discussion thus comes full circle, in that it is only the emphasis on empiricism in method that led social anthropologists to their particular kinds of research discovery in the first place. Their aim always was to cash those findings in sociological terms.

Social anthropology, and community studies, gradually came to use sociological concepts as they progressed and attained enough material for generalization. (Much of this was summarized by Frankenberg.) Furthermore, aspects of communities, rather than whole communities, begin to occupy the whole attention deliberately, such as 'neighbours', 'middle-class families', and 'adolescents in East London'. The real clue to the inherently sociological nature of social anthropology, on top of all that has been said, is found in its original use of and interest in the 'community' as a concept; how in fact groups of people may still have varied features of culture and life, yet remain communal. That quickly becomes a very Durkheimian emphasis, and in Britain a class emphasis; and class, social mobility resulting from changed status, and the effects of this on kinship, all become inevitably drawn out of the empirically-researched background.

I hope these remarks give an adequate enough survey of the main theme of social anthropology as it has appeared over a few decades. But an important development has also occurred with increasing implications for social anthropology, even possibly threatening its existence, and for completeness' sake should be mentioned. In a world where the boundaries of stable communities are eroded by media, technology, immigration and many other things, it becomes increasingly impossible for social anthropologists to keep up the empiricist premise insofar as that results in the unboundedness of the object to be studied. If no *a priori* theoretical position decides what is to be studied, the study must include every aspect of the community: we have said this already. This is (theoretically) easy enough when the object of study is clearly bounded, such as a village or tribe. But with the huge contemporary conurbation or megalopolis the social anthropologist either must curtail the object of study *a priori* after all, or attempt to study the whole thing, a total impossibility if empirical evidence is what is sought. This inability to study the whole community, if it still is one, is parallelled by the inability of the community itself to remain a community on the old bases of isolation, its own economic (often wholly agricultural) underpinning and normative control. Even when a community appears isolated, such as a provincial town, its institutions are increasingly controlled from outside and its population subjected to quick ingoing and outgoing mobility. In a conurbation there is not even that degree of distinctiveness.

Social anthropologists have dealt with this problem in a number of ways. They have first looked at how communal areas such as neighbourhoods have subsisted in the larger conurbation, and secondly at how social groups in the conurbation behave, again, and as always with social anthropology, in terms of their actual (non-social, physical) base. Thus one reads articles like 'A Sociology of the New York Taxi-Driver', and 'Sociology of Football Hooliganism'. The defining characteristic of the subject studied is its relation to the used, physical world, rather than to a sociological category such as role, conflict or on-going account. Other subjects have been for instance jokes, motorbike gangs and blood-donors, as well as the wider but still physically based phenomena of surburbia, leisure and of course industry. But the outcome is still this: that insofar as the social anthropologist still imports sociological concepts to support his or her explanations, the comment on this work is as the earlier comment on social anthropology. On the other hand, insofar as the researcher is himself drawn into the sub-culture studied, so does the study cease strictly to be sociology; it may move toward a loose 'cultural studies'[12] or toward pure anthropology or structuralism.

So social anthropology too, if by a more roundabout route, aspires to contribute toward a fully sociological theory. But in the last decade a kind of sociology has arisen that calls the entire assumptions of all previous sociology into question, and indeed it could therefore less be called a new branch of sociology than a wholly new orientation to it, and within it. For a convenient title I will again call this Reflexive Sociology. It has great importance for this study because of the challenge already mentioned, because it is the most recent large-scale influence, and especially also because it, more than any previous sociology, wants to examine the position of language at the heart of social activity.

This sociology is reflexive rather than positivistic because it takes as its starting-point the recognition that what people think 'society' in its various aspects is, will itself then deeply affect their behaviour in society. And that behaviour is itself clearly a basic constituent of the very society they have their attitudes towards and views about. This furthermore has a profound implication for sociology itself, in that such a sociology is necessarily a consideration of how not only the 'ordinary man' understands society, his activities, his relationships, his day-to-day experience of social reality (and indeed all reality), but how the professional or vocational student of that does too; the social scientist and sociologist. For they too see themselves as members of society, taking socially-originated stances toward the society prior to any professional cast in their overt exploration. The whole analogy between social and natural science, hitherto not by any means unquestioned but certainly presumed by most ordinary sociologists to be tentatively valid, seems to break down. The positivist projection of 'society', as that which is to be studied, suddenly cannot be taken for granted but itself becomes the object or problem to be studied — so, in parallel fashion, does the question of how the so-called (and assumed) ordinary man also takes for granted large areas of social reality in his common-sense attitude.

Not surprisingly, the attempt to challenge positivism in sociology found itself using the theories and ideas of those thinkers who descend largely from the pre-positivist position of Hegel. When that huge shadow of the Absolute Idea ceased to hold sway, and both the objectivities of science and the Marxist inversion occurred, an aspiration to an idealist or transcendental attitude had to re-start from a consideration of cognition as itself subjective and as, so to speak, having initiative. Any credibility that idealism could have would need to stem from some convincing account of how man's actual cognitions, in individual people, were more than mere receptions of sense-impressions. How this line of thought developed to a point where it could help constitute a picture of the social order necessitates a brief comment on the work of Husserl and Merleau-Ponty.[13] These are precursors to the group I see as the centre of gravity of the new reflexive sociology, namely, the ethnomethodologists; not that the latter are necessarily the most convincing, but that they most drastically and radically put the challenge to sociology as hitherto seen. Husserl, in effect, was able to offer an alternative suggestion to that of mere sense-rejection without however resorting to the Hegelian idea or Kantian categorical imperatives, (not that he simply rejected these) by emphasizing the pre-eminence of 'seeing' in itself. Subjective seeing could be regarded as in fact reliable. To see and make a mistake is possible, but to see and deny one has seen anything at all is clearly absurd. The point applies in the realm of ideas, cogitations themselves, as well as physical objects. By eidetic reduction, or 'bracketing' (which may be compared to looking at for example a chair, then closing your eyes and considering the *cogitatum* that remains), the thing seen, that phenomenon, can then be a reliable object of study. The important emphasis in Husserl for later sociologists was this emphasis on positive, subjective (not merely receptive) seeing as itself a fundamental element in human existence. But furthermore the human mind, cogitation, is intentional; it leans forward to its object, it is deliberate toward it. In no other way could we say how the seeing mind 'reaches' the thing seen. These ideas were taken forward by Merleau-Ponty, who also emphasized perception's primary position in our condition in the world. Yet for Merleau-Ponty, although perception is as it were our last reliable activity and apparent perceptions therefore our only trustworthy source of data, this does not mean the world is mere dream. We are immersed in the world, intentional to it. Man is not merely 'in' space; he haunts it. It is not merely 'out there'; we are part and parcel of it.

This brings us to the first sociological phenomenologist,

Alfred Schutz. By Husserl and Merleau-Ponty—not to mention Bergson, Weber and many others—Schutz was furnished with certain orientations to what he called 'the problem of social reality',[14] and to which his between-wars studies directed their entire attention. The common-sense world, whose nature Schutz sought, *is* such a world in the sense that its presence and nature, and how we in it know other men's minds, is never questioned by common-sense man, by everyday man. This is because if seeing is both intentional and carries conviction, and if we feel ourselves to be *within* this world, located and set in it, then we cannot see it detachedly as the scientist does — from a null point, as Schutz puts it — except by a deliberate act of mind. That act will normally not occur, because we normally are and have to be intentional and projective and immersed in the everyday world; that is, the argument is self-defeating and circular. The position is simply that, in Schutz's words, we inhabit the 'vivid present', we bring our biographical situation, our sedimented past, our stock-of-knowledge-at-hand—all Schutz's terms—to actual encounters we experience. We experience the common-sense world by virtue of these conditions it contains which are in no sense discoverable externally, 'scientifically', but in which we find ourselves *ab initio* and into which we are born.

But how do we know this is *social*? How do I not assume my ego to be transcendent, and how do I feel sure that the world containing other people, and those people themselves, are obdurate, constitutive of that real world of people actually there? How do I know this without the positivist, Durkheimian attitude? To answer this we return to a crucial observation of Merleau-Ponty. He suggested that even in observing all phenomena as a kind of homogeneous array, we nevertheless experience entities in that array which seem to treat common phenomena in the way that we do and according to typical behaviours that we ourselves have practised. These other entities — other people, in short — are other subjectivities; they seem born in the midst of my phenomena and seem the only parts that tear at the otherwise seamless phenomenological fabric. As Merleau-Ponty puts it, from the depths of my subjectivity I experience another subjectivity invested with equal rights to myself and thus convincingly fellow to myself.

This experience cannot be denied and is primary; it is as I shall suggest fundamental to the social and sociological idea as attested by the reflexive approach and its phenomenological forbear. Schutz himself took on Merleau-Ponty's idea in the term 'appresentation'. By this Schutz meant that when I experience another person acting in the way that I sometimes do myself from the initiative of my mind, then I 'appresent' a mind to that other person. It is like the way that I 'fill in' the far side or back of a house when I look at it and see only this near side. This ability of the non-positivist, subjective and idealist twentieth-century attitude to become social, that is, to account for and allow the plurality of subjectivities, is a fountain-head for the development of the sociological idea as that on which we remainingly, reliably depend in an otherwise metaphysically barren world, a divinely barren universe. We can, apparently, allow the existence of the Other in a world where all knowledge is suspect and where the nature of knowing is itself the deepest philosophical, existential problem.

But even so, the work of Husserl, Merleau-Ponty and even Schutz, lays out only the bases for the attack of reflexive sociology on sociological positivism; it states its challenge rather than actually infiltrating the other position and disturbing its very heart. The work of Schutz would logically have to be answered, but equally it could merely be left as just another intellectual viewpoint. But the work of Harold Garfinkel and the ethnomethodologists went further. They seemed to take on and subvert sociology itself both as an intellectual enterprise and as a practice within the world. And they did this, or purported to do so, by uncovering the very nature of all social practice, sociology, the common-sense world, and other things included. In this respect this work had an impact on sociology analogous to, though naturally not as finally central as, that of Marxism. For this reason we will pay most attention to it, rather than to (for example) sociologies of formal knowledge, as examples of this kind of sociology.

Ethnomethodology, a term coined by Harold Garfinkel[15] in the late forties, was used by him to mean the study of 'members' practices' — how and in what sense members of society practise the very things that so constitute them as members. In a fair sense Garfinkel's starting-point can be seen as certain inferences from Schutz. If the bases of common-sense life are not questioned by the ordinary man (that very fact enabling it to remain common-sensical), but if also the positivistic stance toward social reality is vapid and necessarily belittling (both points made by Schutz), then what is the basis of any social knowledge we have, what is our social consciousness and self-consciousness? The ethnomethodologists asserted that the common-sense world and knowledge of that world are one and the same thing. Therefore to give an account of what we are doing is itself an in-built accompaniment of the doing of it. The recognition of a common-sense reality is part of, and nearly synonymous with, the socially organized occasion of its use. Thus there is no sense in which for example I can 'go on holiday' or 'get married' without having as part of the very event an account of the event, that account also constituting the event's possibility of reality. Without the accompanying rational account 'I am going on holiday', I could not *be* going on holiday. The ethnomethodologists thus believe that, inseparable from the common-sense activities that do in fact add up to the very ontology of our lives, there is a reflexive account of those activities. Such accounts are themselves constituted and reconstituted into existence as the activities are. Thus also, such acts of constitution are accomplishments, achievements and artful practices. They are rational too, but in this sense: not that they logically and *a priori* work out and predict their steps and then enact them, but rather in the sense that whatever activity is practised by common-sense, simultaneously generates also an account of itself. This account is reasonable for all practical purposes, that generating being also an artful practice.

The crucial point here is that there is no split between the doing and the accounting. The individual is not seen as doing something and also, separately, having knowledge or understanding of it. The account is generated within the circumference of the act itself. Common-sense knowledge is not 'known' but practised, and as such becomes reality, becomes true. The large-scale claim of this is that the social world is constituted and generated by its own members; it is both artful and creative. This claim has led to a parallel belief that sociology is itself creative, indeed, the pinnacle of creativity of our social life, and that the sociological account must itself be creative. It is man's lot, on this argument, not merely to observe or accredit a Platonic Reason, but to make reason; a rational account or *logos* of what he synonymously does. Advocates of this view in its various guises have been Brown, Nisbet and O'Neill.[16] We may say in passing that to describe poetry as giving such accounts would be quite misleading, for the 'account' a poem gives is of nothing other than itself. It is its own 'vivid present'. Yet O'Neill and Brown in particular talk, though not very specifically, of the poetic or poetry of sociology. It is remarkable that the poets who have most shared the basic phenomenological stance — Spenser and Stevens for example — have most emphasized how much poetry is neither factual nor historical, and indeed is a matter of fiction or metaphor. Whereas in the social world the 'account' is taken to be literally true; if it were not, at least to some extent, there would be no social consistency, or reliable action or order.

For our purpose here there are certain implications. The first is that sociologists themselves were held to be artfully practising in giving their accounts of life. Sociologists were members' dupes (sic) if they thought they were giving scientific or objective accounts of activity outside of themselves as constitutive, by their accounts, of such activity. Far from explaining certain practices, sociological accounts very often in effect brought those practices into existence. This, certainly, was not fraudulent or otherwise reprehensible, but might cause prejudgement by framing the phenomenon to be examined. The very framing was itself an achieved account before it started its investigation. The question for the ethnomethodologists was that of what produced the very data to be examined. Thus 'a study of teenage delinquency in disturbed homes' had already generated that account. The suggestions that some teenagers are delinquent and that their homes are disturbed (whatever those adjectives may mean) are themselves accounts, one stage further back, of phenomena already presumed. This very fundamental point suggests that in the constraints of the twentieth century, if this be widely practised, it is the sociological idea that is responsible for our account of ourselves. If sociology is a demonstration of the orderly properties of our achieved social arrangements then it, by demonstrating those orders, itself orders them. Sociology's praxis is our ordering principle.

Thus Garfinkel and the ethnomethodologists too, it turns out, reaffirm the sociological belief. The difference is that instead of postulating it as a huge prior entity, as do the positivists, they say that we incessantly bring it into existence. That does not make it any the less social or any the less permanent. Indeed our final point must be this: that what at first seemed a radical challenge to the sociological idea in the end confirms it as strongly as before. For if sociologists give 'ordinary people' explanations which make use of the sociological idea and those explanations are constitutive of the continuing social reality, then all the more it is true, *because achieved*, that our modern view of the world is indeed premised on this notion of the crucial, fundamental nature of the social dimension and order as opposed to other orders. This point will clearly be fundamental when we consider poetry in Part III, not only in the abstract but in its own relations with and response to the sociological idea as that has grown and become explicit in our time.

Before turning to the fifth aspect of the sociological idea, Marxism, we must briefly consider also the most important contribution of reflexive sociology to the considerations of this book, namely, its view of the place of language. The ethnomethodologists quickly saw that if social reality is basically constituted by the very act of our accounting of it, and yet that account is not positivistic, then an account of the very stuff of accounting, language itself, must be given. Language on this view is not an external reference to inner thoughts, or merely a signal of the interaction it accompanies. It constitutes such interactions. The language of ordinary discourse 'does by saying'; it does not merely pass information but is itself an achieving of the reality to which, in another sense, it might be said to 'refer'. Language is not an external interaction of grammar parallelling social interactions as something separate. It is, as Habermas puts it, wholly woven in with and an acknowledgement by people of each other. It refers not to dictionary meanings (rather they refer to it) but to things those who speak both know about and presume already exist. In short, language is, as sociologists put it, indexical to something already available even if not previously used on the particular occasion when any one language-act, dialogue or discourse occurs. Poetry indexes something never previously available. Language as rooted in ordinary discourse can be contrasted with poetic language which aspires to something wholly other.

And in finally carrying the discussion to Marxism as a fifth area of sociology we have, of course, to change our approach even more than hitherto; for Marxism may not be so much an area of sociological thought as rather — even if we take an academic-liberal position toward it — an event or system in history disposing Western thought toward the very possibility of sociology's existence. Marx did not merely dispute some previous theory, in the way that Durkheim for example suggested that man religiously worshipped not a divinity but society itself. Of course Marx disputed theory, but more importantly he changed, or is regarded by both strong and mild adherents as having changed, the very notion of the conditions of theorizing at all, suggesting not then that this or that philosophy was erroneous but that philosophy itself was inadequate. And yet again not even does that satisfactorily describe it, for the result of Marxist thought and the Marxist event is that philosophy is itself seen as a human praxis inherent in the historical process. This process produced both philosophy's exposure and the Marxist formulation of dialectical materialism itself: so that when Karl Marx himself thought this, he realized that that thought was itself an event in the very process he was describing.

Our concern here is simply to see how the sociological idea results to some degree from Marxism, not merely as something intellectually acceptable as a field of study but as a necessary historical emergence; as indeed an ideology too, legitimate enough when known to those who 'think' it. Marx did not postulate 'society' in the manner of Durkheim and Comte. That would itself have been a new essence-of-man theory like those from which Marx broke away. What Marx did was not merely to postulate but to force into history a certain view or ideology. This was that the struggle between men over the means of production of basic necessities for subsistence such as food and tools, and eventually money and wealth, and the division of men into combating classes, was itself the very thing that shaped history, indeed made possible the fact of history. The first implication is that Marx produced fundamentally not a sociological entity for study but a historical and economic one. From control or otherwise of economic realities men evolved, on the economic base, a political superstructure and at its peak the ideological cultural superstructure which included religious beliefs and 'pure' thought. All this is of course a text-book statement of elementary Marxism. But the result, or at least one result and that which concerns us here, is that if there is no longer an 'essence of man', all things being really reducible to their material base, and if also there is no divinity shaping our ends at some quite different level, then any study of man is left with only the relations between men which occur when this historical struggle between classes is being fought out. There are only relations between men at the social level as directed by relations, in history, at the economic level. If material (generalizable as soil, commodity or money) is all, yet clearly does not contain in itself, as such, consciousness of meaning, and awareness of other men's consciousness and action on that, then it must be social relationships that somehow contain in themselves those things which philosophers for centuries had scrutinized under the heading of pure thought, metaphysical reality, and so on. There is no social consciousness in material itself. The only reality for man other than the material must be the social. This furthermore cannot be individual (and therefore psychological) in any important way, for the separate individual is merely the occasion through which the historical process passes. If an individual misses or refuses his destined activity this merely postpones the inexorable process of history, it does not halt it or alter it radically. As Althusser has put it, Marx founded the science of the history of social formations.[17]

Thus in a sense we have taken Marx at his word. In looking at Marxism in the context of sociology, we have tried to see not what is his 'contribution' to sociology in an academic sense, but how as a process his redirection of thought-in-history helped precipitate the very conditions wherein the sociological idea could arise. Of course Comte and Durkheim also gave us the sociological idea, but they did so within the shape of traditional thinking. From them it was an idea with which one might agree or disagree; Durkheim has won agreement, but within the context of academic sociology. One cannot exactly say that Marx disagrees with Durkheim (and in fact it is the essentially Western quality of Marxism that the literature now increasingly emphasizes);[18] rather he injects energy into our acceptance of how Durkheim, and indeed anyone else, gives a historically-based act of thought in its historical context. We must ask then how Marxism is related to sociology today.

We can perhaps answer this by considering the decline in belief in the predictive value of Marxism. What can be called neo-Marxism seems now almost wholly sceptical of the use of Marx's writings as sacred texts, on no account to be departed from; and both the justifiction of totalitarian regimes by postulating 'The Party' as the guardian of historical process, and at a more local level 'vulgar Marxism' itself, are the object of careful avoidance, if not attack, by many Marxist intellectuals. Yet the *logical* demonstration by such as Popper of the unpredictability of future knowledge, and the actual failure of Marx's predictions to be fulfilled, seem not really the point, and the real point is what the very act of making predictions achieved by generating socialistic energies both politically and in a new, 'post-bourgeois' understanding of the world. (If you warn me a brick is falling on to my head, so that I dodge and it misses, I will thank you rather than say your prediction was wrong.)

Marx predicted a final struggle between upper class and proletariat and thought it was occurring in France. But what is left when one feels, if one does, that such ideas are exposed as illusory hopes? One is left with, not nothing, but the general socialist possibility, the pragmatic version of the sociological idea, the sediment of the more general idea that the economy, in a material and secular world, will in the end be wholly secularized, and that man has his social relations which can result only from his position and his interpretation to himself of that position. And this is surely what did and does happen; the social-democrat movements of Western Europe (as referred to in Chapter I) follow, in however diluted form, from the Marxist idea, or thrust, that *the time has come,* even if the 'class struggle' in social democracy becomes merely the attempt to attain certain equal rights, and 'classlessness' itself means simply democracy. But 'democracy' and 'equality' there can no longer have their original Greek or Rousseauesque connotations. Now they take meaning simply from the pervading point that we are now all susceptible to the laws of social process, social functioning and social interaction. That will be an 'academic' point if we descend from Durkheim or it will be 'ourselves thinking ourselves' if we are more influenced by Marx. Either way we have the sociological idea, and it is curious that the sophisticated later development in Marxism of the idea of ideology as legitimate and necessary, and equally in liberal sociology the reflexive developments already discussed, suggest a new angle on the sociological idea in markedly similar fashion.

This view of Marx can help us to summarize the sociological idea of this chapter more generally. Many writers have recently re-emphasized that Marx wrote within the general principles of his age; that is, the age of the idea of progress, evolution and, with Marxism as the driving-force, revolution. In Paz' formulation,[19] after the centuries-long pact between Christianity and Greek thought, Reason went active. The very capacity of man to exploit matter in ever new ways was itself fundamental to the new momentum in society economically and, in extrapolated ways, in the world of ideology and thought. But, as Paz has again suggested, in our twentieth-century time the difference is that dialectics are built on an abyss; our time is characterized by the search for a foundation. It seems that the sociological idea is the provisional, temporary foundation we now use. In a world devoid of the divine, the 'great chain of being', or the supernatural, and where holocausts have abruptly halted the nineteenth century's optimism, we hold to a conflation of the social residue of Christianity, of positivism collectively applied, and of corporate planning (where there are but degrees of 'free enterprise' from, say, Canada to Poland) which has in its rationale deeply internalized conceptions of social interaction and organization. If this overriding feature is reliably there it would seem its characteristics can also be reliably studied, or held as provisional but legitimate ideology (the formulations are respectively 'academic-sociological' and Althusserian) in all cases. Societies are no longer formless amalgams,[20] and therefore can be seen as, at least, historical formulations of material and economic base, political and ideological superstructure; or, in terms of positivist sociology, structures; or, according to reflexive sociology, our on-going actions and interactions along with our constitutive accounts to ourselves of them. Unlike John Milton (whom in some ways he seems so curiously to resemble) Marx abandoned his early aspirations and decided against writing an epic, nor wanted to 'justifie the wayes of God to Man'. The sociological idea too has 'thought itself'. It has appeared.

PART II

POETRY BEFORE THE SOCIOLOGICAL IDEA

CHAPTER 3

SPENSER AND SOCIAL PHENOMENOLOGY

We suggested the idea of taking five major poets and looking at their work in the light of the five kinds of sociology described in the last chapter. But to show that these poets' interests and achievements were other than those of the sociologists with whom for argument's sake we could match them, might not prove much. The emphasis will therefore be, first, to show how the poems in each case are incompatible not merely with the sociological idea generally but with the particular version of the sociological idea which, on the face of it, they most resemble. Thus for instance Spenser seems to have a phenomenological perspective on reality. In this case it is social phenomenology that would appear to give the strongest challenge to the idea of incompatibility I am suggesting. (To show that Spenser is not interested in social interaction would be child's play.) But, as said in the first chapter, even if this first aim were adequately met it would still not prove our case. For each poet is after all only one poet, and the challenge would then quickly be that the case might have been established for this poet but no other. So secondly, the aim is to show that each poet not only *is* not an implicit adherent of the particular type of sociology apparently relevant to his own case, but could not possibly have been so in any circumstance; that is, that his poetry *is*, in part at least, its incompatibility with the corresponding aspect of the sociological idea, and that what makes us describe his work as poetry is exactly its straining away from, its linguistic tension with, any possible relevant or parallel form of sociological statement.

If the very possibility of formal *poesis* is incompatible with the sociological idea, one might ask how a poet could be valuably discussed in the light of any one kind of sociology more than any other. There are certain underlying realities (perhaps like Kant's categorical imperatives) to which people today usually respond and to which they are related. There is for example the macroscopic and the microscopic dichotomy, the large-scale and the small-scale. There is the subjective and objective, the attention given to the contents of one's own mind or to the outside world. There is the classical and orderly approach and the organic or spontaneous approach. These are comparatively modern, post-Enlightenment distinctions, yet they do also have deeper and older intellectual roots. It seems that it is in terms of such distinctions and groupings that we are likely to say that any intellectual, poet, philosopher or anyone else has certain clear interests and compulsions, or ways of looking at the world. This is not simply a question of their subject-matter, although subject-matter will be seen very differently according to the kind of approach that is chosen. Now what I am suggesting is that when sociology developed its categories and sub-divisions over the last century, it did so according to general kinds of intellectual subdivision such as these. This is certainly no original or remarkable observation, and I do not think many people would dispute it; in fact to mention it is merely to introduce our method of working. But the various distinctions and divisions are not, then, peculiar to sociology alone. They have long and honourable literary and philosophical histories. They are found, as suggested, in the writings of many kinds of imaginative artist or rational intellectual. It should be possible, therefore, to find poets (since they are our interest in this book) who seem to make use of the various intellectual universes that the sociologists also use. If that is so, then by comparing them, poet with sociologist, we can expect to show up all the more clearly the differences between a poetic and a sociological use of these kinds of perspective. We might see a difference between the way a poet and a sociological thinker understand the microscopic and small-scale; or the formal and orderly; or the stable as opposed to the revolutionary, and so on. The themes of common concern that are behind the five poets and kinds of sociology we shall discuss, were briefly summarized on pages 24–25. These common concerns are what I believe we do find.

An excellent example to hand, because with the first poet (Spenser) I would like to discuss, is what we now call phenomenology. Phenomenology is, as the name suggests

Spenser and Social Phenomenology

etymologically, the study of appearances. Phenomenology became a pressing concern in the late nineteenth century (though not, of course, for the first time in Western civilization) because our advances in both philosophical and physical understanding of perception itself made problematic anything perceived. But the point is that the tendency, or compulsion, to see things as appearances, and to feel that the act of seeing is somehow more irreducibly real than is the thing seen — that tendency is possible at any time. The world of faery-romance in the late middle ages seems to have been permeated with it. It is then the significance of the illusions generated in *The Tempest*, re-appears in late nineteenth-century poetry, and has its most recent poetic expression in Wallace Stevens, and perhaps Tolkien. The point is not that the phenomenal-seer is automatically less accurate than the positivist-objectivist. It is that, being more likely to see these things as appearances, he will treat them from a scientific point of view more guardedly, and from a poetic point of view with more freedom to re-dispose them as he wishes. He will not be tied by canon of realism. A surrealist like Magritte paints as accurate, as unmistakeably real-life or perfect, an apple or hairbrush as any realist painter; but he then places the apple in a man's face and the hairbrush in the sky. The point is that the individual with this perspective or view on things, takes things as appearances; and the question for us is, what is the difference when a poet does it from when a sociological theorist does it, and why? And similarly, when an individual sees human embodied life, not now phenomenologically but at the microscopic level: what is the difference between the times when a sociologist (and therefore social interactionist) does it, and when a poet (that is, a poet of love or friendship) does? These are the kinds of question we shall attempt to answer in this second part of the book.

*

Spenser can be shown in uncanny detail to evince a phenomenological view of the world closely parallelling that of modern phenomenology. He wrote *The Faerie Queene* in an allegorical age in which, as C.S. Lewis has classically shown,[1] both religious and allegorical erotic figures had dwindled in the solidity of their representation to the point where they were dreamy, shadowy inventions, more and more open to sheer poetic ornamentation and less the embodiment of actual moral forces. They were thus able to merge with the rather different faery-romance tradition of knights, ladies, castles and dragons, the fantastic, fabulous and supernatural. It has now been commonly said for many years that the world of *The Faerie Queene* is not merely one of wonder and romance, but also has the unreality of dream. (This point is not refuted by the view that many figures in the allegory stand for historical figures contemporary with Spenser.) But, while I see wholly the dreamy unreality of the Spenserian world, I suggest that phenomenology is a more specific and accurate mode of analysis by which to describe it. The nineteenth century, the romantic poets, Hazlitt, and critics such as Greenlaw used the 'dream' description, and phenomenology emerged from that period. We can consider the poem's effect in these phenomenological terms.

In *The Faerie Queene* a characteristic sequence begins, time and again, with a knight appearing seemingly from nowhere (usually 'across the plain') and riding right up to within a few feet of the current hero. This knight is either a villain such as Sir Sansloy (Lawlessness) or is beset by one, as is the ashen-faced young man pursued by Despair (both examples are from Book I.) The hero sets off in pursuit of the villain, and a hand-to-hand battle is fought, with terrific physical and visual detail, much falling on the ground, spilling of blood and tearing of flesh. The hero usually wins, but he finds his own 'maiden' has got lost or been carried off in another direction by another evil, knightly embodiment; that is to say, there is that degree of complexity between sequences and set pieces. And of course there are other settings, such as the well-disposed but pensive Castle of Alma, full of tables and books, and the various more erotic settings of gardens, and maidens undressing by cool waters. But all these are linked through the endless travels of individual knights — sometimes with one companion but often alone — who come across these fixed settings in their travels and whose travels thus constitute a network between them.

In the poem this is a world phenomenologically apprehended. First there is the way that speed (and the covering of huge distances) and absolute stillness in immediacy of space, are combined. The knight is not there, then he is. It is, as commonly observed, like a film cut. It is often very exactly stated; thus:

> far away they spyde
> A varlet ronning towardes hastily,
> Whose flying feet so fast their way applyde,
> That round about a cloud of dust did fly,
> Which mingled all with sweate, did dim his eye.
> He soon approached, panting, breathelesse, whot . . .
>
> (II, iv, xxxvii)

It seems we can see this knight's 'sweate' 'far away', such is the sudden and curious foreshortening of perspective. The foreshortening is equally odd when Una (Truth), the maiden in Book I, travels 'deserts wyde' and then suddenly sees the 'troden gras' where people have apparently been. Similarly in Book III the squire Timias chases Florimel 'through thick and thin, through mountains and through playns', suddenly is tired and 'downe himself he layd/Upon the grassy ground to sleep a throw'. That it is 'sudden' is explicit and extremely important, for this is what makes it like a cut in films, that art of our time that so plays with and rearranges appearances. The word 'suddeine' is one of the commonest in Spenser, and scarcely a page goes by without two or three examples of it.

These knights furthermore are in constant hurry and have great mobility; they 'speed' on their way from one static set-piece to another. 'So they traveil'd, lo! they gan espy/An armed knight towards them gallop fast' (I, ix, xxi, but any of a hundred examples is possible); they 'rush' in to a fight, they 'fly' when any dangerous approach is imminent (which it frequently is), and so on. 'He stayed not for more bidding, but away/Was suddein vanished out of his sight'. Both the speed and the quality of suddenness mean that we can jump directly, and not move by organic progress, from one scene to another.

Next then, these effects come from the poem as visual and

seen, in terms of the five senses. The knight just quoted 'vanished', as do many of the others. Because of the suddenness, the cutting and jumping, just mentioned, we feel we are being referred to manufactured things, not organic ones. For the objects or people in front of us have been cut away from their roots and been placed alongside quite different objects and people. This enables the poet to stress the visual qualities of things, their immediate apprehension, rather than their deeper relations with other things in other terms; such as eating, sleeping, or the industrial and commercial institutions of the real world. Thus, we sense the physical presence there, but we cannot reach out and touch it. Even more oddly, taste and smell are *seen* rather than straightly sensed. A scene is sometimes preceded with a description of great screaming and wailing by some damsel in distress, but this is invariably a prelude to the utterly visual dominance of what follows. Here are two contrasting examples:

> Yet still the Prince pursew'd him close behind,
> Oft making offer him to smite, but found
> No easie meanes according to his mind:
> At last they have all overthrowne to ground
> Quite topside turvy, and the Pagan hound
> Amongst the yron hookes and graples keene
> Torne all to rags, and rent with many a wound;
> That no whole peece of him was to be seene,
> But scattred all about, and strow'd upon the greene.
>
> (V viii xlii)

> In all that rowme was nothing to be seene
> But huge great yron chests, and coffers strong,
> All bard with double bends, that none could weene
> Them to efforce by violence or wrong:
> On every side they placed were along;
> But all the grownd with sculs was scattered,
> And dead men's bones, which round about were flong;
> Whose lives, it seemed, whilome there were shed,
> And their vile carcases now left unburied.
>
> (II vii xxx)

Spenser and Social Phenomenology

The recurrent of what is 'to be seene' seldom lags, and this has, after all, been a theme of Spenser commentary long enough, although the refrain of the phrase itself ('to be seene') is important also. In other passages describing the Seven Deadly Sins, various battles, the miserly store of Malbecco, Una in white for her wedding, and a hundred other places the visuality is equally striking. But equally important for our theme are the resulting modes of seeing by the characters themselves. First, the knights and maidens are repeatedly 'amaz'd', 'astounded' and the like at every arrival, battle or beast they witness, as though they too inhabit this phenomenological dream-world and respond visually to its insubstantiality, and as though their responding emotion is achieved, not exactly in shallowness, but by their own two-dimensionally seen selves. (The *locus classicus* for this theme is *The Tempest*,[2] and we remember that 'astounded' and 'astonished' are etymologically connected with thunder, which happens in tempests. All Prospero's victims are so astounded, for example Sebastian and Antonio, Act III Scene iii.) Second, the seeing is voyeuristic. It is as though if we can see so much we are drawn into that, and with privilege can witness while we (we in the poem as well as outside it) are ourselves unwatched.

> As Guyon hapned by the same to wend,
> Two naked Damzelles he therin espyde,
> Which therein bathing seemed to contend
> And wrestle wantonly, ne car'd to hyde
> Their dainty partes from vew of any which them eyd.
>
> Sometimes the one would lift the other quight
> Above the waters, and then downe again
> Her plong, as over-maystered by might,
> Where both awhile would covered remaine,
> And each the other from to rise restraine;
> The whiles their snowy limbes, as through a vele,
> So through the christall waves appeared plaine:
> Then suddenly both would themselves unhele,
> And th'amarous sweet spoiles to greedy eyes revele.
>
> (II xii lxiii–iv)

Nowhere in *The Faerie Queene* is there the consummation of naked love as is in the third book of *Troilus and Criseyde* for instance. The 'hartlesse' Trompart and 'vaine' Braggadachio similarly witness Belphoebe bathing in Book II; other occasions proliferate elsewhere. But this element of deliberate watching is not confined to the erotic scenes, and it seems that the emphasis on not only the visual but the description of that explicitly, derives almost inevitably from a conception of reality that comes from one sense only. The countless one-stanza Homeric similes are like this, as are the devouring of Kirkrapine, Pyrocles flinging himself into the lake to be rid of the feeling of burning, the Bower of Blisse and Garden of Adonais, and Braggadachio again who 'when fluttering wind does blow/In his light wings, is lifted up to skye', where the moral quality of vain big-headedness is allegorized in a very direct visual picture. Because they are so understood by their surfaces, the observer feels that to try and engage with them — to interact with them — would dispel them. That is voyeurism's nature.

And finally one notices that even the evil, villainous knights and tyrants are static and in any action fail to threaten. Hough has suggested that love and fighting power are present but devoid of their effect.[3] These tyrants rant and rave, but their restraint of their victims is *tableau* only, and their evil seems to consist simply in its own expression, in the ugliness Spenser gives them. This does not mean Spenser cannot render a story movingly (the stories of Malbecco's sad loss, and Britomart's falling in love with Artegall in a mirror, both in Book III, belie that) but the context is still always visual and static. This is clearly illustrated in the description of Duessa, the two-faced one or Falsehood (and, no doubt, papal fraud and usurpation) after her supposed beauty is removed:

> Her crafty head was altogether bald,
> And, as in hate of honorable eld,
> Was overgrowne with scurfe and filthy scald:
> Her teeth out of her rotten gummes were feld,
> And her sowre breath abhominably smeld;
> Her dried dugs, lyke bladders lacking wind,
> Hong downe, and filthy matter from them weld,

Her wrizled skin, as rough as maple rind,
So scabby was that would have loathd all womankind.

(I viii xlvii)

The theme of evil as bodily decay is long in literature, but here it renders the heart of evil power inert, and the stasis is part of Spenser's general method.

Surely it needs little discussion to show how exactly these modes of writing in the poem correspond to the central features of the phenomenological description of reality as described by Husserl, Merleau-Ponty and others, as considered in chapter II. There is one main point and two supporting ones. First is the emphasis on the visual; that is, in Husserl's term, the eidetic, in Spenser's, the endlessly 'seene', so much so in Spenser that the observer is a voyeur, or 'astonished', or rooted to the spot in some other fashion. But the parallel with Spenser is closer. The foreshortening effect by which scenes suddenly change from one to another quite different place, or a present person has suddenly gone, so that scene is cut off at its edges with great finality, makes exactly a frame, a 'bracketing' as Husserl puts it, round the thing experienced. If Husserl's view — and Schutz' and the sociologists' that follow — was of a phenomenon valid by virtue of being bounded in that way, and (as Husserl thought) is the only trustworthy phenomenon for philosophical analysis, then it is interesting that Spenser's scenes are bracketed in the same way. It varies from episode to episode and book to book (being less pronounced in Book V particularly) but the permanent trend is undeniable. The final point concerns the way this seems to draw the sting out of the action, so that even the tyrants are curiously powerless (and the knights' high-velocity movement all over the place is as of sparks or shooting stars rather than real power). For this is an exact parallel to the point made by Giddens about the social ethnomethodologists' examples of social action; namely, that they are 'peculiarly disembodied'.[4] Giddens' discussion attempts to show that the ethnomethodologists' account of human society, stimulating as it is on many fronts, omits the dimension of actual power, order and constraint in the real world which, we are bound to believe, already modifies the phenomenological perceiver at and up to any moment of perceiving. It is just this power dimension, an actual source of initiative and real location of human action, that Spenser's knights and villains are largely without.

We can go on now to ask how the phenomenological poet, and the phenomenological sociologist, use these perceptions. In both cases the difficulty is that of getting across from that which is unreally apprehended to the world of real moral demands. The ethnomethodologist wants to show how, despite our phenomenological stance, we still somehow achieve negotiated intersubjectivity between two isolated positions. Spenser on the other hand wants to win readers into accepting the twleve virtues of Aristotle.[5] Since Spenser follows Aristotle in many matters it is relevant to our discussion briefly to mention this. Aristotle's virtues, as outlined in Book IV of the *Ethics*, have a quality of autonomy. They do not necessarily derive solely from social processes; they are abstractions. They are simply classifications from the twin centrality of the Rational and the Moral and their sub-divisions. Following from this, Aristotle argues that virtues are not feelings or capacities but states. Therefore, and this is very important in comparison with Spenser, their argument is circular and self-contained. The way to be just is to practise justice. As Aristotle says, 'The work of a good man is to do these things well and nobly. . . .' 'The work of a good harp-player is to play the harp well'.[6] This means that the poet following Aristotle can only make Guyon and Britomart symbolize Temperance and Chastity by having them temperate and chaste, which they duly are. But how then can this have any dynamic force at all, and how can we want to follow it? If Temperance is good solely in that it makes us temperate, what is the appeal by which that is accepted? Not at all by demonstrating social processes that necessarily lead to those things, for, as we have said, the phenomenological view is enervated against encompassing such things, it does not have those energies. The answer, of course, is aesthetic. The poet makes the virtues delightful and the vices ugly. The virtuous and the phenomenological can, apparently, be reconciled. We stand, astounded observers rooted to the spot, and witness virtue in action, albeit virtue allegorized. As Aristotle again says, the poet is a maker.

Spenser's own introduction to *The Faerie Queene* tells us more about his reasons for this:

> To some, I know, this Methode will seem displeasaunt, which had rather have good discipline delivered plainly in way of precepts, or sermoned at large, as they use, than thus clowdily enwrapped in allegorical devises. But such, me seeme, should be satisfied with the use of these dayes, seeing all things accounted for by their showes, and nothing esteemed of, that is not delightfull and pleasing to commune sense. For this cause is Xenophon preferred before Plato, for that the one, in the exquisite depth of his judgement, formed a Commune welth, such as it should be; but the other in the person of Cyrus, and the Persians, fashioned a government, such as might best be: so much more profitable and gratious is doctrine by ensampe, than by rule.

The position is extremely similar to that of Spenser's contemporary, Sidney, of whose *Apologie for Poetrie* Peter Bayley says 'at times it is almost as if he is actually describing *The Faerie Queene*....'[7] For Sidney writes; 'Onely the poet, disdayning to be tied to any such subjection' (i.e. 'sticking to the facts') 'lifted up with the vigor of his owne invention, dooth growe in effect, another nature....' It is Sidney's emphasis also that poets value delighting above merely teaching (though they value both) and finally, and in most Aristotelian fashion, 'those things which in themselves are horrible, as cruell battailes, unnatural Monsters, are made in poeticall imitation delightfull.' This last point, taken from the *Poetics,* makes quite clear that no *mere* facile nice/nasty distinction between virtue and vice is being offered, but a generally aesthetic mode of apprehension of things altogether; and thus, moved by the poet's successful 'making' of them by invention (and not just reproducing them, however accurately, as social processes), we are convinced.

But the whole inference, I would argue, is that this explicitly aesthetic method is only available to a poet who, by detaching language from subordination to a preconceived idea of social interaction, sets it free. If we make social interaction obdurately real, we must let language follow the requirements of what we think are the social norms and values that control it. The crux of the argument is that Spenser is only able to go for a hedonistically-seen, subjective, invented presentation of the moral reality by adopting some other different account of human behaviour than is suggested by such terms as institution, negotiated reality, or interpretation of role. For if he believed in those he would necessarily have to show virtue (moral quality) in the context of those very things; he could simply not avoid using the language of subjective perception in that context, and that would not set free the possibilities of invention. Instead, he 'makes' rather than describes what is already there; he does not just embellish and adorn. Aristotle means what he says. We are not saying that Spenser did not believe institutions exist, which is manifestly wrong, but that a description of them according to the sociological idea would have been anathema to one such as him, even supposing such a description had been available.

For their 'gratious' quality (that they too might win allegiance 'by ensample rather than by rule') cannot be presented by the sociological idea. And this is inseparable from the nature of language as seen by the phenomenologist. For whereas the social phenomenologist must see language as an attempt to overcome our isolation in order to reach intersubjectivity — and therefore morality and 'vertue' — Spenser precisely capitalizes on what he believes to be language's phenomenological isolation. He can use it to invent what he likes, trusting 'vertue' (unanalysed) to do its work, and his poetry then *is* his rendering of these inventions in a language phenomenologically freed from its otherwise social obligation or context. Spenser's honified harmonies, sweet ladies, bowers, wonderful alliterations and movements of line like soft breeze or gentle birdsong or insect hum, all utterly impossible in ordinary discourse or institution-supportive prose, *is* the freedom he gains from not being tied to a collective idea.

This aesthetic use, finally, can be seen to be not merely possible when phenomenologically outside a social use; it is essential. For no other organizing principle remains to language when the social demand of interaction or institutionalized normative structure is gone. With other kinds of poetry the poetic tension comes from the strain away from a social use which nevertheless underpins it. But because of the subjectivity of the phenomenological stance, and the deep feeling in it that the Other is appearance only, that strain has already been slackened and cut free before the writing starts. And so any poetry from that stance must lie in what the poet can do with language according to a wholly autonomous kind of harmony or organizing principle. It is not from moral conviction (social process), but from language made simply beautiful, that the voyeuristic and astonished reader will be overwhelmed and want to be virtuous. The poetry does not, as poetry, depend on a reality seen as dominantly social at all; it depends precisely on an escape from such reality.

The extraordinary thing is that the phenomenological-aesthetic tie is found with the sociologists too. It is the ethnomethodological school, and no other, that spawns offspring such as 'Wild Sociology' or 'open and playful attitudes toward sociological writing'.[8] In much of Garfinkel's work there is a certain tone of the ludicrous. That word itself is of course etymologically tied to the idea of play. In Garfinkel's experiments this sense of the whimsical is seldom far away; the woman who changes sex, the jurors' modes of reaching decisions, but most of all his students' experiments, show this. For instance one student will go home having inwardly committed himself to the role of lodger rather than son (to his parents' consternation). Another will board a street-car pretending not to know the universally-known fare. But since this, unlike poetry, is still tied to its sociological legitimation, it is mere whimsy, and never full-bodiedly harmonious or aesthetic, and it leads to the sense of disembodiment Giddens mentioned. For this reason the sociologist is sooner or later drawn back from that disembodiment (whereas Spenser, and Shakespeare in *The Tempest*, exploit it more and more) to their sociological, account-giving aim. And when he is not drawn back thus, acrimonious discussion occurs among sociologists on the point whether it still is genuinely sociology.[9]

There are two other points to mention. The first is that not only Spenser but any poet of the phenomenological stance is in this position. We have mentioned *The Tempest*, and the island setting for that work exactly allegorizes this aesthetic separation from normal social and binding activity, so that 'sounds and sweet airs, that give delight and hurt not' have no socially constraining power for that reason, and equally by that fact become as it were the very principle of meaningful utterance.

Wallace Stevens, heavily influenced by Husserl and Bergson, espoused the notion of poetry as fiction hand in hand with his cardinal principle that such poetry 'must give pleasure'. But the second point is most important of all. For if Spenser's language is indeed cut off from its sociologically-defined use, and is phenomenologically so set free from those constraints as to follow a wholly aesthetic principle, is not the resulting poetry simply verbal confetti and pretty nothingness? Not at all, surely. In the poem we repeatedly encounter things with which we can identify in a full human sense; courage, love, fear and pleasure, and very tangible (if not realistic) embodiments of the occasions on which to savour such things. But we are not at all justified in simply extrapolating social values, sociological inferences, from them, because the poet totally integrates those human qualities and events and the non-human (physical, magical, mystical, natural) appurtenances of them. The union of these two orders of reality is precisely the poet's integration and, with that, his integrity. We have absolutely no right, when reading Book VI and Spenser's poem on Friendship (to take the most sociologically 'convertible' of the six virtues Spenser completed) to extract from it those features subsumable under the sociological idea, and then pronounce that Spenser's attitudes or views are necessarily sociological. On the contrary, the fact that Spenser's imagination sees Chastity, Holiness and Friendship as wholly inseparable from their natural appurtenances, the beautiful or ugly aspects, the light or dark that hangs over them, the fruit, clothing, armour and other things that accompany them, means that it is impossible to avoid facing that his response to them is of that kind. For us to extrapolate the sociological dimension of these is reductionism. These 'vertues', which are not analytical qualities, find themselves synonymous with their poetic body, and that cannot be transposed into something else. But this does not merely mean that poetry is one thing, sociological theory another. As we have already suggested, poetry would appear to have a special inverse relationship with the sociological idea of language; for poetry cannot omit the non-sociological, (non-interactive, non-institutional) features of language; indeed the poet loves and cherishes those very features. To trace how the real virtues of chastity, holiness and friendship could make their way down into Spenser's mind, down separately into words, and then into the combination of those two things which make Spenser's poetry, would be the subject of a separate book, but it could be written without benefit of the strictly sociological version of those virtuous values. Spenser could write as he did, and include — who denies it? — any amount of material from his own time (such as the papacy or the Irish question), because the sociological idea had not yet insisted that our language is at its humanly most important when expressing or describing the avowedly structural or interactive abstracted qualities of our social relationships. We shall consider what does happen in that event, in Part III. And Spenser did also, of course, set himself unusually free poetically by taking out the phenomenological option. What of a poet who does not do that, and indeed whose language does at first glance seem to be addressing someone very intimately? We can now consider that in the case of Donne.

CHAPTER 4

DONNE AND SOCIAL INTERACTIONISM

Donne, and his *Songs and Sonets* in particular, provides a comparison with the social interaction school of sociology. These poems are apparently about a very intimate form of what we would now call social interaction, namely, sexual love, its emotions and consummation. Indeed one suspects that the relation between our perception of the love passion and that of intimate and microscopic social interactionism could be traced from the Oedipus tradition, through courtly love to Donne, Freud, Mead and others with many interesting results. For our purpose Donne is in many ways an obvious choice, but clearly what we say here might, with qualifications, be taken to refer to other love poetry, although metaphysical love poetry is significantly different from other kinds. But first, and this is a difference from the other comparisons between poetry and sociology we are making, we have here not one but two questions to answer. I would like to show not only that the poems are not 'about' social interaction after all, but also that they are not themselves social interactions, or parties to interaction, even when they seem to address mistresses and loved women. Of course we are suggesting this is true of any poetry, not just this kind, but the challenge that there is a case to answer seems, in this instance, to present itself more strongly.

The first thing to be said is that, while today we who hold the sociological idea think of erotic love as social interaction, for Donne it seems more like the end of interaction, and the consummation that occurs when the interactions of love are complete. It would seem that 'interaction' is precisely what is *not* the act and consummation of love. For 'love' is consummated when interaction, in any sociological and even any dynamic sense, is over; when there is silence; when, as twentieth-century love-songs revealingly put it, there is 'no need for words', and when, most intriguingly of all, we 'die', that word being a common reference in Donne's time to orgasm — that moment when society, interaction, association, or whatever we may call it, are wholly suspended, at most an irrelevant blur. In Donne, this is expressed as the experience of love as union; indeed, for Donne love is union. But union, by definition, cannot contain interaction. Interaction of necessity requires two parties, and thus the total unity ends the possibility of our describing them as interacting. The interactions of lovers lead up to that, but the thing itself, as Donne expresses it, and indeed certain moments often well prior to it (for example consider 'The Extasie', stanzas 1–5) contain no interactive dynamic but, rather, motionlessness. The flavour and nature of this union is presented by Donne in a number of ways.

To start with, he says it directly. 'The Extasie' and 'A Valediction: Forbidding mourning' are both more explicit on this theme than most of his poems. The first fifty lines of 'The Extasie' are an intense probing into the stages by which this unity occurs. At first 'to intergraft our hands . . . was all our means to make us one', and later the imaginary bystander 'knew not which soul spake/Because both meant, both spake the same' — a situation which renders interaction's dialectic impossible. As a result of souls' 'mixing' the lovers 'are this new soul', and at the poem's end the stages of love have been called 'this dialogue of one', which changes only slightly when it reaches actual bodily union. In the 'Valediction' poem even physical separation brought about by a journey means that 'our two souls . . . which are one . . . endure not yet a breach but an expansion', and in 'The Canonization' the poet exults: 'The phoenix riddle hath more wit/by us: we two, being one, are it'. Evidence neatly arranged like that gives us, naturally, only an introductory formula; yet I think that the great controversy over 'The Extasie' means simply that those who (unconsciously perhaps) are contemporary enough to hold the interactive view may be led to think those early stanzas are a burlesque, while others (myself naturally too) take that extraordinary monosyllabic stillness of lines 19–20 and elsewhere to mean a heightened expression of real experience.[1]

> All day, the same our postures were,
> And we said nothing, all the day.

That two people who love can thereby be, literally, one, is not in Donne a merely sentimental notion. It is the termination of logical processes, even if we think the logic suspect.

The idea that love is too homogeneous to be a mode of articulation is suggested, wittily, spontaneously, sadly and exultantly, in ways that enrich the idea further. The conceits Donne uses to get at love's nature themselves tend to be homogeneous. In 'Love's Alchemy' it is a substance, a continuous material one gets from down a mine, and one can only add more; it is not a matter of variations on a process fundamentally dynamic by nature. There is almost an exasperation, if a happy one, in the preceding poem 'Lovers' Infiniteness', in which Donne can only question and worry at the matter of *how much* love he and the woman have. 'If yet I have not all thy love,/Dear, I shall never have it all' is the first statement of this: he then plays on the matter of her love being 'partial', more of it being created, and the general implication of love, taken or withheld, as a totality. Thus, despite the wish to 'have a way more liberal', he is left — not unwillingly — with his own first conception of love's union when all is said: 'we shall be one, and one another's all'. And in 'Love's Growth', and perhaps 'The Primrose' too, we have what might be called an algebra of love as, simply, growing or shrinking, rather than diversifying inner parts in an organic relation.

But all of this idea of love as a unity, and perhaps a substance, clearly derives from that other very old idea, also present in Donne, of Love (and we now capitalize the word) as a deity, or at minumum an autonomous personification. Donne is of course an inheritor, if in a changing world, of the medieval idea of love-religion, courtly love and the worship of Eros, a name which then had a different meaning from that of our time.[2] The implication of this can be put as follows. Our modern view, entailing socially interactive processes, is that desire of the beloved leads through proliferating interactions to love, whereas for Donne, inheriting this from earlier ages, it is that Love generates desire for the beloved. In one or two passages Donne is explicit on the matter, actually addressing love ('I bid love ask . . .'— 'Air and Angels'), and in 'The Will', where every stanza ends with the same refrain ('Thou, Love, taught'st me. . . .') It seems that the survival of Love as deity specifically is something Donne does not quite escape.

The couplet

> I long to talk with some old lover's ghost
> Who died before the god of love was born

begins, in 'Love's Deity', a somewhat sad examination of that god's functions, and the autonomy of the source of power so remains to constrain the lovers that the very variations of its expression merely give more exasperation that 'love' cannot always be what, at its true heart, it must be: union itself. In 'Farewell to Love', even though what he refers to is past, there is no denying the literal way it is meant to be interpreted:

> Whilst yet to prove,
> I thought there was some deity in love
> So did I reverence, and gave
> Worship; as atheists at their dying hour
> Call, what they cannot name, an unknown power,
> As ignorantly did I crave . . .

And it is clear furthermore than Donne's uncertainty on the matter does not suggest doubt that 'Love' autonomously exists, at least in some way. Rather there is a tone of profoundly quiet joy and security precisely when the uncertainty of what Love actually consists of (what that 'substance' is) is most clearly faced: where we have 'a love, so much refined,/That our selves know not what it is', (a note found also in 'The Relic', lines 23–4). This idea of Love as a divine entity has extension, of course, in the idea of lovers as cut off from the world, martyrs to love, and distinct from the 'laity' and the 'profane' ('The Canonization', 'The Undertaking' and elsewhere). It is, I take it, close to the idea expressed in our time in Rilke's fifth Duino Elegy.[3]

The idea of love as religion might be thought to be connected with another theme that runs through Donne's apprehension of love; namely, death. But I suggest it is different, and again it seems that the metaphor of death really refers to a severance of love from the specific human interaction that could be seen as leading to love, and is therefore left over, as it were, a now useless means only, when love is gone. Donne repeatedly expresses his bitterness that, when a mistress is false, he will die. More poignantly he has only death when a loved woman is herself dead. If love were a relationship between two people, then when one died or departed the other would simply survive, to live another day and with new occasions of interaction appearing. But if love is union, then the death or departure of the beloved tears the total union apart so that the other party to it must metaphorically bleed, and die too. The greatness of the loss is most totally and deeply given to us in the 'Nocturnal upon S. Lucies Day'. 'I am every dead thing . . . I am re-begot/Of absence, darkness, death; things which are not. . . .' 'I am by her death (which word wrongs her)/Of the first nothing. . . .' In the modern world, however wounded or unwanted we might feel as a result of rejection in love, it is likely that any period of recuperation would take place in the form of analysis — self-abasing and despairing perhaps — of the relationship that had occurred, and what went wrong with it; and this is likely to be inseparable from consideration of similar relationships we knew of among friends, or our own relationships with colleagues and family. But Donne's idea that he is buried in his grave, as in 'Farewell to Love' or his black feeling that what love he did have might as well not have existed ('The Paradox'— 'I cannot say I loved, for who can say/He was killed yesterday?') are both couched in this idea that he is dead. The belief, widely accepted in our culture, that love is a product of something more general, namely, the human interactive possibility itself — that belief would not have existed for Donne to resort to, and therefore death as the end of love is his only analogy. Most interestingly of all, it seems we cannot regard these expressions as merely black bitterness, for the idea of blankness outside of love can be a most happy one. 'I wonder by my troth, what thou, and I/Did, till we loved. . .?' Next to love nothing else is comparable, or even capable of recall. When two lovers, wholly happy, have to separate temporarily, there is no suggestion that other friendships or 'relationships' are even candidates for substitution. Rather, '... think that we/Are but turned aside to sleep....'

But what then is the implication of all this for poetry? Love for Donne may be union rather than interaction, but how does this affect our general argument? The point is surely that if there is no interaction there can be no language of that interaction, with which to express its nature. Between friends, neighbours and colleagues or work-mates there is necessarily the discourse by which the interactions that make the relationship are constituted. (For this reason there is little poetry of those things, a point to which I shall return.) Between lovers, there is no such language. Of course lovers talk to each other, and indeed affectionately and wooingly, but that is not the love itself, at least not according to Donne, nor does any such language tell us love's nature. It is not at all words, but eyes, hair and hearts, through which love is mediated. Love's nature is not revealed, nor characteristically love established, by the language of interaction, for love as union has no interaction. Therefore if Donne would come at the nature of love, as he so irresistibly seems to need to do, he must find a different kind of language for it, and so he is disposed to poetry. No woman, ever, speaks, or is alluded to as speaking, in Donne's poems. There is not the smallest hint of language passing between two lovers in moments of love (there is one reference to 'letters'). On the contrary, lovers are either silent and still, as in the passage from 'The Extasie' already cited, or placed in set-pieces where love simply, as it were, exists, as in 'The Sun Rising', where in even so immediate a picture as of lovers in bed with sun coming in through the window, we are told only 'She is all states, and all princes I./Nothing else is'. There is no dialogue, no interchange.

To come at the nature of this mysterious, elusive, divine, non-worded (if not always silent) love, is the substance of Donne's main love-poetry. It is the incessant probing of love's nature from the point of view of someone in — immersed jointly in — love. But that cannot be explained in any language conceived of as explaining it between the lovers themselves, because, in so far as they are loving, they are not interacting, but are 'one'. How then can that love be explained or captured?

As said, it is certainly not through its words. Perhaps it is in hearts. Donne turns and tries the matter of what happens when hearts are given in love. If they are given, they cannot then have been retained. Perhaps a heart can stay in one place with the beloved while its owner travels away. ('The Blossom'). Perhaps, as in 'The Legacy', the heart of the lover and that of his beloved can become confused. Musing sadly and speculatively on the 'heart' is one possible probe, one way, both to love and to explain love. But equally, Donne seems to say, it may be in eyes that we can find the union of love. In love, we can stare at the eyes of the beloved in a total union, for what we see there is our own image, reflected as in a mirror. 'My face in thine eye, thine in mine appears'. Could it be then that this is the cause, or very embodiment of that union? 'The Extasie', line 12, seems to suggest so. Again, perhaps it is tears, which behave something like eyes in that they too reflect the other's image (and so can be compared to coins bearing a king's effigy, and equally 'of worth' — 'A Valediction; of Weeping'), but which can also be 'mingled', like love's union itself, and again too express the sorrow at separation, or the lover's unrequited love.

These probes, and several others, and the various levels of joy, despair, bitterness and doubt with which Donne the lover inseparably expressed them, *are* his poetry. A poetic rather than discursive language is needed, because the central experience — 'that we two are one' — is not interactive but a paradox. It is one which turns out to be the germ of paradox's entire proliferation in this poetry, or at least the opening through which Donne's aptitude for that intellectual characteristic can be released. The further, compounding paradoxes resulting from this fact are that, although we two are one, the woman may be 'false'; but also that love may continue during physical separation (when the lover has journeyed far away) even though love depends apparently on things present, such as hearts, eyes and tears. Donne then uses any means he can find to come at this mysterious thing, which is not explicable, it seems, in the language of ordinary interaction. The language to express this mystery or paradox is of necessity mysterious or paradoxical itself; in fact, poetic. What we call Donne's metaphysical or extravagant imagery is, in fact, his attempt to come at this mystery by however far-fetched means. His soul will catch up his mistress's by its greater power, though dying later, just as 'bullets flown before/A latter bullet may o'ertake, the powder being more'. The one soul when its bodies are separated is like gold 'to airy thinnesse beat', and the justification of bodily love may be that a flea has already given precedent to it by mingling the lovers' two bloods in itself. You can no more 'judge woman's thoughts by tears/Than by her shadow, what she wears'. Much as this imagery — or kind of conceit — has often been called 'extravagant', that hardly seems sufficient comment when one considers the great, meticulous care with which Donne effects the expression of such conceits, and the intricately worked, often slow and cautious, movement by which they are tightly rhymed and worked out. Rather it is surely that, in an age whose sensibility was still influenced by the idea of an overall metaphysical unity in reality, a 'great chain of being' with its several parts all interrelated, Donne thought that an apparently far-fetched connection would all the more expand our perceptions about reality's nature (by naming unexpected connections within it), and thus give a greater intellectual surety that the mysterious thing, Love, which he probed was indeed all the more actually understood. Certainly the dominance of the chain-of-being (or 'Elizabethan world picture') conceptions have been challenged, but they survive enough to suggest that Donne's comparisons are not merely intriguing analogies, but do try to suggest actual likenesses at a more fundamental level. The fact that a geographer covering a bare globe with a map can be compared to a simple tear reflecting a lover's face, is not merely an interesting comparison that appeals; it suggests some real affinity between the two examples in the very order and nature of things.

But this same argument, and its implication for our argument about poetry and social interaction generally, can now be taken a stage further. The endless probing and self-questioning, and even intellectual self-torment (in one that 'lov'st to be/Subtile to plague thyself'); the trying to cope with both contradictory and painful experience; the pressing on further, then starting again, then winding the argument back on itself, and then thinking of a new factor not yet accounted for; and furthermore, all this too played with great variation, so that at times the poet gives up and is simply whimsical or bitter, then more truly sad, then on another occasion trying gently and fancifully to further love itself by logic, both to have that love and to see if the logic works ('. . . since thou thought'st it best/Not to dream all my dream, let's act the rest'); — all of this, surely, would be wholly out of control if it were not contained and held in a tight, tensive state from which it cannot overflow or seep away. For this reason, it seems, the poems are held in tight rhyme schemes, with thick textures of economical ambiguity, and with much grammatical inversion and infolding. The result is poems like tight wire, as though ready to burst apart if their tensions went too far one way or the other. These techniques both hold the tenuously reached position tight (as Martz puts it, they 'suffice')[4] and again, therefore, simultaneously and inseparably from that, render themselves quite unsayable in ordinary discourse or as words in ordinary interaction. Rather they achieve and contain a certain *awe* at Love's reality (a 'hush of sanctity', in Roston's phrase),[5] and at their own quality in what they do express.

These three things — tight rhyme, inverted and convoluted grammar, and ambiguity or at least redoubling of meaning in one phrase — are ubiquitous in Donne. He will make an argument almost three-dimensional by his inversion of ordinary grammar:

> If our loves faint, and westwardly decline,
>   To me thou, falsely, thine,
> And I to thee mine actions shall disguise.
>
> (Lecture on the Shadow')

The reader is made to wait until 'actions' comes to bolt the whole thing together. There are no less than eleven separate clauses in the one sentence which is the second stanza of 'The Funeral', and we cannot know the key to the whole complex until the last clause is reached:

> For if the sinewy thread my brain lets fall
>   Through every part,
> Can tie those parts, and make me one of all;

> These hairs which upward grew, and strength and art
>   Have from a better brain,
> Can better do it; except she meant that I
>   By this should know my pain,
> As prisoners then are manacled, when
>   they are condemned to die.

Similarly, as Empson has shown, the middle pair of lines in each stanza of 'A Valediction of Weeping' may refer equally back or forward yielding at least two meanings (and many shades of meaning, by this device), so that we have almost two poems, two pieces of paper one on top of the other.[6] This cannot conceivably refer to or be part of ordinary discourse, ordinary interaction. All the arguments which might be offered — but even then with difficulty — in a discourse about love, or in love, are captured and contained, and made tensive and multiple, one with their shape, imagery and rhyme. On the matter of rhyme itself, it seems in Donne as it were a proof, a confirmation, that what he is saying is solid and existent, the rhyme seeming to make it so by coming down on the important word and tying that back to the earlier (rhyming) context next to which it matters. By stressing the aural connection of 'fears' with 'tears', for example, in 'Lovers' Infiniteness', Donne emphasizes the second word more strongly in a way no one can answer: 'Which have their stocks entire, and can in tears/In sighs, in oaths, and letters outbid me,/This new love may beget new fears. . . .' Again the statement is clinched by the simultaneous arrival of the second 'new' and the locking rhyme. My argument is not that this proves Donne right — in so far as he could be held to be making statements, right or wrong, in any event — but rather that, right or wrong, his words are so wrapped into each other as to be rendered permanently insulated from the outside. To use such words in ordinary discourse would be to make a presumptuous claim; but in poetry, the unnaturalness is justified, for the poet gives us his emotive source for such usage, simultaneously with the usage itself.

And finally, to say that language locked into poetry cannot be said in discourse, is not enough. For that is self-evident. It is also that, by being so locked in, it must be that something other than interactive discourse is occurring; something else is being expressed, something physical, mental, metaphysical, mysterious, or something further. It is some event of an order not recapturable into the social order at all; it is untranslatable, permanently itself, an incessant reminder of the empty spaces outside the pattern of merely social interactions and institutions; a hint that the empty spaces may not be so empty after all.

Donne has been described by various critics as elaborating paradox for its own sake; relieving mental disturbance; comparing erotic with divine love; or as chasing false syllogistic processes to their own end, either to convince himself or precisely to demonstrate that, where reason and logic fail, a more remote metaphysical certainty in the universe is the only reliable entity, the very balance of harmonious thinking itself, aside from the virtue or otherwise of any one example. If we can combine what we have said already about the desperate need to probe the nature of the union that is love, with Eliot's idea that Donne savoured a thought like other men savour a rose, then we might say, too aphoristically perhaps, that he studied Love intellectually and the intellect lovingly; and that this connected with his amorous activity in the real world in that failure to understand love intellectually was synonymous with failure in love itself. Either way, we must seemingly argue, Donne's poetry does not, ever, 'address' the mistress, as commentaries so often seem to suggest. Rather, it teases out amazing conceits, redoubled levels of meaning, strange inversions of grammar and logic, and shifting levels of mood, to present a mind from which at present outside activity is excluded.

Yet a further question remains. Even if the foregoing argument be accepted, why should it not be the love relationship alone, rather than all relationships, to which it is applicable? How can we be sure it also applies to interaction that occurs in friendship, for example, or between colleagues at work?

My answer is precisely that those other relationships do not aspire to union. They therefore continue to be negotiated by language in ordinary discourse; and for this reason they do not have a poetic tradition. That is to say, there is no body of friendship-poetry of this order, or of neighbour-poetry or colleague-poetry, and yet there is a poetry of love. The sociology of interaction uses the same analyses and analytical tools (role, norm, interaction, superordination and relationship) for all interactions, yet in the palpable world the significant matter is the distinction between these other kinds of interaction; and that lies in what the parties to them share. In friendship it is, in the deepest sense, shared interests; beliefs, attitudes, cultural matters, as well as activities, sports and scientific interests. In the relation of neighbours it is the shared, or at least tangential and cordially comparable, territory; home, garden, street and their physical and tangible details and natural or made objects. In the relation of colleagues or work-mates it is the sharing of tools or industrial or factory space, or shop-floor or office. It is those things, not the interaction itself, that yield the interaction's context and embodiment, and therefore, when it occurs in poetry, its imagery and affection. If the interaction itself (as seen by theoretical sociology) rather than its incidental embodiments, is what the poet thinks important, then discursive language will be attempted in the poem; but it is invariably stilted and dull, for the poet, although of necessity a single voice, is presumptuously attempting to speak for himself and others. The poetic epistle, though quite an established convention, has a very small number of poems indeed which command a permanent estimate of value. When they do have that, the convention of addressing someone is usually being used to have a sort of channel wherein the poet may publicly soliloquize. Donne has a poem to Mr Tilman, earnestly recording that gentleman's ordination into the church, and how solemn that is; but we simply cannot forget the real Mr Tilman in the background, inglorious, unmysterious, so that any image is too big and sacred for him, and the tone is just a little ridiculous, however legitimate the sentiments of which he is the subject. (Much of Wordsworth's worst poetry was of this kind). A person can be spoken of, rather than to, in a poem, but this is an elegiac, not interactive, tradition, and is consummated in the cases where the poem's subject is dead and being honoured. When alive, such characters are treated roundly, in their fleshly embodiment and in their surroundings, community, and place of work. The interactive voice is not present. In some poetic *genres* both parties to what we call an interaction may be present, rather than just one addressed by the poet; but in those cases either the parties as a pair are caught up in some larger spirit or atmosphere, which is the poem's true subject (and charmingly, as in pastoral, or more speculatively, as in Arnold's 'Sohrab and Rustum', where both characters are dominated by a certain brooding cosmic presence); or the two characters begin to split from each other and speak independently, so that we are quickly moving away from poetry and into drama. But the relationship of erotic love, in Donne's vision, is that of union, so that the interactive difficulty does not arise. In our time, where it is popularly (perhaps rightly) held that erotic love is indeed nothing other than social interaction accompanied by bodily meeting at a different level, then either the poet is one-sidedly speaking for both sides again, as in our earlier example, so that the poet explains to the beloved what the interaction is like, and it seems embarrassing and mealy-mouthed; or else the physical details *must* force their way into the poetic range of imagery far more directly than Donne needed, and we quickly have the paraphernalia of immediate genitalia and mammalia, tits, cunts and everything else. This indeed may be quite legitimate, and argues against the idea that contemporary love-poetry is merely pornographic. On the contrary, without notion of love as union, it is exactly what we should expect.

Two other matters must be briefly mentioned. The first is that wider body of traditional love poetry which rather conventionally praises the mistress and woos her. These may be lyrics, songs or sonnet-sequences. It seems to me that such poems are best seen as gifts. They become objects, an admittedly inadequate word. As such they are analogous to flowers or rings, and indeed often seem to become identified with the object that, vicariously for the mistress, they address. Donne's 'Elegy to his Bracelet' (No. 11) is an example. Many of Herrick's lyrical invitations become detachable songs, presents to his mistress, or simply usable by singers and directed outward to the air, away from any particular woman who may have brought about their origin. Such is Jonson's 'Drink to me only with thine eyes'. Marvell's 'To His Coy Mistress' seems also to be rather public in tone, addressing a general idea or hypothesis for general consideration. But the prototype is perhaps Waller's 'Go Lovely Rose'. It seems to address the rose as an opportunity to address the woman ('Sacharissa') Waller is said to have admired. But when we see the poem itself as the rose, it leaps into the richness of meaning of poetry truly; it insulates itself from social interaction by addressing itself, and the poem is asking the poem to take the poem's message.

The other matter is Donne's divine poems. The power of the best of these derives from a passion arguably close to that which inspires the songs and sonnets, as the second line of the couplet quoted below suggests. But the object of attention, the poem's subject, is itself what generates the words, emotions and deepest spiritual turbulence in the poet himself. It is as though the poem's subject itself is not merely a source of inspiration, but the poem's originating power and initiative, almost more than the poet is. It is as though that force had directed and commanded the poem to be written. Again then, there is the confounding of the poem's subject, and itself as message, as the same thing. The poem tells of a second message, that its subject also gave the instruction that it be written:

>   For I
> Except you enthral me, never shall be free,
> Nor ever chaste, except you ravish me.

CHAPTER 5

MILTON AND MARXIST SOCIOLOGY

Paradise Lost offers an extraordinary parallel to Marxism, the revolutionary sociology that sees society as stemming from the interplay of the material and history. The poem is dialectical in that it would 'justifie the wayes of God to man'. It is materialist in base in that the solid quality of the language is prior to all else, a position I hope to argue. It is centred on power and struggle for control of the world. It is historical in that, although using a myth-type source, its supernatural events do not have the ring of the mysterious but come over as temporal unique happenings which alter the course of events to come. It is also historical in the different sense that, like Marxism, it itself enters history (in our case literary history) in such a way as radically to alter that, not merely by introducing this or that new style of writing, but by bringing on its own obsolescence. Finally it is revolutionary, in the literal sense that it is about a huge, central event that itself renders impossible a repeat of its own mode or subject thereafter.

The important thing is the matter of Milton's language. Much of what I say has doubtless been said elsewhere; it is necessary to recast it for this argument's purpose. The language we speak in social intercourse is made to stimulate us into preparing our answers while the other party speaks. This is not so in poetry, least of all in this poem. Because the language of *Paradise Lost* seems external to the speaker, the poem has clear, hard edges; it does not 'flop over' into or link with normal experience of feeling or spontaneous comment, as does the language of Shakespeare. Shakespeare thus makes us think what we might have said as well, or after him, as perhaps does Eliot. But Milton's central language is a diversification from a single universally charged source, not of the language's entire resources, but those of its substantives (in Chomsky's terms, the nominal, adjectival and adverbial.) This does not mean nouns only, yet the frequent absence of main verbs in Milton, and the absence of those of any force or substance, and the substitution of participle, means that his force lies not in the common-sense narrative of 'What happened next'? (a matter of verbs) but of the content those described events is made of in each case. It is as though the events are only the expression of those power-packed contents. Most certainly there is narrative, but it is contained tight within that nominal framework and condition. Thus the language expresses the fact of the solid obduracy of the cosmos and its origin; that is to say, the language seems to emanate from that aspect of the world.

The story Milton tells does not produce the language, it feels rather as though it follows from the language. The language itself is Milton's prior *logos*, enabling him then to commit himself to the story's most huge and arbitrary events. Here is an excerpt, randomly chosen except that it is not from a speech:

> . . . at length
> Saw where the sword of *Michael* smote, and fell'd
> Squadrons at once, with huge two-handed sway
> Brandisht aloft the horrid edge came down
> Wide wasting; such destruction to withstand
> He hasted, and oppos'd the rockie Orb
> Of tenfold Adamant, his ample shield
> A vast circumference: At his approach
> The great Arch-Angel from his warlike toile
> Surceas'd, and glad as hoping here to end
> Intestine war in Heav'n, the arch foe subdu'd
> Or Captive drag'd in Chains, with hostile frown
> And visage all inflam'd first thus began.
>
> (VI 249–261)

We get here not only the massive force of packed substantives (linked by the briefest particles — as, on, to, when, etc.), we also get those substantives unrepeated. Even counting right back to line 230, 'seem'd' comes three times, 'fight' and 'air' twice and 'fighting' once, and 'arch'd' twice. Otherwise the 240-odd words occur once each only, every one adding a new nucleus of solidity and tangible sensuous reality, which themselves take the narrative on by having an energizing relation with one another. They thus constitute both the 'story' and, more profoundly, the vibrant, empowered nature of the material universe from which the story is made and in which, and with which, it is enacted. This energized materialism is parallel to Marxism itself, for, in Marxism too, matter is the fundamental reality. If we go back furthermore to the immediately preceding phase (ll. 189–225 approximately) we find the same, but more; for not only is that passage also largely devoid of substantive repetition, it does not even greatly anticipate the vocabulary of the next passage, already quoted. It seems that Milton can go on and on, as indeed he does, adding new contents, substantives, realities, never however as a mere list, for the grammar of their association with each other — a matter of nouns, verb-nouns and adverb-nouns — gives the tense power by the clash and vigorous sinuosity which pervades the poem's twelve books.

Such language allows no interruption (as Johnson said, 'such is the power of his poetry, that his call is obeyed without resistance') but we cannot resent this because it is not a man but a language itself which seems to be speaking; a voice incarnated. In several passages it is not Milton, nor even the voice, but the language itself, which seems to approve of the content, for it is generating into existence from its own nominal-dynamic nature what it then says. (This is made interestingly clear when we compare such writing with those other passages where Milton too obviously inserts matter of prior choosing, such as Raphael's description of the creation of the world. It echoes Genesis too exactly, so that the language no longer seems the autonomous source, and Milton the man seems to loom back into the picture.) And the proliferation of vowel-sound also, making for a total plurality and variety so that every vowel seems to sound like a new one, is the aural counterpart to the tangible nominal qualities of the language's other aspects. The obvious example is the famous opening passage: Of man's first disobedience — fruit — tree — mortal — taste — death — world — woe — Eden — greater Man: that is to say, Milton so pluralizes these sounds, and makes it seem as though every one is different except for some special purpose (as with 'greater Man' repeating and thus contrasting the first 'man', who are of course Adam and Christ) that a uniqueness is given to the substantive nature of each noun, adverb and adjective all the more. The language itself conveys with endless diversification aspects of sensuous reality. For this reason Milton is not a 'rhymer', (so that again Johnson, though preferring rhyme, 'could not wish his work other than it is',) for rhyming would of course militate against the singularity of the several vowel sounds achieved. And it is this confidence that gives the poem the unlovable quality it is thought, by some, to have, for it refuses compromise, and is resistant, heavy and ferocious, as a direct result of Milton's vast knowledge of the language, vast vocabulary and great confidence in its use. It is as though, having this huge resource, the writer proceeds to demonstrate the fact very directly rather than with oblique gentleness; yet we cannot deny the power, for it just is the case — showing the futility of anyone who 'durst defy th'Omnipotent to arms'.

This is the language of materiality itself: the language of substance, matter, the object referred to in theories of materialism. Because of such new perception (which the poem anticipated) a culture is possible based on the exploitation of science and the possession of property not just as terrain but also as commodity. The poem in its solid black outlines, its huge distances and vivid earthy and airy landscape, seen so strongly in terms of light and dark, is itself a piece of property or real estate, if one could whimsically give it that description. This material furthermore is no longer sacred or animistic, but it is not just dead and inert either; rather it is highly energized and charged in a way that enables matter itself indeed to be the first item in a fundamental later theory (materialism) of the world and man, and man's consciousness. In the so-called Latinate language of *Paradise Lost* the energies of capitalism, Freudianism, natural science and Marxism are all present. Consider for example the extraordinary Freudian appeal of the passage where Satan finds the serpent sleeping: 'in at his mouth the Devil enter'd', and the libidinous, anal, olfactory passage that follows. There are also the quasi-scientific obsessions and cautions, 'no fear lest dinner coole', and the piece curiously reminiscent of modern transport timetabling: 'since the morning hour set out from heav'n . . . and ere mid-day arrived in Eden'. The real nature of the cosmos Milton gives us has ceased to be traditionally theological.

Because of this underlying quality of immense materiality, energy and power achieved by the substantive language described, the question arises of the part played within it by actual people and characters, and their speeches, *their* language. The poem is split, in a sense, between the language of Milton alone and the language of Milton in speeches. My argument will be that in all but one case the second type of language more or less continues the first; but, more important for now, here is the obvious analogy with the distinctions between matter and consciousness, and between base and superstructure, in Marxism. If Milton's solid substantive language is his material base, the speeches correspond to the ideological superstructure and the fact of consciousness from which, as was argued in Chapter 2, the sociological idea comes. Obviously this analogy cannot be pushed very far, but it offers a starting-point for considering the speeches themselves and what they achieve, and how Man too is seen against this material base. The crucial outcome, of course, is the action of the first man and woman who find themselves in such a world.

To take Man first, he is structurally microscopic in the poem's cosmos, and in *Paradise Lost* that means the poem's language also. Against the vast spaces of heaven and hell, and the distances the angels fell, (these Copernican references also seeming prophetic of light-year calculations in the modern world), Adam and Eve are located in a couple of overgrown acres west of Seleucia. They have gardening jobs to do. This 'gardening' has at times been ridiculed by critics, but it helps render Adam and Eve pitifully tiny, not only next to the size of Satan in Books I and II but also, in coldly different mode, as against God and the Son. In short, Adam and Eve are at first simply dwarfed by their cosmic positions, which contrasts with their sociality.

But then there are the speeches. Much of the poem is taken up with words from the mouths of imagined characters: indeed most of the best description, the material and substantive language already indicated, is from speeches. According to our argument about poetry's non-sociological nature generally, these speeches will in the main have a non-interactive (and, therefore, in Marxist terms, material) quality. With one important exception this seems to me true of *Paradise Lost*; not that the 'speeches' necessarily always work but that they remain within the tenor of the poetic unity. Broadly, there are five categories of speech in the poem: a) God and the Son, b) the fallen angels, c) Raphael and Michael to Adam and Eve, d) Adam and Eve innocent, e) Adam and Eve after the Fall. All of these except the last are able to render discourse transfigured in that the speakers are not humans in the world we know. Only Adam and Eve are human, and they are pre-lapsarian in the fourth category. Thus Adam and Eve after the Fall are the only characters in the poem remotely comparable with ordinary humans in the world as we know it, a point that will be crucial.

First there are the speeches of God and the Son, and they have been drastically criticised. Whatever the justice of that, Milton's weird God now seems simply the voice of a ten-foot cube of concrete; matter itself; or, theologically more generously, serene omnipotence rendered so by Milton's designation of him, deliberately surely in that mode. He (God) can do anything at any time, but with no physical or visual characteristics; merely 'th'Eternal Eye' (V 711), and never a God on a throne, rather 'A voice/from midst a Golden Cloud thus milde was heard. . . .' The 'God' in the poem, and the complementary Son also, are thus the transfigured expression of a rightness or fitness only.

> O Father, O Supream of heav'nly Thrones,
> First, Highest, Holiest, Best, thou alwayes seekst
> To glorifie thy Son, I alwayes thee,
> As is most just; this I my Glorie account,
> My exaltation and my whole delight . . .
>
> (VI 723–7)

They anticipate metaphysical materialism by two centuries. They are devoid of even metaphorically social characteristics. This is not true of the angels on either side. They taunt and jeer in battle, and on God's side are correctly stern, virtuous and brave. But here, as in the speeches in the 'great consult' in

Books I and II, the speeches are merely a continuance — certainly a stupendous one — of the action, and not, even then, as in drama where what the characters say emanates from themselves as original persons bringing the action into existence. In Milton the voice, the substantive language, brings the speech into existence, and there is no break in the language-use already analysed when these speakers talk. But, if this is true, the result is that the speakers are only understandable to the extent that they have access to that central voice, and equally the speakers themselves only have understanding through that means. The speeches in the Pandemonium debate are divisions, alternative readings in an already integrated argument. Their colossal power contains no set-backs, crises in the debate, or 'personal involvements', and the debate therefore proceeds to the great pronouncement of Beelzebub with some inevitability. And when a really new and dramatic element enters, that of Satan's news about the making of earth, the debate is over.

Raphael's speeches to Adam, to take the next category, are didactic, and as such tedious to many people. But again they all aspire correctly back toward Milton's central poetic. Not being a confrontation even in a formal sense they thus merely convey heavy information or moral counsel. But surely they would be infinitely worse without the thing for which Milton has usually been faulted; the tense, weighted cadences. The point is made most clearly in the whole description of the war in Heaven in Books V and VI. Raphael offers to tell that story, and after a brief introduction starts at V 577. This continues to VI 892 — over one thousand and two hundred lines — when Raphael winds up with some brief counsel. But I suggest it is the reader's experience that after a while he has forgotten who is speaking: it is in fact Milton, or Milton's language. That these passages are comprehensible and powerful is largely irrelevant to their emergence from the angel's mouth in the story. For a time Adam is the reader, and the reader Adam.

Fourthly, the earlier speeches of Adam and Eve before the Fall, in Book IV are similar. Again there is criticism, for example that Adam sounds sententious and priggish. Even so the cause is not a failure of the poetry but the unrealizability of the subject. The case that most offends most readers is IV

610–88. Adam discourses to Eve on the nature of night and day and their tasks. Eve admits her weaker female status, and humbly asks (like a student addressing a teacher) scientific questions about space and the sky; Adam answers. Surely any objection we feel is caused not by the poetry's failure but by its success, Milton endowing Eve with lines not only of great economy, clarity and ease of movement, but this still in the materially-activated mode already suggested:

> To whom thus Eve with perfet beauty adornd.
> My author and Disposer, what thou bidst
> Unargu'd I obey; so God ordains,
> God is thy Law, thou mine, to know no more
> Is womans happiest knowledge and her praise . . .
>
> (IV 634–8)

It is the sense, not the language, that is impossible to accept, for Milton is writing within a convention, accepted by him, of male domination. Since these speeches of Adam and Eve merely declare this, in however effective and controlled cadences, it follows that the pair make only ritual declamations and do not constitute interaction. But where the speech is prayer, a proper subject of ritual, it is very beautiful:

> . . . promis'd from us two a Race
> To fill the Earth, who shall with us extoll
> Thy goodness infinite, both when we wake,
> And when we seek, as now, thy gift of sleep.
>
> (IV 732–35)

But after the Fall it is different. It is after the Fall that the argument about poetry's non-social nature might seem, *prima facie*, most challenged. We say 'after' the Fall, but, as some critics have pointed out, Eve really 'falls' earlier;[1] and within the poem's context her sins of disobedience, and wilful bridling at Adam's injunctions, doom her before Satan's arrival. And it is at that point exactly that the interchanges are actually drawn into the characteristics analysable now as 'social relationships'. The exchange where Eve, with cunning combination of winsomeness and archness, persuaded Adam to let her wander alone is not merely substantive. The 'speeches' here are not merely speeches; they are as close to real interactive speech as poetry can allow, and each is brought out by the one before it. The first explicit event is Eve's arch remark that Adam's apparent lack of trust in her is something 'I expected not to hear'. She goes off and meets the serpent (containing Satan) who tries to persuade her; she hesitates, muses, is won over, and eats the fruit. A seed of doubt and anxiety however makes her wonder how to break this to Adam, and when she meets him again she tries to make light of it. When Adam eats the fruit the new socio-psychological realism unritualized continues; he and she feel a new uninnocent lust, and they make love. Then as in post-sexual remorse he recriminates, they cover their nakedness and bitterly and spitefully quarrel. In the next book Adam rolls on the ground in self-abnegation, and then spurns Eve's approaches while she tearfully pleads and takes all blame on herself. When he finally softens to her and takes the lead again they decide on a prayer for forgiveness in their humiliation, and the very immediate and realistic quality of their interaction, spread over two books, ends.

All this is very fascinating, and quite unlike anything in previous epics — unlike for example the highly formal exchange of Odysseus and Nausicaa in Book VI of the *Odyssey*, or the loves of Troilus and Criseyde (deceptively 'psychological' in perception but actually idealized and suffused with a golden chamberlight of other-worldliness and innocence). Furthermore this group of passages in recent years has more and more been taken to be the poem's imaginative core. Bergonzi puts this explicitly:

> [We might] propose that the theme of *Paradise Lost* is indeed 'loss of Eden', and that the imaginative centre of the poem is to be found in Books IV and IX: its meaning might well have to do with what Freudians call the birth trauma, the expulsion from the womb into a world where life and death are inextricably mixed.[2]

The question of Satan's goodness or badness which so exercized earlier critics, now fades from significance. The relationship in the poem, for the first time, is clearly and deliberately social; that is, in terms of the sociological idea already suggested; it is mimetic, if in formalized fashion, of what may actually happen between two people, unconstrained by ritual, myth or the supernatural, and following the interactive course so that what each one says is prompted by the sidelong demur or defensive answer of the preceding talk in each case. It is 'social' in the modern analytical sense; it is enacted at the level of the relationship between the parties concerned. Eve, as soon as she ceases to accept her position as designated by that of a larger order (a theological one) is forced to 'make a relationship' with Adam if she is to get her way, and he in turn must establish a new interactive position if she is to be controlled. They have entered the modern world.

In contrast to all this even the Satan–Abdiel exchanges in Books V and VI, the most realistic to be found elsewhere, are set pieces. Those are certainly powerful, and in a sense depict character, but such character does not itself evolve in the interchanges and has no way of doing so from such positions. Abdiel in both senses is illustrative of this. He does not derive from any notion of reality stemming from the nature of interaction itself. With the Adam and Eve passages the progress to the Fall is channelled through that first tilt between Eve and Adam. The Fall is made contingent on that event. The traditional framework of the first succumbing of the woman followed by the man, the new feeling of nakedness as shameful, and the 'What is this that thou hast done?' house a present event which is not traditional at all.

And the language has changed also; the words are limper, the nominals less substantial, and there is more repetition of words in themselves not solid; all for the first time. The weak copulative verbs are put under strain by being made to do more work.

> Hast thou not wonderd, *Adam*, at my stay?
> Thee I have misst, and thought it long, depriv'd
> Thy presence, agonie of love till now
> Not felt, nor shall be twice, for ever more
> Mean I to trie, what rash untri'd I sought
> The paine of absence from thy sight. But strange

> Hath bin the cause, and wonderful to heare;
> This Tree is not as we are told, a Tree
> Of danger tasted . . .

(IX 856–64)

It is as though Eve is not understanding the nature of things, and the Eve of Milton's poem is suddenly not using Milton's language in recognition of the uncomprisingly solid nature of the only world which that language must of its nature express. She is drawn to modify the language so that she can establish a social relationship with Adam as that is seen in the modern way, that is, according to the sociological idea; to express herself as an Ego to his Alter, since by taking the fruit she has stripped herself of all non-social, natural, divine resource. She has 'realised that she is naked'. From that point her language must negotiate or manipulate a relationship, which is not what the devils do in the debate. Evilly they distort argument, but not relationhip. They are not human and do not relate or need to relate in that way. Beelzebub and Moloch remain what they are.

This change to a social acceptance is what I take to be Milton's revolution. I mean that the poetic limitation of the created world as Milton sees it is the basis of his language; that this, like any other poetry, is prior to and constraining on the 'social' as we see that now; but most important, that Milton finds himself having to alter this when he needs to depict a social relationship for a sudden, surprising purpose. We might then say that, by putting their social relationship first, and acting within the constraints of the sociological idea, our first parents laid themselves open to the Fall; and the comedy of that notion is possible just because Milton wrote of lapsarian matters in these new conditions. Milton has anticipated from his Puritan-sensuous stance a modern world where the social dimension is the only conscious reality we have at a non-material level, and finds that the 'wayes' of God he has to 'justifie' are now of a wholly different order. This, alone, seems the sense in which Milton was of the devil's party without knowing it.

Furthermore, when the Fall occurs and the Adam–Eve

relationsip is established in the new terms suggested, the essential action and business of the poem are over. That may sound a strange contention, for the angel Michael then spends many hundreds of lines telling Adam and Eve the dreadful outcome of their weakness and folly, by showing them the catastrophic unfolding of the history of the entire human race. But that, however long it takes to say, is the result of the action, not the action itself; it is given as predictive not palpable reality as told second-hand by a narrator; and it underlines all the more strongly that the epic poem, the *Aeneid* or the *Iliad* or *Paradise Lost*, has always to give, as account of human existence, not a present theoretical scheme but an original, primaeval event or set of events, particular not general in nature, and from which the society, nation or world addressed is said to come. The earlier protagonists in *Paradise Lost* cease to affect the situation at all. Satan, with at least some theatre about his exit, becomes a serpent as do all his applauding rebel devils, while God and the Son are no longer mentioned and simply fade away. There are, of course, wonderful later passages, particularly at the very end, but Milton's poetry cannot essentially carry this matter now gone secular and social any further. The language of social interaction has no relation to the cosmic voice. And yet Adam and Eve can live on earth in a new, secular way, for the eating of the fruit leads not to death but to 'higher degree of life. . . .' 'to be Gods, or Angels demi-gods'. The hint is of a world whose chief constraints other than matter must be men alone.

It is an extraordinary, an amazing, implication. Milton's central voice was the poem's core, and he abolishes it. With it, he abolishes the epic in its traditional form, and there have been no successful attempts since. Pope did not do it; the Romantics' idea that it was a poet's vocation to produce a great epic in the Homer-Vergil-Milton line was disastrous, and the various descriptions of *The Waste Land* and *The Cantos* as 'plotless epic' or 'of epic scope' demonstrate all the more the movement to something wholly different. That is a cursory summary, but that epic has declined in the post-Enlightenment world is surely a matter of agreement. Karl Marx, having early on aspired to become a great poet, turned against it,[3] and instead wrote a historical work of immense force and, if we like, epic scope which studies the secular implications in the real world of the fact that we have nothing but the material of our consciousness. Milton's revolutionary temperament, making for the event in the poem—the Fall—is structurally similar to Marx's event—the proletarian revolution—and is historically unique in poetic terms as Marx's work is in political-economic terms. Both writers thus not only write but insert by force of will their writing into history (in Milton's case, poetic history, insofar as we can separate them) and so abolish and transcend (*aufhebung*) what went before: prehistory with Marx, the epic with Milton.

The 'Fall' into a secular relationship. one amenable furthermore to the sociological idea, is equally the fall of the poem, for there cannot be a poetic epic of secular social relationships. The Fall, poetically speaking, is the fall into the secular account of social relationships according to the sociological idea. Once Milton has (unwittingly) done this, the poem is over. But Milton's own poem brings itself to that position. His newly materialistic, scientifically-seen world, however purportedly run by God, yields (as Marxism yields) the sociological dimension as the only other reality.

The impossibility of epic in our time is inversely related to the sociological idea. That idea relentlessly pushes poetry back to the point where poetry's own concern is first and last with language itself. That is the condition when the sociological idea is in the ascendant, and will be considered in Part III. Whether, as has been argued, Milton was really writing about the England of the Civil War does not seem such an important question.[4] Where the poet gets his ideas from is important only insofar as it helps answer the question of precisely what art it is that enables us to forget that source.

CHAPTER 6

POPE AND SOCIAL FUNCTIONALISM

If any poet could be described as social in emphasis and content it might seem to be Pope. He entertains and soothes in *The Rape of the Lock*, gives advice in the *Essay on Criticism*, justifies himself in the *Prologue to the Satires*, taunts in the *Dunciad* and argues in the *Essay on Man*. He treats furthermore of actual people rather than invented ones and appears to get to grips with them as Alexander Pope, an actual person in a time and place. Finally his poetry is apparently supportive of society not only in the optimistic picture of the *Essay on Man* but in another sense as well. As is well recognized, the satirist is commonly also the conservative, deeply the desirer and upholder of the order he sees threatened. He sees that order threatened not by enmity but by the evil of stupidity, that which would destroy because it is incapable of comprehending the banked riches of civilization.

There is in fact a striking similarity also in cast of mind between Pope and the 'grand theorists' or macrosociologists, Durkheim, Parsons and others. In these sociologists and their followers a quality of orderly, patterned analysis, on at times a near-geometrical model, is evident, with central conceptions then sub-divided into their components and those parts then sub-divided further to make an interlocking conceptual scheme. Durkheim's classificatory system of totem types in *Elementary Forms of the Religious Life* and his fundamental duality in *The Division of Labour in Society* leads on to the similar but more elaborated duality of Tonnies in his classic work.[1] There the Gemeinschaft-Gesellschaft distinction is broken down into the Gemeinschaft of blood, home and friendship, and the Gesellschaft of town, city and city-state. Weber's traditional-rational distinction is analogous. With Parsons the entire work is a highly complex elaboration of similar distinctions, characteristically in pairs and fours, in effect a series of binary operations, as we put it in Chapter 2. The fundamental 'four functional requisites' system articulates with the 'pattern-variables' system to make an overall whole. The patterns of choices made across large samples decide the central social qualities of the society.

This is of course a kind of classical rationalism — less prominent in Durkheim, certainly — and is exactly paralleled in Pope. Pope's couplet with its internal antithesis and variations on that has been extensively analysed.[2] But we can also suggest that, if we do insist that Pope's poetry has a social context, (as it clearly does in one sense), then that context itself gets subjected to the couplet's mathematical, rhythmic and thus poetic nature, and not to a reality of society itself. From Pope our thought about society is deeply shaped by the balance and emphases the couplet gives, and by *its* order, not any social order. Wimsatt described the basic principle as 'distinction', something we can again see as binary.[3] The run of a passage again and again suggests, 'This is this. That is that. Now see this too, now that too . . .' and so on. In the *Essay on Criticism* many passages run through a set of couplets which have a weighting like $A, A^2; B, B^2; A, B; AB^2$, and then the final flourish of 'C', an unantithetical line.

> Whoever thinks a faultless piece to see,
> Thinks what ne'er was, nor is, nor e'er shall be,
> In every work regard the writer's end,
> Since none can compass more than they intend;
> And if the means be just, the conduct true,
> Applause, in spite of trivial faults, is due.
> As men of breeding, sometimes men of wit,
> To avoid great errors, must the less commit:
> Neglect the rules each verbal critic lays,
> For not to know some trifles, is a praise.
> Most critics, fond of some subservient art,
> Still make the whole depend upon a part:
> They talk of principles, but notions prize,
> And all to one loved folly sacrifice.
>
> *Essay on Criticism*, II, 253–66

The implication is that the profound conservatism of this

psychological stance is shared by the poets and sociologists of this kind, so that we have a basis of comparison.

The question to be asked is this: if the sociological idea is anathema to poets, how can a poet with this rationalistic and even mathematical kind of mind, now apparently consistent with one aspect of that idea, still contradict the idea overall? The *prima facie* answer might be, quite simply, that the poet is a satirist, and therefore simply defies or taunts the object, 'society', of which the classical sociologists purport to give a systematic description. But the point then is, how is that possible? Why does one of Pope's orderly mentality and rationality aspire to ridicule society, and how is it achieved? My answer is not that a poet cannot support society (as described by the sociological idea) but that he cannot do so poetically; his poetry satirizes what is bad rather than cherishing what is good, and where he does offer a social blueprint (as in the *Essay on Man*) we find that its successful parts are precisely those which are dependent on poetic mataphor not social analysis. Let us consider how this seems to be done in Pope.

The point is first compounded when we ask how that which is ridiculous or small-minded can be the object of attention and still provide the worthwhile interest poetry is traditionally supposed to provide. For it would appear that the poet must try to keep the reader's attention on the object of the satire, the society itself and the details satirized, so that the full implication — that his society actually was as terrible and fatuous as made out — would strike the reader as strongly as possible. This is invariably done by parodying the social phenomenon in its own modes. A magazine like *Private Eye* apes newspaper columns by approaching their own style as closely as possible, ridiculing headlines with headlines and advertisements with advertisements. The nearer the satirizing production can be to the original the more the reader will feel the original has been exposed. In other words, and surprisingly, invention and imagination, insofar as they bring in new figures and formulations less connected with the object satirized, must *not* be too compelling if they are not to distract from their real object, the ridiculed society, precisely by attracting too much attention away from that and on to themselves. This may be done, but it is not strictly satire. Rather, it is parody, which gets laughs, or it is mock-heroic which can even lead attention right away so that we are amused and entertained, not warned and lacerated. In a yet further mode a book like *Animal Farm* would seem to employ great imaginative originality to become not really satire but a sort of cautionary fable. But poetry — that which 'makes' — is presumably unable to take either of these directions, that of staying near the thing satirized and that of eschewing the imagination. It is of the nature of poetry to do otherwise in both cases. What then is open to the would-be satirist who would satirize poetically? If the poet is indeed in some sense outside the social, and his deepest tendencies are not toward that, how is satirical poetry possible?

The logical answer would first be that if the social thing itself is unworthy of attention then any poetry satirical in aim must be a matter, in rhythm, of intellect or wit. The structural arrangements and falsely declared values of society will be deranged by superior intellectual penetration so that a practice, or the justification given for it, is exposed as absurd or fallacious, and for this to be done poetically it will have to be a matter of verbal economy and rhythm rather than imagery. Imagery may well be employed (there has been argument over this matter in Pope) but, as Kenner says of Pope, this manifests itself not as an original or beautiful creation but the perversion of an already standard image expected to be otherwise.[4] Thus when Pope writes 'While pensive poets painful vigils keep/ Sleepless themselves to give their readers sleep' the unoriginal idea of writers staying up late to finish their work is given the sting that the sleep they miss is made up for by the drowsiness their work induces in others; but the effect is also made by the pleasing elegance of the line's balance, beginning and ending with 'sleep' neatly paired, so that the notion seems inevitable, and therefore understood and controlled by the mind that writes it. This elegance can become permanent and borrowable, so that everyone can later mutter ironically of any journalist or committee man, that they are 'sleepless themselves to give their readers sleep'. Such is the very absence of importance, in one sense, of the detail, that 'hearers' can stand in for 'readers' with the same result; for 'sleep' is what is important (and is incidentally nice and safe, in the way that imagery of torture and violence would not be). Not only is this so, I would suggest of Pope, but it could not be otherwise, for to achieve such balances at the intellectual level of construction only, would leave us with sniping comments about society social but not poetic. It is the turning of the social into something other than itself, a deranging or perverting formulation, which we remember and prefer, and it occurs when the disparagement is encased in the form of balance and rhythm.

But this first characteristic of satirical poetry is inseparably accompanied by another. This is to do with the physical dimension of reality. Society itself is expressed and embodied in the actions of people physically in the sense that, however much 'things' be left out of the picture in order to reach as purely and theoretically 'social' a subject as possible, there is still left the minimum of people's actual bodies as universally the medium through which the social is enacted and negotiated. Equally, poetry is itself made of words which are at root physical, they take space on the page and time to say or hear, and they are underpinned in their physical origins in the parts of the material world that gave rise to them. Therefore if poetry is incompatible with the social, (leaning away from the language of discourse and the affirmation of institution as social) and yearns and aspires elsewhere, then the satirical poet, who must have one eye on the thing he is disparaging, will be likely to give attention to that aspect of people as the answer to his problem; that is, their physical qualities. Again though, the poet cannot let imagination go too far, and expect to remain a satirist, or let his reference to such qualities be too positive, for that would distract us too much from the force of the satire. Yet equally if I am correct he cannot as poet present the embodiment in human flesh of social reality as it more or less is. The poet's only way is to accompany the debunking of social realities with a debunking of the physical forms in which they are found. In Pope, as in much satire, this is done by decomposing matter, human matter included, to its lowest form where it becomes undifferentiated, fragmented and decayed. In short, there is preoccupation with the messy, stinking, broken-up appearances of matter, and with excrement and its many associations in particular. In *The Dunciad* this is the context of all the physical action. Lines like 'where as he fished her nether realms for wit' and couplets such as

'Vigorous he rises, from the effluvia strong/Imbibes new life, and scours and stinks along' surround and support a central presence of the poem, the black mud in which the scribblers and poetasters and hacks wallow throughout, and particularly in the games in Book II. The same reasons are behind the same preoccupation in the *Moral Essays* and *Satires,* with lines like 'Astride his cheese Sir Morgan may we meet', and the extended and renowned portrait of Lord Hervey in the figure of Sporus, 'This painted child of dirt, that stinks and stings. . . .' who 'half froth, half venom, spits himself abroad', the whole picture amounting to something in fact superficially attractive (with 'gilded wings') but really deeply corrupted, and physically so, as fundamental to the metaphor: 'A cherub's face, a reptile all the rest'. Imagery certainly, but it is always the imagery of decomposition, never distracting us from the poet's intellectual base.

The preoccupation with many varieties of sticky or glutinous matter and their associations is pronounced, and at one point in the second book of *The Dunciad* provides material for the concluding line of several paragraphs almost successively: 'Signed with that Ichor which from gods distils', 'Nor heeds the brown dishonours of his face', 'And the fresh vomit run for ever green!' But there is another point too. The close connection between these emphases and the permeation of intellectual over other forms of attention is found where such associations are themselves the occasion of wit or pun: 'And now had Fame's posterior trumpet blown'. In other words, the reasons suggested for satire at the meaningful level (intellectual wit and binary operation emphasis) and at the physical level (ultimately excremental emphasis) turn out to be one and the same. In both cases it is a matter of *reducing* otherwise complex, structured, and potentially fruitful and imaginative thought and matter to a single stratum which is homogeneous. This is an important characteristic of nearly all Pope's poetry. If everything is seen not as capable of emotional or imaginative celebration but only as to how the intellectual faculty alone can get from it a verbal balance or spark, then everything, all mental phenomena, human experiences, suffering and feeling are levelled and made to seem part of a single, very thin plane of vision. Everything is assessed from and by the outside, leaving it (deliberately) no individual and unique heart or gut. But in an exactly parallel way, if all matter and substance get analogous treatment, then all matter, too, is levelled to waste, discharge, and dismantled or putrefying substance. The mere wind given off by stupid humanity is like the discharges that same word describes in material cases.

But here is the incompatibility with the sociological project. When the rationalistic minds of such as Parsons and to a lesser extent Merton go to work on 'society', they are able to do so, and arrive at abstract coherence, only by *omitting* reference to society's tangible manifestations in their actual form. For those references would conjure up irrelevant and inconvenient other categories. It is remarkable that Parsons provides not one physical illustration of what he is saying in the entire five hundred and fifty pages of *The Social System*. He cannot afford to. When Merton discovers features which disturb the social system outside the consciousnesses of the actors, he calls them — rightly enough — 'latent functions' and the disturbances 'unintended consequences'. For Pope unintended consequences are caused by banana skins and mud at the bottom of the Fleet. In this way these things can be arranged to suit the intellectual structure of the heroic couplet and the mind that produced it. If these things retained their organic structure they would burst the couplet at the seams. Material has to be collapsed if it is to be manipulated by binary operation. It is exactly from this point of view that the organic version of grand theory — Durkheim's and even the later, evolutionary Parsons' — can be seen as vulnerable to satire's decomposing force. Pope's collapse of (and therefore his satire on) 'society' *is* his rendering of of its matter as amenable to the control of his binary couplet; that is, his poetry. Parsons' equally binary treatment of society to make it seem orderly, means he must leave out matter altogether.

The final step after the decomposition of the base itself is the mode of rebuilding that can then occur. This I would describe as accretion, and it is the antithesis of the organic. It is accretive in contrast to the more four-square constructions of Parsons and Tonnies because by that means it can incorporate the components, the physical and cultural artfacts, it wants to ridicule by having them broken up and then leaving them in that state in what follows. The reconstruction is cerebral addition,[5] and it is the exuberance with which Pope energizes this which is itself the poetry. The same binary mind that in the macrosociologists produces the sociological idea, in Pope collapses the society it actually sees, leaving that social object ridiculously sprawled out behind us, the fine poise of its poetic description having been retrieved and taken away:

> How hints, like spawn, scarce quick in embryo lie,
> How newborn nonsense first is taught to cry...
> How tragedy and comedy embrace;
> How farce and epic get a jumbled race;
> How time itself stands still at her command...
>
> (*The Dunciad*, I, 59–60, 69–71)

The accretive characteristic needs no comment. The first two hundred lines of *The Dunciad* are almost a list of such accretions, a mounting demonstration of additive exultation. No body of poetry could be nothing but this, and its diversification is part of Pope's brilliance. The thoughtless layout of the composite 'Timon's villa' — too long to quote here — is equally listed in its parts in the fourth of the *Moral Essays*; there are many other examples of the accretive rush. At one point only, at last, does Pope commit himself to his own overview:

> As one by one, at dread Medea's strain
> The sick'ning stars fade off th'ethereal plain
> As Argus' eyes by Hermes' wand opprest,
> Closed one by one to everlasting rest;
> Thus at her felt approach, and secret might,
> Art after art goes out, and all is night...
>
> (IV, 635–640)

The 'one by one' and 'art after art' are his own comments on the accretions. The atoms and fragments of the brittle kingdom of Dulness are gathered to a larger order of generality: the great modes of knowledge are themselves wheeled off; 'skulking Truth', 'Philosophy', 'religion blushing', physic, metaphysic and the rest disappear, leaving for the first time a clearance, within which also for the first time Pope gives us a genuine intricate and organic image, no longer shattered at its heart but toughly resonant, this time however not of society or the civilized world but its grim obverse:

> Lo! thy dread empire, Chaos! is restored;
> Light dies before thy uncreating word;
> Thy hand, great Anarch! lets the curtain fall,
> And universal darkness buries all.
>
> (IV, 653–6)

*

But of course many of Pope's poems are not destructively satirical and therefore need further comment. We can only briefly refer to *The Rape of the Lock* and the *Essay on Man*. In the context of what has been said the aspirations of the *Rape* away from the affirmation of a real world seem clear enough. It mixes levels in a faery, almost phenomenological way, so that a mock-universal meeting of sylphs at an ethereal level can instantly be switched to a microscopic close-up of a game of cards in which the participants are so much larger than life that we feel ourselves to be down almost below table-level witnessing how the King of Hearts 'falls like thunder on the prostrate Ace'. More importantly, the actual snipping of the lock feels about four inches away, so sweetly and exactly is it described (Who has not inadvertently dissected a wasp with the breadknife in warm September?):

> The peer now spreads the glitt'ring forfex wide,
> T' inclose the lock; now joins it, to divide.
> Ev'n then, before the fatal engine closed,
> A wretched sylph too fondly interposed;
> Fate urged the shears, and cut the sylph in twain,
> (But airy substance soon unites again)
> The meeting points the sacred hair dissever
> From the fair head, for ever, and for ever!
>
> (III, 147–54)

The passage shows exactly how poetry defies the sociological idea, for it is exactly this microscopic foreshortening into sub-reality in this particular poem that takes from the poet any need to defy, alter or collapse society in the way he later must in *The Dunciad*, where the real is more robustly seen.

The *Essay on Man*, however, might at last appear to be a wholly social poem. It declares its interest in man's social nature, and it argues in as nearly positivist and functional terms as the eighteenth century might seem able to offer. Its central precepts, 'Whatever is, is right', 'The Universal Cause/Acts to one end, but acts by various laws', and 'True self-love and social are the same', would do credit to Talcott Parsons himself.

Here are two passages:

> God loves from whole to parts: but human soul
> Must rise from individual to the whole.
> Self-love but serves the virtuous mind to wake,
> As the small pebble stirs the peaceful lake;
> The centre moved, a circle straight succeeds,
> Another still, and still another spreads;
> Friend, parent, neighbour, first it will embrace;
> His country next; and next all human race;
> Wide and more wide, the o'erflowings of the mind
> Take every creature in, of every kind;
> Earth smiles around, with boundless beauty blest,
> And Heaven beholds its image in its breast.
>
> (IV 361–72)

> Order is Heav'n's first law; and this confess'd,
> Some are, and must be, greater than the rest,
> More rich, more wise; but who infers from hence
> That some are happier, shocks all common sense.
> Heaven to mankind impartial we confess,
> If all are equal in their happiness:
> But mutual wants this happiness increase;
> All nature's difference keeps all nature's peace.
> Condition, circumstance is not the thing,
> Bliss is the same in subject or in king . . .
>
> (IV 49–58)

Pope and Social Functionalism 113

The first passage succeeds as poetry, while the second is a versification in metre and rhyme of a number of very explicit social conceptions. The first passage registers the social event it is talking about in the succinct natural analogy of the fourth line, and then elaborates its theme in terms not of society but of that analogy: and the social process is thus caught in terms of that outwardly rippling progression which the lines themselves ('another still, and still another. . . .', 'next; and next. . .') exactly capture. That is to say, the social process of affectual increase (so to call it) is captured, and only captured, in the complete integration between the physical image and the flow of words. There is no separate sociological idea at all. In the second passage Pope confines himself (in eighteenth-century terms) to order, stratification, affluence, intelligence and experience, satisfaction, equality, reciprocity and the environment. Here we have rhymed and level dissertation, in which small tremors of human engagement and felt knowledge (like the end-of-line hiatus in '. . . greater than the rest,/More rich, more wise . . .') testify to the deep power of the individual's feeling, and to the necessity of a spiritual source for any worthwhile sense of ourselves if a dead recitation of formula about our condition is to be avoided. For the barrenness of the middle three lines from 'Heaven . . .' to '. . . increase', and the dreadful betrayal of that repetition of 'confess', show Pope not merely in disputation, but surrendering to disputation. It reduces the mystery of what we are, to that activity. Can so utterly profound and numinous a thing as the relation of 'Heaven' — no less — to 'mankind' — no less — be merely 'confessed' and ticked off as a debating point?

Insofar as the *Essay on Man* is memorable — and opinions vary about it from Pope's contemporary Welsted (fulsome praise) to Byron ('comfortable metaphysics') it is not through any union of social and poetic by which the second deeply delights while the first remains intact. Rather, we mainly remember those very words and lines, I suggest, that jump out from that elegant but bland presentation of orderly thesis — lines like 'A mighty maze! but not without a plan'; the zeugma in 'And now a bubble burst, and now a world'; and the sudden power of a single word tensing against the line's mathematical relation rather than supporting it: 'All are but parts of one stupendous whole'. Finally there are the longer swelling passages in which we come across apostrophe or extravagant awe rather than accuracy of classification of social parts:

Force first made conquest, and that conquest, law;
Till Superstition taught that tyrant awe,
Then shared the tyranny, then lent it aid,
And gods of conquerors, slaves of subjects made:
She midst the lightning's blaze, and thunder's sound,
When rock'd the mountains, and when groan'd the ground,
She taught the weak to bend, the proud to pray,
To power unseen, and mightier far than they . . .

(III 245–52)

Marshall McLuhan held the view that Pope's real object of attention was not his nasty rivals but a world mesmerized and stupefied by the printing press and the threat of mass communication.[6] In that light I speculate whether that 'quaking mud' in *The Dunciad* is not really a thick sea of black ink. Pope is immersed not in society, even a serenely ordered and yearned-for one; rather his forbears 'dipp'd me in ink' at birth.

CHAPTER 7

WORDSWORTH AND SOCIAL ANTHROPOLOGY

I have tried to show that each poet goes away from rather than towards a fundamentally social interest even in the tradition of sociology to which he might seem closest. Wordsworth seems drawn most nearly to the things to which social anthropologists are drawn. But, before thinking of that, it must be said that in writing of Wordsworth we face the question of the relation of poetry with sociological thought at a new level. This is because we can no longer omit the presence of sociology itself, and the idea of a sociological attitude beginning to be present in the society in which the poet himself writes. The conditions which released the Romantic poets into the world are the conditions which similarly released sociology. Later in the chapter this will be considered specifically.

The materials of Wordsworth's universe are near to those that interest social anthropologists. Social anthropologists are commonsensical in attitude rather than theoretical or paradigmatic, they see people in the actual and tangible circumstances and environment in which they live, and as a result find their criteria for evidence about social behaviour spreading wider and wider to include nature, agriculture, artefacts and domestic detail, as well as sociological concepts. Wordsworth's gaze is directed toward a very large actual place (in effect the Lake District, although this spreads in periods to take in London, France, Salisbury Plain, Cambridge and elsewhere), seen as yielding a reality which must be viewed organically and whole, and in which the central throb of the reality is not a system on a mathematical model but an actuality, something which just is there and must be investigated, feared, 'researched' or lived in for what it is. There is nothing like the invented romantic or cosmic worlds of Spenser, Dante or Milton, or the fading of the real world into that of the spheres, as in Vaughan. And similarly, social anthropologists do not have a theoretical purpose *a priori*, as do Marxists, structural-functionalists or social interactionists. The spread from the centre, the need to give a description that includes everything, poetically or scientifically, in the light of what we do tangibly experience, is the orientation of this sort of poet and sociologist. For as we said in the earlier chapter, the social anthropologist has to consider any evidence no matter what, and not merely that relating to concepts already decided on. Equally the sensitive poet of this kind cannot stop, but will ask any questions of himself or his environment, no matter what arises. In the *Preface to the Lyrical Ballads* Wordsworth's open-ended attitude to the place of a poet is made clear. The description is not specific and technical but general. The poet is a man like other men, and in the same fashion he has, not some specialized quality or interest, but 'more lively sensibility, more enthusiasm and tenderness, a greater knowledge of human nature, and a more comprehensive soul'. The sense that striving for total understanding comes from one's very qualities in all their magnificence is, needless to say, considerably different in tone from the common-sense and workaday approach of a researcher investigating the communal life of a twentieth-century industrial town; but the feeling for the place and its wholeness — the lakes and mountains of Cumbria, and the actual back streets, pubs and parish halls of Banbury and Bethnal Green — stands out very clearly in contrast to the exact profile of sociological theories on the one hand and, for example, the heroic couplet of Pope and the black-edged universe of Milton on the other.

These seem to be the similarities between the social anthropologists and Wordsworth. If we now want to show the differences between them, the course of the argument might seem obvious. Although their evidence comes from the natural world and men in it, the social anthropologists want to order it according to sociological categories, whereas Wordsworth sees nature as more fundamental than man, and man as a product of nature. But in Wordsworth we actually find something much more startling. He is not only less interested in people communally, but his interest appears deliberately to hurt and destroy them, or at least to express a compulsive fascination with such hurt and distortion.[1] This furthermore occurs almost invariably when a kin connection (the ultimate basis of community structure) is present. Wordsworth's poetry teems with characters, yet it never feels so, and this is because they never amount to a community in the way they do in the major novels of, for example, Dickens, Tolstoy and George Eliot. Wordsworth's characters are solitary, dislocated, and often the victim of some dreadful mischance or deeply earthly distortion. It is as though the natural order, the very thing in which he and social anthropologists are most interested, has gone appallingly wrong, or has wreaked some dire punishment. The well-known examples are the ghastly soldier who appears, desolate and unfamilied, round the corner of a lane; there is Leonard whose brother fell over a cliff, and the dead man in Book V of *The Prelude* who came bolt upright out of the lake like a black pole surging up from the water. There is also the man hanging from a gibbet, and the sailor in 'Guilt and Sorrow' who finds that the suffering woman he has accompanied through many trials is the widow of a man he himself murdered many years before. And there are the children Lucy, Alice Fell, the Winander Boy, the baby buried by the thorn, all of whom die young and abnormally or are bereaved by such a death. There is something wrong, it seems, not only with humanity in general but with humanity specifically in its communal aspects. These characters altogether miss exactly the features of life that are so central to community; namely, kinship and residence.[2] The solitary characters are homeless and wandering, they do not reside. On the few occasions that they do, as in 'Michael' or 'The Ruined Cottage', it is indeed a matter of ruin and gloom; but more often they are on the hills, on the road, or rumoured to have travelled far across the sea. If they have any resting-place it is in the soil itself, they are buried in the graves and the stones. Furthermore they do not at all seem the result of disaster at the 'social problem' level. They come from nowhere but the earth and stones and hills. The disturbance is not everyday or institutional; it feels cosmic. Similarly Wordsworth's deeply disturbed attitude to kinship is inescapably suggested by the children in his poems. It is children who most deeply symbolize and also actually cement kinship ties, since they are biological links between individuals in families — a point which, with its necessary reference to the physical (that is biological) rather than social dimension of human reality, is what has enabled social anthropologists more than other sociologists to centre their work on the subject of kinship. But Wordsworth's children imply the bleakest wound in the body of kinship. They die, or they sit beside the graves of those who are dead.

The question therefore arises as to how this stark and frightening aspect of Wordsworth's thought is related to our subject. One feature of communities of the traditional kind, not yet mentioned, seems to me important. Compared to the idea of society, community is finite, bounded, clearly anchored to a certain territory. The finiteness of the community is reinforced by the network of relations of stratification and the well-known fact that such divisions and conflicts actually bind the social structure more tightly, sealing it with rituals and sanctions by which such divisions are held in tension and which themselves constitute actual events, ceremonies, patterns of symbol and ways of living in the culture. Through such factors a degree of ignorance, as it has been suggested,[3] must exist for a traditional community to be secure. And such is traditional community theory. But Wordsworth — for many people still simply the nature poet — has as different an outlook from that suggested by this picture as it is possible to have. His yearning toward the infinite, vast, unknown and, most importantly, unspecific, that without clearly marked edges, is what permeates his work, both outwardly and in terms of the mind. It is not necessary to quote the well-known passages at length, but we can note the way that physical roaming ('like a roe/I bounded oe'r the mountains . . . wherever nature led') ties in with the dependence from the earliest part of *The Prelude* on 'dear Liberty' to produce the passages of unbounded space both in terrain and meditation:

> No familiar shapes
> Remained, no pleasant images of trees,
> Of sea or sky, no colours of green fields;
> But huge and mighty forms, that do not live
> Like living men, moved slowly through the mind
> By day, and were a trouble to my dreams . . .
>
> (I, 395–400)

This is indeed the expression of the 'growth of the poet's mind'; 'the eternity of thought' and 'the mind's abyss'. The immensity of what is available to, or itself constitutive of, the mind prior to the community of its location is the subject also of the 'Immortality' Ode.

Formally Wordsworth explored this infinity of knowledge in associationism, Godwinism, rationalism, the ideas of Newton and from other sources. But his expression of what the mind feels itself to *be*, giving us those passages about the poet as 'neither sick nor well', having 'broodings, obstinate questionings', and that this is in nature itself so that 'even the stones . . . I gave a moral life: I saw them feel, or linked them to some feeling'; and that the mind does 'half create' as well as perceive — all of this suggests a direct apprehension of things we might now think of as the province, in the intellectual world, of structural anthropology, and the relationship between thought, myth and nature. If then Wordsworth is not interested in myth out of that trio (and he positively disclaims it, when stating in Book I of *The Prelude* his decision to put aside themes from the ancient or chivalric world), we can ask how it works, through what means, that he does not identify with actual, tangible places in their social and communal aspect. Why does he, rather, go to the dark origins of the natural mind, a mind whose broodings, depths, turbulences, fears and sicknesses are given the embodiment of lonely and bereaved women, dying children and sick beggars? For that surely — and it could be elaborated very exactly, I think, in Freudian terms — is what those characters we considered turn out to be. Why does Wordsworth do this and what has it to do with the nature of his poetry?

Here are some representative passages:

> There was a time when meadow, grove and stream . . .
>   To me did seem . . .
>
>   . . . with purpose of its own
>   And measured motion like a living thing
>   Strode after me. With trembling oars I turned . . .

> . . . How I have felt,
> Not seldom even in that tempestuous time,
> Those hallowed and pure motions of the sense
> Which seem, in their simplicity, to own
> An intellectual charm; that calm delight
> Which, if I err not, surely must belong
> To those first-born affinities . . .
>
> Mine was it in the fields both day and night,
> And by the waters, all the summer long.

What stands out very clearly from these passages is the degree to which Wordsworth's sonority of thought, and the union of sound and thought, depends on the nasal consonantal sounds, 'n', 'm', and 'ng'. It seems certain that they occur in Wordsworth more than in other poets, although I have not counted them, but the impression they make survives whatever such a count could prove; and it is the use and placing of those consonants, as well as their frequency, that is at the heart of the spontaneous overflow. This is one of those cases that is seen more than ever to be an unprovable critical claim; doubtless many other people have noticed it, but it is not mentioned in the major Wordsworth studies I have read, or certainly not emphasized. I can only say it is remarkable how often the eye falling on the page in Book I of *The Prelude* picks on a line that seems to reinforce the impression: 'Into the tumult sent an alien sound', 'In common things, the endless store of things', 'To brace myself to some determined aim/Reading or thinking'. Often also it is the placing of these sounds that makes them the phrase's centre of gravity: 'Even then I felt/Gleams like the flashing of a shield . . .' or when the poet is enumerating his gifts; 'Nor am I naked of external things,/Forms, images, nor numerous other aids. . . .' The first two lines of the Ode, quoted above, stress the 'm' word in each case with 'grove' the only exception. And the 'ng' sound is often found at the end of a line, where it seems to magnetize other emphases towards it.

If a person closes his mouth and attempts to make a sound, these consonants are the only ones available. Certain other noises can be made in the shut mouth, squelches and salivations and so on, but these are essentially external in that their source is not the heart of the physiology, the visceral rhythms of the body itself. No vowels can be distinguished when the mouth is shut, yet when it is open the vowels too proceed not simply from the tongue, cheek or lips but from the body itself. The gutturals, labials and explosives in the consonants k,t,g,p,d,b, are equally impossible when the mouth is closed and they, although expressive of more than mere noise or physical event, tend to be aggressive and in fact specialized in their application. It seems that Wordsworth's incessant recourse to the nasal group of consonants is the raw material of his expression of the mind itself. This is quite a large claim, and in a generation that prefers structural to physical linguistics it may seem eccentric, a lean toward not merely Chomsky but even Bloomfield. But if we are interested in the relation between body and mind, as we necessarily are in considering Wordsworth's connection between thought and nature, we cannot avoid asking at exactly what point thinking and its physical expression in sound actually occurs. What *is* the embryo, the first sound, of thought and mind at their most basic, as their innermost selves? The question has had more force since the work of Ryle, for we cannot now even disentangle 'mind' as a distinct entity. (In reverse, a similar question would be that of the stage at which an embryo in the womb could be said to be thinking.) Wordsworth is not explicit about this matter in the sense of actually analysing it, but that seems all the more to make his poetry synonymous with that expression, the thing actually happening. Furthermore, in no sense does Wordsworth use these sounds as a template, an external parallel to the thoughts he expresses. The sounds and their proliferation *are* the thoughts' expression of the thinking and feeling mind. Wordsworth's repeated reference to song, number and music, as well as wider terms such as brooding, feeling, being, restless motion, and those seen in nature too ('low breathings coming after me, and sounds/Of undistinguishable motion. . .') suggest that he has actually got into and down to the tap-root where feeling meets and is one with sound so that spontaneous overflow rather than just cerebral consideration is possible. His phrase 'a dim and undetermined sense/Of unknown modes of being' seems almost to hum, to throb, with this material, and to become mind in the very sounds it utters, at the same moment as comprehensibly describing it.

It would be idle to say that Wordsworth can do this only because the words employing these sounds already meant something in his culture ('socially' in fact), for the reason why that was so would then need to be asked. Equally if these words had meant something else then Wordsworth would not have used them as he did, and his poetry would not exist. It is perhaps more interesting to consider these uses as an example of the metaphoric mode in the metaphoric/metonymic distinction made by Jakobson and the structural linguists. In Lacan's very appropriate terms (in the context of Wordsworth) these metaphoric uses would be acts of repression, the repressed layers of mind being expressed consonantally, as suggested by for example sense, mind, motion, moon, meaning, man and being.[4] And this repression would yield that deep pathological (in the literal and etymological sense) 'hum', and profoundly affected and suffered incantation in the vivid and symbolic characters of the subconscious (waifs, old people, victims and tramps) who 'surface' in Wordsworth's narrative right away from the communal order, in their solitary state and at the mercy of the elements. Poetry's self-referring quality allows the poet to reach such language without the pressure of sustaining roles in discourse, or of supporting or affirming the normative structure of an institution.

Again then I would argue that the poet defies the sociological idea even in that version of it which he seems at first sight most closely to parallel. The suggestion is that Wordsworth not only is not identified with the sociological version of the community and its use of nature, but in no way could have been so and remained a poet; for the very nature and texture of his poetry, what constitutes it as poetry, is the exact matching of its mental activity and almost physiological motion. This is a relation which social anthropology cannot by its nature entertain, for it must use, not the terms that ring from the very rhythms our mind-body organisms offer, but those derived from abstract sociological theory and public description. In Wordsworth's case we have the unique confirmation of this in that, when after his earlier period he did finally turn his poetic attention to more public, social and institutional concerns, all this hidden power drained away.

*

We can now consider the question raised at the start of this section. Wordsworth not only as it were contests social anthropology; he is also the first poet of the five we have discussed at length who wrote in the period in which sociological thought itself first arose.

Of course, the whole of Romantic poetry is at one level a response to the collapse of old forms of thought in the early nineteenth century. But with the exception of Coleridge this poetry is still of clear, hard-edged subject-matter (however the Romantics treated it) and does not, even in Blake, actually embody the modifications of mind at the deepest level, as Wordsworth did, in a way that helps explain intellectual development in our own time. I am bound to oversimplify, but Keats and Shelley can be said to have written on clear topics, autumn, skylark and west wind, the Greek legends and in 'Adonais' a death, where pure ecstasy of feeling or remarkably refined sensuality are achieved. Blake's visions stem from a mental black-and-white energy, and Shelley seems to have a singly energized voice. It is Wordsworth alone who took the mind itself as explicit topic, and precisely by retaining the blurred edge of half-thought (the very thing to which Pound objected), more clearly illustrates the concern with what was still tenuous and unknown. Wordsworth is both less and more than revolutionary because this unspecificity is by its nature embryonic; it is the once-off attempt by a poet to examine his own mind in the light of the deep changes by which that same mind is being modified. His long description in *The Prelude* (Book I), already referred to, where he explains how he came to put aside old themes, legends, a possibly Arthurian epic, in favour of 'some philosophic song/Of Truth that cherishes our daily life' is a new sort of poetry in a number of ways. It demonstrates the Romantic poet's cessation of interest in history rather than present consciousness, it takes the topic of mind itself for theme, and it also interestingly incorporates into the poem itself a hesitant, critical description of how its theme was reached. The inclusion in the poem of the wandering steps toward it are both symptomatic of the modern age's self-conscious sensibilities, and also of the modern tendency for a work of art to declare criteria for its own evaluation.

So Wordsworth is the most explicit and self-conscious of the Romantic poets, and the Romantic movement was generated by the same conditions that generated sociology. What would be more likely, then, if we were moving into a sociological world, than that his poetry would anticipate and lead that interest? It does nothing of the kind. Wordsworth does not at all find in language a pull outwards to an expression of the nature of society; he finds a pull *inward* to a presentation, an embodiment by his poetry, of the language-mind relation which is a precursor of the entire tradition of the philosophy of mind in the twentieth century. Of course he must in part use, as material, trends and disturbing events which sociologists, in a separate way, reduce to the 'social'; but in the poetry they have shed that possibility, they have rejoined nature, and are subordinate to the *poesis* of the object that results. In this light we can see that a romantic protestation like Shelley's poem 'On Liberty' is a side-effect of Shelley's main poetic impulse, and that Blake's also publicly apocalyptic concerns are the subordination of the social to something wholly visionary, eschatalogical and angelic.

The astonishing thing is that Wordsworth in *The Prelude* does explicitly raise the question of 'society' in the strictly sociological sense.[5] He uses the word in that way a dozen or so times, always in the spirit of a search as to whether it will yield a satisfactory answer to his problem of man and nature. That he finds it does not, is clear enough:

> I summoned my best skill, and toiled intent
> To anatomise the frame of social life;
> Yea the whole body of society
> Searched to its heart. . . . Endlessly perplexed
> With impulse, motive, right and wrong, the ground
> Of obligation, what the rule and whence
> The sanction; till, demanding *proof*

> And seeking it in everything I lost
> All feeling of conviction and, in fine,
> Sick, wearied out with contrarieties,
> Yielded up moral questions in despair.
>
> (XI 279–82; 298–305)

It is not simply that that is of no great inspiration poetically, nor that Wordsworth is no sociologist, though both those seem true. Rather it is precisely Wordsworth's contact with more clearly-defined and intense human society (in London, France and elsewhere) that precede his poetic decline and loss of confidence. In the end his poetic failing was co-extensive with his increasing attempt in later life to extol society's central institutions such as the established Church and government. These take him away from the intense oneness with language itself that enabled his unique (historically unique) poetry, that unique poetic event, so that increasingly his verses became artificial pieties expressing the externally accepted institutional or normative structures. His earlier idea of 'the language of men' does not contradict this, for the source of that language to Wordsworth was not social interaction or normative structure, but the oneness of language and nature. The 'language of men' is inherently poetic (needing therefore no additional 'poetic diction') because the source of man's humanity is deep in the mind and below the line of visibility above which 'interaction' and 'institution' parade in our everyday lives. The source of language, for Wordsworth but not for sociology, is not in interactions or institutions but nature, in bodies, feelings, and minds. When therefore Wordsworth began to register the influence of the new sociological concerns, his poetry died. When sociology is about to become explicit, the Romantics (even Shelley and Blake with their apparently public absorptions) cannot grasp it directly but must find a visionary, mythological or physical objective correlative. Wordsworth, who did grasp it more explicitly, took an entirely different direction. The result is that sociology cannot claim poetry as even so much as a distant, chance or incidental forbear.

PART III

POETRY CONTEMPORARY WITH THE SOCIOLOGICAL IDEA

CHAPTER 8

INTRODUCTION AND BAUDELAIRE

In the first part I tried to argue that earlier poetry and sociological thought are in some sense incompatible. Poetry's potential, what it can do and be, cannot be borrowed to support sociological theory, nor is it illustrative of such theory. Equally it does not support or eulogize 'society' as sociological thought understands that, though it may certainly eulogize people's good qualities and their actions. I argued this by outlining the five kinds of sociological thought that seem seminal and pre-eminent, and then considered five poets next to one of each of those five sociological kinds. I tried to argue, then, that the five poets in some way strained away from rather than toward any sociological kind of orientation.

But, although we also briefly suggested ways in which these poets stemmed from intellectual and cultural roots which are also the intellectual roots of different kinds of sociology, that exercise was necessarily in the main ahistorical. I think it was legitimate, and indeed gained such analytical advantages as it had because of our freedom, in it, to consider the bodies of poetry and the variations of the sociological idea detached from most other considerations. But we must now consider the obvious second question without which this investigation would be incomplete. What happens when the sociological idea does appear in the world, and poets, like everyone else, have to cope with it? That is the subject of this part of the book.

Surely it is clear that when such an idea appears it is bound to bring about some response from poetry, if poetry, as I am arguing, strains away from that idea and indeed is virtually constituted by its using language in a way antipathetic to the way that sociology argues it must be used. I think we do find that response. The entire tenor of poetry in the last hundred years, in many different ways, has exactly the self-consciousness, and sense of deliberateness about making (or 'remaking') poetry, that we would expect to find in an art suddenly up against a socially central and overwhelming mode of thought with which it finds itself at odds. There is furthermore a sense of strain, a permanent tussle or weariness, or alternatively a too-ready and over-expressed eagerness and confidence, as though the poet feels the difficulty is being overcome. This strain is entirely absent from the openness of Homer, from the spiritual serenity of Herbert, from the chastity of Shakespeare's sonnets, and even from the nervous ecstasies of Shelley and Keats.

Once again I will examine a number of poets, although this time it seems wiser to group them according to certain characteristics rather than to consider them one by one, and to suggest various answers these poets adopt to the overriding problems facing them. Before doing so, there are two general points to be made. The first is that this new orientation of poetry to the sociological idea itself is closely tied to what we usually call Modernism.[1] Modernism itself is not confined to poetry, but again that need not refute our argument, for the arrival of the sociological idea is of such importance that every art, and a good many other things besides, has had to come to terms with it. The visual arts, music, the novel and perhaps most explicitly drama have responded to the idea of the actual human relationship and to the individual as 'the cog in the wheel' in a number of fashions from protest to close psychological analysis. But poetry can be described as having a special inverse relationship with the sociological idea in that its very medium, language, is argued by supporters of that idea to be the central means of social interaction, of social institutionalization and wider social coherence, and of our symbolic and cognitive life.

The second point concerns technology and positivistic science. It might be argued that while poetry has certainly undergone an overwhelming change in the last hundred years this has been a response not to the sociological perspective on humanity and the world, but to positivistic science. In short, poetry used to be the expression of myth and legend, with a non-literal mimesis of nature and behaviour, and this has had to change. The modern world also presents a radically different aspect through the proliferation of man-made artefacts based on electricity, petrol and other forms and sources of energy, so that these not only themselves change the natural topology but also put us into a different relation with it in terms of the vastly different rates of speed we use, and the frequency of communication we have with different races and geographical locations. And our perspective on these, as well as our increased witnessing of them, has changed, giving to poetry a whole new source of imagery, rhythm, echo, and existentiality of thought. In addition, man himself has very largely become an existentially operating creature, that is, seeing himself scientifically, so that his very means of symbolism, expression and communication would be expected to be of a wholly different order in such a world.

I think it is tenable to state that it is that same positivistic science that has projected the sociological attitude into the world. By the reduction of all matter to something purportedly inert which we can at least in principle control, and which at least in principle is not mysterious and certainly not animated with other forms of intelligence or spirit which may control us, the nineteenth century left us in effect with two dimensions of reality only. These were physical matter, and our own consciousnesses which (whatever science says) we do experience as living in us and in the others with whom we relate. Since the other human discipline of our time, namely psychology, is itself reducible, again at least in principle, to something physiological and to a matter ultimately of physical responses and stimuli, then it follows that the only other dimension of reality left to us of any distinct nature was the sociological idea, the idea of what relationships constrain us over and above our individual physical characteristics. Insofar as other modes of human knowledge such as economics and anthropology differ from sociology in their descriptions of our conditions, they do so by tending to include in their theories, equally material things in a way parallel to that of psychology: land, money, property and the objects of cultural activity. In short the sociological idea was the one mode of description the modern world had left when theology, metaphysical philosophy, myth, and other large descriptions of something other than a merely physical level of being were found wanting.

This distinction is made here because it seems to be the sociological idea that has permeated people's consciousnesses as an everyday description or accompanying account of what they do. Positivist natural science is taken by most people to describe the underlying conditions of the experiences we have, not the experiences themselves. Most people do not think a physical-scientific account of reality adequate. The centre of the experience, its meaning, is thought to be social and conscious. The reasons why I enjoy last night's party or my job, or why my sister's family is unhappy, are thought to be fully captured only in terms to do with experience. Certainly it may be relevant that a room is warm or a person physically beautiful, but a wholly physical account is never adequate. But the account of a marriage as being a 'bad relationship' for example, or of a joke being well told so that the company laughs, is social. It is that which is at the heart of our idea of meaning in reality. The physical components of the world only set the conditions or the raw materials which we as social beings, as people from this or that family or class or group, then use for our lives. And this surely means that if poetry is still to satisfy it has to do so at nothing less than that level; that is, at an alternative or competitive but parallel level. A poem solely about the physical experience of a jet flight or the sea or even love-making, does not satisfy. It must at least express the consciousness of a human being in experiencing those things, and it must do so in a way that we recognize.

The difficulty is that many people might respond to these remarks by exclaiming, 'Exactly! So poetry is social after all!' Quite the contrary, I would argue. Poetry combats the sociological idea precisely by converting into language alone, a greater fullness of experience than that with which the sociological idea claims to deal. Poetry deals with all our experience, often by producing new experiences for us, and not only fictive ones. It does not attempt to account for it, or explain it. It claims, implicitly at least, to produce experiences, as well as recall them, in the way that the sociological idea can never do, and its claim is made with the same medium as sociology uses: language. The natural sciences do not make this claim. They may purport to say at one level why I enjoyed something, but not what that enjoyment means, and they mainly claim to plot the physical experiences that occurred. Sociological thought very often claims exactly such meaningful description, and it is this which poetry, implicitly or otherwise, seems always to go beyond.

*

We can now begin to ask what defiant responses, so to call them, poetry has made to the sociological idea. We can trace roughly three general areas of response. The ways a poet responds in this intellectual situation may concern the poem as such ('the poem itself' as the phrase goes); or society as such, however widely we interpret that; or thirdly the person who is the poet. Thus the *poetry, society* and the *poet* are the three central components in whatever analysis or description we can give of poetry in the context of a world that largely assumes the sociological idea. And I think we can point to those three areas of interest and concentration as providing broadly three large movements or kinds of poetry that have appeared in the modern period.

It seems clear first that poetry which makes explicit the idea of the *poem* has been a response to the intellectual process which would make poetry no more than a sociological phenomenon. This is the poetry of imagism and symbolism, of the poem as icon, as symbol of invisible reality, as supreme fiction and as the first idea. The important examples are Mallarmé and Stevens, Valéry and Hulme, to a great extent Yeats, William Carlos Williams, Roethke and e.e. cummings. We can also suggest the concrete poets of the last decade and, if in a wholly different way, Dylan Thomas. The pervading idea seems to be that a poem, unlike a letter, a piece of conversation, or a play or novel, is autonomous and self-sustaining, needing no reference to outside events except as material for what is said or made. The idea of poem as icon has early if rather effete expression in D.G. Rossetti: 'A sonnet is a coin . . . Carve it in ivory or in ebony'. This idea is not wholly synonymous with the idea of the 'well-wrought urn', for that kind of poem may encapsulate a human feeling, even a very social circumstance, in a strict form, as for instance Larkin does in 'The Whitsun

Weddings'. The interesting thing about the modern idea of 'the poem itself' is again its repeated absorption with the question of its own independence. Mallarmé and many critics are always talking about it, and Stevens refers to it repeatedly within his poems. But the idea of the 'pure poem' is central, defying us to answer it or see it as part of discourse, institutionally identified or otherwise engaged in social activity.

A second poetic reaction to the sociological idea is found in the employment of history, or material drawn from past civilizations or groups within them. Such poetry defies the sociological idea by offering an alternative, equally sizable, representation of those historical raw materials from which the sociological idea itself was also drawn. Or this kind of poem may be (implicitly) arguing that the sociological idea is not valid, and that some other large-scale cultural complex such as Christianity, rural life, Imperial Rome, Scotland, Wales or Russia is what is to be evoked or recaptured. The obvious examples are Eliot and Pound, but other poets we might mention are Allen Tate, John Betjeman, C.H. Sisson, Basil Bunting, Brecht, MacDiarmid, Auden and David Jones. The disparity of that list indicates that it is not a sharing of political or social beliefs that is significant, but of something deeper. These poets seem unwilling to rule out any language reference whatever which may be poetically apprehended. The resulting poetry, often very large, has great complexity and scope and is very detailed. And again it is the conscious and explicit and even defensive absorption in the nature of what they are doing which is important. With David Jones there is, certainly, a tenderness and love for the heap of past references he compiles for his huge poem *The Anathemata*, and less concern to do this for any reason slavishly followed; his predisposition is toward gentleness, which itself seems sufficient premise for what he does. With Eliot it is the weight of weariness, the huge need to cope with civilizations seen retrospectively in the face of a vast newly self-conscious world that pervades his major work. Although at the other political extreme the socialist and Marxist poets like Brecht, Neruda and MacDiarmid have an equal aspiration to a world which contains everything, where all human richnesses and satisfactions are possible. Eliot and Pound in particular seem to be saying two things: first, that any civilization's store-house of goods can be employed and sampled and furthermore left as it is in the sampling, so that no reductive abstracting is necessary for its understanding; second, that the individual who writes the poem, though he must be repressed in terms of his 'personality' (a common theme in Eliot and Pound), will write uniquely. It is the uniqueness of the social offering that is experienced, not — and necessarily not — its sociological quality.

The third group of poets who have arisen to respond to the sociological idea centre their poetry on the poet. They seem to aim at an irreducible expression of the individual, often agonized, human condition they themselves feel. They determine to show that the most powerful use of language occurs when a lonely and isolated, perhaps madness-prone or suicidal person, expresses that condition. The poetry of this century occurs precisely when it is the least socially-central, the least group-situated or group-explicable phenomena that are at the back of the agonized cry. Or, if a group is in question, it is a group of victims, one with therefore no power of social function or collective (or individual) action. I hope to show, perhaps surprisingly, that it is Hardy who first makes a poetry of the joining of language to such feelings, although in his case death, rather than the self, is the first point of identification. Such poets are Berryman, Lowell, Edward Thomas, Rilke and many others. They seem to suggest also that their poem will, ideally and in the end, be a silence, as though language cannot be trusted to be social and to do a social job. Commonly this is thought to be a post-Auschwitz quality of language, that our language now debased beyond hope does not let the poem dare or presume actually to say itself, to make a noise, but must simply be. This however is not an iconic quality of aspiration as with the imagists, but a result, as it were at the end of the line. Certain poems of Edward Thomas have this quality, and he too speaks often of whispering and silence.

It may sound strange to talk of Lowell, Berryman and Hardy in terms of silence. But that merely shows that these three categories cannot be separated too much, and often are not separated by the poets. Of course one could argue that the noise or voice in Lowell, Rilke and others is a sort of cover for silence, like one's last talk or shriek in the face of death, and this may be so. With Larkin, as I think with Hardy, there is no such serious or uncompromising dallying with death itself, so that Larkin shows a certain libido in the expertly used forms of his successful poems like 'Dockery and Son' or 'Church Going'. Hardy's death-attitude is a temporary stance rather than a naked, bleak and black attitude of the poet himself. I think that there is in Eliot something of this tone, although he does it as it were on behalf of civilization, and so straddles the gap to another of our three themes. With the third group, if all language is social but poetry is not, then the poem must get his or her own self into a 'non-social' position, however separate. It may in the end be death.

Which stance the poet takes will depend on his or her view of the world encountered. I suggest that either because the poet's sensitivities rouse language, or because the attachment to language raises for the poet certain areas of thought, the poet will come to a position where the poetic use of language *is* the countering of the sociological idea along one of the lines suggested. The poet will turn to language itself in the face of the modern world's tendency to reduce it to sociological formulae or cliché. Or he will look at large-scale versions of reality (such as history, religion, or other whole literatures) other than the sociological version and find richness of language inseparably a part of those. Or thirdly the poet will feel that the separation of his own self from security and serenity necessarily gives rise to an intensity of language which demands release, but which cannot find that in interaction with others.

I will not try to analyse in detail even half the poets named, but will discuss only a few. I will not refer to the sociological idea in terms of its stricter divisions, as I did in the first half of the book, but rather think of the sociological idea itself, I hope now satisfactorily outlined in its general features. The various kinds of sociological thought are certain to intrude, as for instance the socially phenomenological in the case of Stevens (an avid reader of Bergson and Husserl) and the grand-theoretical in the case of Eliot (who as far as I know certainly never quoted, and hardly read, a sociological work.)

*

The suggestion of three areas of poetic response to our age is important in the light of the first poet to be considered, Baudelaire. For I think we can show that he, uniquely, works these three things to a total, and very tense, fusion, giving each equal importance; and that this compulsive unity of emphasis on *poem, society* and *poet* accounts for the intensity and impressiveness of Baudelaire's achievement. If it is true that other Modernist poets find themselves magnetized toward one or other of those areas as of the first importance, then it is all the more remarkable that Baudelaire, the first poet of this era, should feel the significance of these three things so exactly as to strain to unite them in such hypertension. Furthermore he does this in a small space (for his *oeuvre* is not great) and this is what accounts for his poetry's effect, his electric intensity, almost as though three electric wires were meeting at one point, his poetry constituting nothing other than the resulting massive spark. This view can be squared with many themes usually regarded as important in Baudelaire, and with the ways in which we commonly talk about him.

For example, in using the prototypes of Evil, Satan and Death, Baudelaire uses what are necessarily figures of extremity and indivisibility. That Evil should be explored in no matter what occasion it offers itself, and that sin as a general category is normal, not abnormal human behaviour that can, as it were, cover everything, means that the poetry that expresses this may have little room for qualification, or change of mind, and little variation of emphasis, passion or emotion. Its power will be likely to be single. There is also the prominence Baudelaire gives, among the five senses, to that of smell. This has commonly been noted. But it is well worth observing that smells and odours, unlike sights or sounds, are singular. One can seldom detect more than two or three, at most, 'aspects' of a scent, cooking savour or bad smell, and in fact they are likely to mingle; but anyone can discern any number of objects, and boundaries between them, in a room or on the street. (I think this is why all smells are either intoxicatingly evocative, or funny.) Again then there is no tendency for Baudelaire to have to diversify what he is saying, or to account for plural parts by pluralizing his own voice, or force of emotion. The presence of things smelt and scented in Baudelaire is thus strongly associated with the unified charge of the poetry itself. And again, the many objects and people that litter Baudelaire's poems, and seem to be inert as simply more and more examples of the material — the kitchens, women's hair, savours, Lesbians and corpses — all these would be of little significance without this unifying force shot through them, bringing them to life in the same way that a handful of strings, pulled all at once below a table, jerks limp puppets to their feet. As Mario Praz put it, Baudelaire 'sent a wave of electricity through the shapeless *putridero* which has been gathering into a mass since 1820'.[2] Raymond also uses the analogy with electricity, and for the same purpose: ' [Baudelaire aimed] to eliminate the dross, the *impedimenta* which tarnish [poetry's] brilliance or encumber its movement . . . so as to preserve only the spiritual fluid or high tension current that will convey the suggestive powers inherent in poetry with the highest chance of success'.[3] His lines tremble as they go, and always in the same manner. It is in this sense that Baudelaire is the enabler of modern poetry, for he provided the energizing charge which started it all.

This I think should be shown in greater detail, and we can do so by the direct exercise of comparing the combinations of the three categories and considering them — thus; society and self; poem and self; society and poem. This may seem rather mechanical, but it guarantees that we take our own argument seriously. If we take the first of these pairs, we see that Baudelaire seems obsessed with what we call 'society' in his fascination with the city; it is always that rather than nature ('these sanctified vegetables') which is his source of imagery, and he grapples with Paris at dawn and at evening; his poems are often set in kitchens, salons, luxurious apartments and cafes, and occasionally on the street. Furthermore the setting, or pattern of imagery, is not usually changed within any one poem, and so each poem remains coherent and objective, and does not seem simply the turbulences within a mind. They are the civilized artefacts that the mind, however intensely, engages with outside itself. Yet at the same time they are too isolated and domestic to seem a whole apprehension of a modern city the poet is commenting on comprehensively, as do Pope or Auden. Baudelaire's 'Parisian Scenes', even when they are scenes at all, are galvanizings of his own *horreur,* a word often repeated. The one passer-by and red-haired beggar-woman, and the old men, old women, gamblers and blind, are subjective projections. In one sense, then, Baudelaire is socially powerful, perhaps revolutionary; in another way, one can see neither his self-flagellations nor his cats, mulattoes, perfumes, bottles and furs as the implements of anything like a revolution. The mind is working on something outside itself, yet the mind's intensity as though for its own sake is what we remember of the effect.

Again, on the one hand Baudelaire is little concerned with 'poetry' as something autonomous on a pedestal, and it is Mallarmé and Gottfried Benn after him who speak much more of the self-sufficient poem as the aspiration of modern poetry itself. Baudelaire was wholly impatient with the Art for Art's Sake movement, and his poetry has an uncompromising integrity which is quite different from, for example, the pre-Raphaelite mode of his contemporaries in Britain. His poetry scarcely refers to poetry itself; he refers to the poet but not to poetry, and his references even to the poet are rather unoriginally correct views of the poet's separation from society, as in 'The Albatross' and 'Benediction'. But on the other hand, none of this makes his poetry that of the 'self' in the later sense of the confessional poets. It is too concerned with the quality of hedonistic experience (as of wine or hair) to take the straight road of pure self-abasement, neurosis, and death. He experiences reality rather than acts on it, and this is too often a matter of sensual receptivity, of odours, textures and sheens of clothes, fur of cats, and wine. This *receptivity* of sensual experience seems very important in Baudelaire. His sexual references are acquiescent not dominating, the breast is the feminine symbol and his sexuality is notably unpenetrative. He touches the woman's breast 'comme un hameau paisable au pied d'une montagne' — like a small hamlet at the foot of a mountain. He does not, then, extol the poem as such, yet equally the enjoyment of tactile and olfactory experience is an aesthetic rather than only personal equivalent, to some extent, of the iconic attitude of many moderns to the poem itself.

There is thirdly an equal fusion between Baudelaire's Satanism, his 'Mal' (that is, his external category where we might look for 'society') and its expression in the poems themselves.

On the one hand 'Mal' is a theological, external idea and therefore convertible to a social one in the secular world. That is to say, it is not a psychologically analytical term as Baudelaire uses it, but rather a general criterion. On the other hand in the poetry itself it is captured as an immediate, sensuous experience which almost invariably occurs in a tight, regular form that conveys the experience the poet is recording or recommending. This use of regular form is ubiquitous and deliberate. Because of it, we can take seriously Baudelaire's deceptively bad and vicious interests precisely because we are forced to respect the degree of conviction that the orderliness of outward and classical form imply and embody. Again then two things are present and fused; Evil and its appurtenances here as a general category that interests the poet, but also 'the poem itself' as an autonomous aspiration by virtue of the tightness of the regular rhyme containing the very breath of the poem's experience.

This, then, argues the unity of Baudelaire's power, and his claim to be the first modern poet. But how does it also argue the poet's rejection of the sociological idea? We can consider this question by referring to the very famous essay by the Marxist critic Walter Benjamin.[4] Benjamin's approach, which is stimulating, convoluted, brilliant and eccentric by turns (Hannah Arendt described him as 'the most peculiar Marxist ever produced by this movement') naturally enough wants to place the poet historically and in terms of his response to the material productions of his time. Benjamin's argument — somewhat oversimplified — is that Baudelaire responded directly and without mediation to the central characteristic of the new, modern world; its very high level of shock experience. 'Shock' in this sense is the effect of the instantaneousness of the arrival of events, and Benjamin does not mean it in a merely cheap or melodramatic sense. Shock is the effect of such diverse technologies as the telephone, the camera, the ordinary striking match, the factory production line, the act of gambling (the 'coup'), and many other things. Shock, in a thousand microscopic manifestations, is the defining characteristic of a mechanized world. And obviously, this 'shock' concept is close to the source of the electric quality of Baudelaire which we have already discussed.

Now Baudelaire, forswearing reason and coldly determining to find a mode of expression of pure passion itself, actually embodies the shock experience. He does not attempt to respond to it with rational (in our context, sociological) explanation; and this embodiment, furthermore, is synonymous with his poetry. His words are the charged, co-extensive expression of his own body in the actual state of experiencing, of receiving experiences. This is very directly illustrated by his references to breathing; both breathing in, which is exactly what is entailed in receiving 'odeur', 'parfum' and the rest; but also the many occasions of breathing out (*exhalant*), and the way his lines themselves seem to do that:

> Tu marches sur des morts, Beauté, dont tu te moques;
> De tes bijoux l'Horreur n'est pas le moins charmant,
> Et le Meutre, parmi tes plus chères breloques,
> Sur ton ventre orgueilleux danse amoreusement.
>
> ('Hymne A La Beauté')

The lines are 'exhalant' themselves, an expulsion of breath to the slower last syllable. This breathing is itself the experience. This is important in Baudelaire in the way that the consonantal sounds were important in Wordsworth. If Donne can say of a woman, 'one might almost say, her body thought', then we might say that Baudelaire's body — his whole self — quivered and trembled with self-sufficient passionate utterance. It is of no importance to Baudelaire merely to say something that can be read off, as it were, as a 'comment' about this new form of experience. What matters in Baudelaire's poetry is the unified, unchanging and uncompromising force by which the shock-waves from immediate reality are picked up by his antennac and re-emitted as, themselves, a matter of shocking expression.

Now because this 'shock' that constitutes Baudelaire's poetry is a unity, it constitutes an opposition, not so much to this or that aspect of the sociological orientation, as to its very possibility, and the very centre of it. But here is the final reason, and, I think, the clinching of the argument as to why this shock expression is at once poetic and antithetical to the sociological response to the things shock is caused by. For Benjamin the Marxist, this 'shock' is a historical occasion. For Baudelaire, the association *is with evil*, that is, in secular terms, the most anti-social conception one could possibly imagine. Baudelaire's poetic 'Mal' is the intellectual dimension of the physical (linguistic and poetic) shock, is equally indivisible and unified, but is also a linguistic embodiment and poetic energizing of the very opposite remedy to that which the sociological idea would seek. As Lowell's interesting translation of Baudelaire's line has it, 'Only when we drink poison are we well':

> O Mort, vieux capitaine, il est temps! levons l'ancre.
> Ce pays nous ennuie, ô Mort! Appareillons!
> Si le ciel et la mer sont noirs comme de l'encre,
> Nos cœurs que tu connais sont remplis de rayons!
>
> Verse-nous ton poison pour qu'il nous réconforte!
> Nous voulons, tant ce feu nous brûle le cerveau,
> Plonger au fond du gouffre, Enfer ou Ciel, qu'importe?
> Au fond de l'Inconnu pour trouver du *nouveau*!

> It's time. Old Captain, lift anchor, sink!
> The land rots; we shall sail into the night;
> if now the sky and sea are black as ink
> our hearts, as you must know, are filled with light.
>
> Only when we drink poison are we well —
> we want, this fire so burns our brain tissue,
> to drown in the abyss — heaven or hell,
> who cares? Through the unknown, we'll find the *new*.

('Le Voyage', translation by Robert Lowell)

If evil exists, the poetry seems to say, we cannot speak of it without having known it, seen it from its own side, and perhaps having done it. This exactly opposes the view of Durkheim. Durkheim (born in France two years before the publication of *Les Fleurs du Mal*) acknowledges that crime is a permanent component of human society, and this was a revolutionary attitude.[5] But Durkheim could never allow it to be society's central principle (he could never ask 'Enfer ou Ciel, qu'importe?') for he is trying to state in cold prose the key to orderly social coherence. Baudelaire's poetry on the other hand shows language energized — language electrically charged, Evil, shocking — as alone able to express the subversion of the language which aspires to give the social order an orderly description.

Having established Baudelaire's centrality to modern poetry in this way, we can now consider the separate and more special ways in which later poetry coped with man's new sort of social self-consciousness.

CHAPTER 9

THE POEM ITSELF – MALLARME, STEVENS, WILLIAMS, YEATS

The first kind of poetic response to the sociological idea was an attempt to produce 'pure' poetry, 'the poem itself'. The most explicit statement of poetic purpose on this front comes from Mallarmé.

Baudelaire qualifies as the first poet of the new age because he faces the same world as the new sociology faces; the spreading of the city and the confounding of moral positions. But Baudelaire's utterly non-sociological answer — as different from sociology as oil from water — is central exactly in that it is not explicit about the separate things the sociological world gradually affirms. With Mallarmé it is different. Mallarmé's view of the new role of poetry, whether he thought of it as such or not, certainly does contain specific elements which at the deepest level oppose the sociological view of those elements, and these largely concern language. The simplest thing to do is directly to list them. They are: the view that language's true nature is not to do with its use in social interaction; that its true nature is found in poetry and that poetry, which is not a description of man, is the supreme linguistic achievement; also, most surprisingly and challengingly, that this supreme use is fictitious; that all but poetry is chance; that language must be brought back to its essential rhythms. None of these statements is remotely compatible with the sociological idea or use of language.

In this light Mallarmé's most important point is his distinction between an immediate and an essential word.[1] An immediate word is like a coin put silently in another's hand, so that as soon as it is understood it has done its job. An essential word, however, creates a void round itself and pushes its environs out of sight. It is an instrument of power and its meaning is less than the form, colour, scent and affinities it diffuses. It is words in this second sense that Mallarmé thought of as making his poetry. What matters is not whether we think he was right; in fact he cannot be said to have been right or wrong since he is explaining how his poetry was written. What matters is that many poets of the modern world should have felt the need to adopt this specifically non-discursive, non-interactive, non-sociological view of language. For Mallarmé's suggestion about the word as coin which, when understood, must lose its value, squares exactly with any view of language as merely a means or medium for the carrying out of social interactions or the maintaining of social institutions. Once the interaction is over or the institutional norm upheld (or successfully countered) it does not matter what words are used; what could be less interesting? The poet's answer is: 'I agree; the way the social science mind thinks of words could not be less interesting. Furthermore it is an abuse and an annihilation of words to limit them and their reality, and their potential, in that way'. It is therefore the poet's task, says Mallarmé, to take words right back to a pure condition, to render them free of the vagaries of chance (their being blown like leaves wherever some holder of power at a different dimension diverts them) and fix them, beautifully, for ever. This makes poetry the supreme reality and achievement for man, 'la seule tâche spirituelle', the only spiritual task.

A passage from Paz summarizes this:

Modern poetry is an attempt to do away with all conventional meanings because poetry itself becomes the ultimate meaning of life and of man; therefore it is at once the destruction and creation of language — the destruction of words and meanings, the realm of silence, but at the same time, words in search of the Word. Those who dismiss this quest as 'utter madness' are legion. Nevertheless, for more than a century a few solitary spirits, among them the noblest and most gifted who have ever trod this earth, have unhesitatingly devoted their entire lives to this absurd undertaking.[2]

If that 'madness' Paz refers to is taken literally, we find ourselves talking of poets like Rimbaud (whom Paz also mentions) who deliberately derange not only language but also their own minds so as literally to alter the historic mind of man. In that sense Rimbaud belongs to the group of twentieth century poets who use poetry to express the condition of the poet. In fact Mallarmé himself avoided madness in that literal sense (despite one serious crisis) because his pursuit of these ideas was across a narrow cerebral band, so that he did not allow it to affect his entire personality. As he said after the crisis, 'My Thought has thought itself, and reached a pure Conception'. But that Hegelian echo can serve as an introduction to his poetry itself, and this is a necessary next step in that it shows just how his ideas of language work out.

Mallarmé's difference from Baudelaire lies in his aspiration away from gross materiality rather than toward it. We referred to 'breathing' in Baudelaire, and this doubtless influenced Mallarmé as did the very qualities of the thinner, lighter French language as compared to English. But Mallarmé's 'breath' is almost unbreathed, almost simply air itself. 'Aimai-je un rêve?' he asks, at the start of 'L'Après-Midi D'Une Faune'. It is scarcely a movement on the air outside us, and one which translations like 'Did I love a dream?' cannot be expected to capture. The subsequent lines of that poem are a gathering of such notions in which language and breath are one; 'soupirs', 'brise', 'lasse pâmoison', 'le seul vent', 'Le souffle artificiel' and so on. It is a commonplace about Mallarmé that it is the foam, air, hair, feathers, and the lightest of things which are employed as images in the attempt to create the spiritual essence the poem must embody. If the words are, very nearly, simply breaths, or breathing itself in this disembodied sense (in that the very word itself is thought of as breathed, whispered by breeze or air themselves, and not necessarily by people); and if we think of the connection, etymologically also, of the ideas of breath and spirit, then we can argue that Mallarmé's poetry attempts to embody existence itself apart from its real, material or social trappings. He necessarily cannot do this because words always have some traces of material reference. But our contemporary studies confirming the ordinary nature of language still show all the more clearly how Mallarmé's language escapes social context or reference.

The point is finally confirmed if one looks at Mallarmé's recurring use in his poetry of the image of whiteness. By a consensus, I think, this is at its finest in the sonnet about the swan:

> Le vierge, le vivace et le bel aujourd'hui
> Va-t-il nous déchirer avec un coup d'aile ivre
> Ce lac dur oublié que hante sous le givre
> Le transparent glacier des vols qui n'ont pas fui!
>
> Un cygne d'autrefois se souvient que c'est lui
> Magnifique mais qui sans espoir se délivre
> Pour n'avoir pas chanté la région où vivre
> Quand du stérile hiver a resplendi l'ennui.
>
> Tout son col secouera cette blanche agonie
> Par l'espace infligeé à l'oiseau qui le nie,
> Mais non l'horreur du sol où le plumage est pris.
>
> Fantôme qu'à ce lieu son pur éclat assigne,
> Il s'immobilise au songe froid de mépris
> Que vêt parmi l'exil inutile le Cygne.

The movement of such masterful lines exists beyond the 'content' to which they refer. It is a matter not of reference but of aspiration (again a word whose etymological connection with breathing seems to underline the integration of Mallarmé's project). Mallarmé's dictum, that 'the whole world exists to be written in a book', is underpinned by the recurrence of both the image of a book, and of whiteness, in his poems. The book is a series of white pages which, in the poetry Mallarmé wanted, give us the distillation of writing, 'l'écriture'. The sonnet about the purity of the frozen swan seems to aim for such distillation. The swan's feathers seem to merge with the book's white pages as both location for and result of 'l'écriture'. It is analogous, though with very different effect, to Baudelaire's electrified intensity. 'Writing' is a kind of spiritual substance and is shot through words, their gross materiality transfigured and transcended. In short, the idea that the whole world exists to be written in a book can be rephrased to say that the apparently central use of language, the social discourse that confirms social interaction and organization, is not central at all. The effect of Mallarmé's poetry is this distillation of words from their feel in our ordinary lives in dialogue, class or other reference. That again constitutes the poetry, and again Mallarmé's insistence upon it is contemporaneous with the emergence in our civilization of the sociological idea.

*

The next poet in this category we can consider is Wallace Stevens. Like Mallarmé, Stevens came to see poetry as the 'supreme fiction', and it is because Stevens' language is so different from Mallarmé's that we have an opportunity to see all the more how our main contentions work out. When Mallarmé died in 1896 Stevens was already nineteen.

In Stevens the supreme fiction is a replacement of the religious traditions and trappings he rejected. But in their place the materials of those fictions which Stevens is left with turn out to be what is available to the senses; the eye particularly, but with a cast of thousands from the bird kingdom and its weird cries and odd little noises:

> Deer walk upon our mountains, and the quail
> Whistle about us their spontaneous cries;
> Sweet berries ripen in the wilderness;
> And, in the isolation of the sky,
> At evening, casual flocks of pigeons make
> Ambiguous undulations as they sink,
> Downward to darkness, on extended wings.
>
> ('Sunday Morning')

The eye and ear of Stevens together, and especially in the earlier work, give us an unforgettable realm and paradise of objects directly presented; the choppy sea off Florida, brightly-coloured birds, sloppy wet fruit such as pineapple and watermelon, the 'bird with the coppery, keen claws', the frog that 'boomed from his very belly odious chords', insects:

> For me, the firefly's quick, electric stroke
> Ticks tediously the time of one more year.
> And you? Remember how the crickets came
> Out of their mother grass, like little kin,
> In the pale nights, when your first imagery
> Found inklings of your bond to all that dust.
>
> ('Le Monocle de Mon Oncle')

There is also the more manufactured but still luxuriant world of things as different as gowned grammarians, the 'tense machine of ocean', and the 'celestial ennui of apartments'. The great play of sunlight across these in an atmosphere of puffy clouds and blue sky seems to enhance more clearly the sense of these things as surfaces; not pessimistically, for a spicy vapour of sensuality is experienced from all that these things give off at their edges.

> The sea-clouds whitened far below the calm
> And moved, as blooms move, in the swimming green
> And in its watery radiance, while the hue
>
> Of heaven in an antique reflection rolled
> Round those flotillas. And sometimes the sea
> Poured brilliant iris on the glistening blue.
>
> ('Sea Surface Full of Clouds')

As well as these are the obsessively evoked musical instruments, the guitar, bassoon, claviar, oboe, 'hoobla-hoobla-hoobla-how' and countless others. The question is of how and from where these things are produced.

Rather than indulge in what he called the evasions of metaphor, by which one thing is attractively but rather pointlessly compared with another, Stevens' view was that poetry should present objects by a direct reduction to a sensitive perception of them. These perceptions will change, and the sensitive expression of such changes is what makes us call the poet a creator. Any description at all, of the world, that does this is thus metaphorical; more fundamentally so than the traditional metaphor that notices a chance, interesting but really unimportant comparison. As Stevens says, 'The pineapple is reduced from the sum of its complications'. In Stevens then we get mere pineapple, mere bird, slopping sea, or sun on bowl of flowers. The point is made most explicitly in 'Sea Surface Full Of Clouds' from which we have just quoted, where the same set of objects changes, as in a kaleidoscope, to a different but equally succulent version of itself in each section, to go on and on for ever, as the poet says with a final remarkable onomatopoeia of sea waves, in 'fresh transfigurings of freshest blue'.

The aim of this kind of poetry is to give pleasure, and in talking of Spenser we have already suggested the necessary connection between the phenomenologically seen and the playful or pleasurable. (The ludicrous is as present in Stevens as in the sociology of Garfinkel. A watermelon is almost inevitably ludicrous. Titles like 'Frogs Eat Butterflies' or 'Large Red Man Reading' have the same spirit.) The pleasure-principle here seems to stem from a certain use of language. If we think that what we see 'out there' is only framed or ordered by our language, our naming, then conversely it follows that in our names and words are all that objective realities in essence have. Thus if I say 'ice-cream', there is nothing about that substance the word does not refer to, for our word has named it in the first place. Stevens is always naming in this fashion; 'prodigious scholar', 'good eel', 'odious chords'. The central statement and explicit expression of this is found in the remarkable achievement of 'The Idea Of Order At Key West'.

This reduction of things from 'the sum of their complications', the direct presentation of objects to be seen through words, has profound implications when the reduction is carried out using the criterion of subjective perception. All Stevens' objects, from his fruit to his sunlit 'President' seem, though wholly real, also isolated, made; simply there without theory or history. His flowers, fruit and objects seem to be as we see them in the supermarket. Of course a supermarket is a social place governed by norms, values and so on, and the character of the physical things in supermarkets may be modified by that fact; but that merely sets them up for the poet to regard, and how he regards them is then the question. Stevens' objects are fresh, certainly, not wrapped or made of plastic—

in fact they seem positively dripping with dew and freshness — but they do not derive from seed, nor the bowls and chairs from manufacture. There is admittedly a repeated insistence that they are subject to rot and decay, and this goes along with the need to 'change', another tenet in Stevens' theory of poetic fiction. But they change to the future from the present, and the past does not seem to be there. Like Whitman, who also greatly influenced him, Stevens wanted a poetry which did not descend from the past, either from the heritage of a traditional religious belief or symbolism, or that of traditional poetic practice. But this fact now raises the central question to be asked in the context of this book. Why, eschewing the past, did Stevens not take on a social and sociological perspective for his world? Why is Stevens' world of perceptions so entirely exclusive of social perceptions? Or to put it another way, why did the poet not make the same jump as Merleau-Ponty (see Chapter 2) and recognize, even fictionally, the special reality of that subjective perception which is said (by sociological phenomenologists) to occur when I perceive the one thing exactly like myself; another human being? The point is important both for a theory of poetry's non-social nature and for the accompanying view that in a sociological world poetry's non-social nature will emerge explicitly so that the poet protests it, or at least has an internal dialogue about it.

'Have an internal dialogue about it' is, I suggest, just what Stevens eventually did. His later work is well known to have diminished its hedonistic stances in favour of an increasingly explicit examination of poetry's own nature, and the pressure toward this came from the world Stevens found himself in. Martz has argued that the poem 'Farewell to Florida' in effect spells out Stevens' decision to leave his isolation behind him and to 'plunge somehow into the turmoil of the thirties, to engage it somehow in his poetry'.[3] Stevens did absolutely nothing of the kind. Rather, he engaged in a meditation which left poetry more and more secure as a fictive matter and as having 'no social obligation whatever';[4] just what, I would argue, poetry's nature would lead us to expect. But what must be emphasized here is that Stevens did not make the jump Merleau-Ponty made, and the fact that he did not is not a political or moral decision of Stevens the man; it can be shown to be the constraint in him of his own poetic voice. Here we come to Stevens' 'music'; the Muse, the synonymity of Muse, music and meditative musing which the later poetry more and more projects and which is obsessive, and which is not compatible with the language of society as seen by the sociological idea.

The earlier poetry has some of this, but in rather formal fashion (as in 'To The One Of Fictive Music'). In 'The Man With The Blue Guitar' the Stevens mode of letting the music play *him*, and virtually dictate the underlying rhythms of his mind and direction of his thought, is used to the fullest extent for the first time. The ideas and thoughts do not produce the strumming of the guitar, nor are 'accompanied' by strumming; the strumming generates the idea. One is reminded of Lévi-Strauss' dictum that the heart of any culture is its music, the very form of its thought itself. If a poet is subjected to this rhythm, this Muse, then the language that is projected simply cannot be the language that asks and answers in social discourse, for the source of that language, according to the sociological idea, is the constraint by our social situation to play roles, to interpret and re-interpret what is said to us, to bargain, to uphold (or subvert) social institutions in all their sociological fullness. But the Muse plays her own music in the poet's mind. He only 'answers', antiphonally, himself. The result is a meditation from music's nature — affected as that is by autonomous non-social sources; the kinds of material available for making musical instruments, the kinds of noises in the air where musicians work and write. The refrains in Stevens' poem, 'Things as they are/Are changed upon the blue guitar' is pursued through the poem, the rhyme 'ar' wheeled away from and repeatedly returned to stanza after stanza as some new aspect, qualification or rumination is nudged forward, or strummed into the open, by the poem's twanging — 'twang' being one of the many words of actual physicality that recur and describe this thinking process:

> I know my lazy, leaden twang
> Is like the reason in a storm;
>
> And yet it brings the storm to bear.
> I twang it out and leave it there.

He is even more explicit in his identification:

> Tom-tom, c'est moi. The blue guitar
> And I are one. The orchestra
>
> Fills the high hall with shuffling men . . .

It is this poem, 'The Man With The Blue Guitar', written in Stevens' middle period and indeed constituting the pivot of his poetic career, which generates from its quiet, notated meditation Stevens' central dictum:

> Poetry is the subject of the poem,
> From this the poem issues and
>
> To this returns. Between the two,
> Between issue and return, there is
>
> An absence in reality . . .

If Stevens at this stage leaves the plainly hedonistic mode expressed so well in 'Sea Surface Full Of Clouds', 'To The One Of Fictive Music', and 'Le Monocle De Mon Oncle', then it is to thought wholly inseparable from certain other mental enjoyments, turnings, playings, that he turns, even though he rejects the traditional past and so might have been expected to concern himself with the actual life of the contemporary world. Stevens finds himself increasingly pursuing the idea, in poetry itself, of what poetry must be. We can illustrate this meditative musing, and its reflexivity:

> The death of one god is the death of all.
> Let purple Phoebus lie in umber harvest,
> Let Phoebus slumber and die in autumn umber,
>
> Phoebus is dead, ephebe. But Phoebus was
> A name for something that never could be named.
> There was a project for the sun and is.
>
> There is a project for the sun . . .

This, from Stevens' late and ambitious 'Notes Toward A Supreme Fiction', shows how the exoticism is now achieved by the way the poetry slides and winds and coils in and about itself; a two-forward-one-back-then-on-again process, a dance. The poem moves towards its climax:

>   But to impose is not
> To discover. To discover an order as of
> A season, to discover summer and know it,
>
> To discover winter and know it well, to find,
> Not to impose, not to have reasoned at all,
> Out of nothing to have come on major weather,
>
> It is possible, possible, possible . . .

and we see that the musical references need no longer be visible, as in 'The Man With The Blue Guitar', for they now lie very deep. One could illustrate Stevens' fictive conclusions in terms of his own postulations, 'the first idea', 'Major man', 'the supreme fiction', and so on; but it seems surely that his true fiction is the use of words in this circular and self-referring manner, in order to reach a hypothesis which is no hypothesis (we can never reach or formulate 'the first idea'), but which exists simply in the movement of the uninterrupted, self-generating and self-ending language:

> The poem refreshes life so that we share,
> For a moment, the first idea. . . . It satisfies
> Belief in an immaculate beginning
>
> And sends us, winged by an unconscious will,
> To an immaculate end. We move between these points . . .

*

Another mode of the poem as icon is found in the work, particularly the early work, of William Carlos Williams. Here, rendering 'the poem itself' iconically seems like putting something directly under a microscope, so that the thing the poem apparently refers to is what becomes the icon. Williams' down-to-earth orientation as a scientist and realist, and his wish for poetry to be contemporary and to refer to the artefacts of actual life in his time — sidewalks, newspapers, just everything around us — prevents these iconic items he arrives at from being 'beautiful' in a too obvious or traditional fashion. That is, they normally are not about myths or paintings or sunsets according to some already aesthetic or pleasurable connotation. But this does not prevent them ending up iconic. They are insulated in exactly the same way as anything taken from nature and examined in the laboratory in positive science. As an example of this effect the well-known poems about the paper rolling over and over, and the fruit in the ice-box, could be cited; but here is another (in full), less often quoted but surely just as good:

>   with big breasts
>   under a blue sweater
>
>   bareheaded —
>   crossing the street
>
>   reading a newspaper
>   stops, turns
>
>   and looks down
>   as though
>
>   she had seen a dime
>   on the pavement

What do we make of this? With Williams, as J. Hillis Miller puts it, the words move from being a mode of representation of reality to being simply one more piece of reality.[5] They are not merely not mimetic; they do not even capture (*symboliste* fashion) some invisible, ineffable idea or fiction behind themselves. They name themselves, and they refer only to themselves. As a result the poem is not 'social' for it is not mimetic of the social. To some, that assertion may sound simply absurd. The poem is so vivid, so immediate, that we instantly recognize the thing it appears to describe. But what *do* we recognize? We do not know, and never shall, who the girl or woman was, what she did beforehand, what she did afterwards, or what she thought of it. Ninety per cent of what we may think we get from it, we ourselves read into it: it is the poet's skill to make that so. For if we say that references like 'big breasts', 'newspaper', 'dime on pavement' are social in that they imply values, modes of communication or sex relationships, the answer is that of course they do, but they do so hardly less when those same words are simply listed in the dictionary. The poetry of the piece, the fact that it is poetry, *is* the way the language renders this apparently social thing pure and self-contained, like water in a sealed bowl.

In Williams' view then, imagination neither copies reality nor creates it. It simply re-arranges it, or recombines it like stirring water into ripples or shifting grains of sand to different places. The words are put into different places. This is not rearrangement pure and simple; on the other hand such re-arrangement is not directed by some essential, ideal or other prior reality. The criterion seems to be that the words are repositioned to places in which, carrying a meaning (namely themselves successfully; not just as in Chomsky's 'colorless green ideas sleep furiously') they are new to words' use or reality in our culture simply because they stand in a new isolation. And this means they do not function as go-betweens for sociality in sociological terms.

The effect is as well described by comparing these short poems to the stopping of film. Time is stopped and an instant, or even a quantum of zero time (if such is not too impossibly fanciful) is held fast for our attention.[6] These short poems are still and silent. They therefore also become objects made of words because they are not in an organic process or sequence although they, those word-objects, are a legitimate part of reality and so *post hoc* could take their places in reality. But the 'stopping of the clock' (or film) seems to square exactly with Williams' own statement about society and people, particularly in answer to the criticisms he received about his own work. 'I love my fellow creature. Jesus, how I love him! But he doesn't exist'. When the film stops the social process stops, and its participants and used objects take on a silent, almost eerie glow. For this is the atomizing of reality lovingly done.

There is little space to speak of *Paterson*, Williams' immense contemporary epic which uses these ideas (particularly that of the rearrangement of reality); the wholesale introduction of letters, newspaper clippings and hardware store bills; also little poems like the one quoted above; much association-of-ideas rambling, and many passages and indeed whole sequences of passages 'scarcely readable' as Eric Homberger candidly expresses it.[7] It is clearly a large-scale work containing multitudinous observations, and in parts what one would strictly call poetry. But the enterprise seems to be self-defeating precisely because the attempt to make a contemporary epic from contemporary materials prices itself out of the market. If the material is so much its raw original self, left as it was prior to any handling for use in the poem, what has been achieved? The contrast is clearly with Eliot and Pound, whose collage effects are achieved from materials of different cultures and civilizations, so that the interplay between them is from the start potentially more fruitful. Williams' aspiration to emulate Whitman and cut off the past, while at the same time eschewing Whitman's 'single broomstroke' method, is immensely significant, but is not itself consummated. I can hardly claim that these few remarks deal adequately with the poem, but they suggest the lines I would argue, given space, in this book's context and its wider argument. In the end the attempt to capture society without alteration is just that: without alteration. Williams said, 'Only the imagination is real', a view Paterson seems ironically to bear out.

*

I would like to consider Yeats as the final example of this kind of poet, and one is tempted to call him the greatest of them all. I mean that unlike the other poets of 'the poem' he seems more to include the other sectors of reality — the obdurate wider world, and the self of the poet — as themselves among the things which must in some way be packed into the iconic result. In short, Yeats 'hammered his thoughts into a unity' and those thoughts include myth, theosophy, Ireland in many guises and at a crucial stage of its history; and also the poet's own separate selves, his personae, both 'the man and the mask'. (The 'personae' of Eliot and Pound stay apart because the poets make whole cultures, not their individual selves, central.) Yeats' 'unity', his 'image', is analogous to Stevens' First Idea and Mallarmé's Pure Conception. Again this unity can be seen as incompatible with the unity expressed in the sociological idea, for it was Yeats himself who stressed, with contempt, the nature of the world that could not but yield such an idea in the result. As he put it, Descartes, Locke and Newton took away that world leaving us only its excrement.[8] That is to say, when the world was rendered mere matter, mere resource for human use, the only sentient or conscious reality left was the collectively human. To see that as the only or main reality is something every grain of Yeats' work refutes.

We can look at how this works out in his poetry. In the second period of his writing, epitomized by the collection *The Wild Swans at Coole*, he copes directly with clearly specified 'opposites' in the form of pairs of antitheses such as mind and body, or male and female. The most important poems here are such as 'Ego Dominus Tuus' and 'The Phases Of The Moon'. From our point of view this period is the crucial one, for the opposites with which Yeats wrestles are those which, some would argue, appear to derive from the contradictions within his own personality and which stem from exactly those features of social existence that so strongly characterize the modern world. By these I mean the pressure for role-taking ('the man and the mask') and the individual's sense that he is not complete but partial; that he is also susceptible to and a product of environment and social background; 'all complexities of mire and blood', as well as the nature and demands of constructed institutions. In the third period, epitomized by *The Tower* and especially the poem of that name, the two Byzantium poems and 'Among School Children', Yeats achieves the sought-after unity between those apparent opposites.

From a reading of at least one very important poem of this second period, 'Ego Dominus Tuus', it might seem that since two speakers are imagined in discussion, the way they speak is interactive and thus necessarily social. Indeed Yeats imitates the graces of civilized dialogue very happily:

> Ille.   By the help of an image
> I call to my own opposite, summon all
> That I have handled least, least looked upon.
>
> Hic.   And I would find myself and not an image.
>
> Ille.   That is our modern hope, and by its light
> We have lit upon the gentle, sensitive mind
> And lost the old nonchalance of the hand;
> Whether we have chosen chisel, pen or brush,
> We are but critics, or but half create,
> Timid, entangled, empty and abashed,
> Lacking the countenance of our friends.

The reply in Ille's second speech clearly avoids a harsh rejoinder like 'You're wrong you fool! I don't agree!' It is itself gentle and sensitive. Such imitation of interaction, at one level, occurs also in 'Michael Robartes And The Dancer', the first poem in the next book: 'You mean they argued./Put it so. . . .' And Yeats does use the dialogue form in many poems in this period. But surely if this were the heart of his poetry, and the basis of his aesthetic, then he could not possibly have believed the very point made in the poem from which comes the passage just quoted: 'I seek an image, not a book'. The whole argument — so to call it, for Yeats is really working through positions — is against the position of Hic that the object of the search would be himself, that is to say his personality, his character. Dante, says Hic, sought himself, but Ille refutes this, saying that what Dante sought was 'the apple on the bough-/Most out of reach'. The passage becomes explicit about the significance of the sociological idea when Hic argues that poets have been 'lovers of life' and happiness, who 'sing when they have found it'. Ille's answer is Yeats':

> No, not sing,
> For those that love the world serve it in action,
> Grow rich, popular and full of influence,
> And should they paint or write, still it is action:

— but Ille makes clear what he thinks of such work:

> The struggle of the fly in marmalade.
> The rhetorician would deceive his neighbours,
> The sentimentalist himself; while art
> Is but a vision of reality . . .

— and the whole weight of the poem is thrown forward to the final passage, in which the poet's activity is claimed to result from something quite different altogether — 'I call to the mysterious one who yet/Shall walk the wet sands by the edge of the stream/And look most like me. . . .'

Thus the important notions of the image, the book, the light in the tower, and the anti-self, are all clearly marshalled for the more categorical treatment they receive in the next poem, 'The Phases of The Moon'. In that poem the dark, trembling presentation of the poet's vision is directly possible because the two envisaged characters in the dialogue, Aherne and Robartes, are this time really standing side by side, effecting not interactive argument, as over something in dispute or exchange, but rather a split incantation:

> Aherne.   Sing out the song: sing to the end, and sing
> The strange reward of all that discipline.
>
> Robartes. All thought becomes an image and the soul
> Becomes a body: that body and that soul
> Too perfect at the full to lie in a cradle,
> Too lonely for the traffic of the world:
> Body and soul cast out and cast away
> Beyond the visible world . . .

The heart of Yeats' poetry is his search for an image of all reality, not a search for himself or for a book. ('Book' here is quite different from Mallarmé's book, for Mallarmé's image *is* his book.) But such a view denies any idea that the self's opposite could be merely some other contrasting personality-configuration, such as might result from the taking of a confronting role or merely different social circumstances. Yeats did not see the self as even connected with those matters. As he once wrote, 'My character is so little myself that all my life it has thwarted me and affected my poems, my true self, no more than the character of a dancer affects the movement of a dance'. The sociologist might simply disagree (as Yeats' father disagreed), and will possibly dismiss the poet as self-deluded. But that is irrelevant, for the question is what connection exists between these views of Yeats and his poetry. In fact, they are the very heart of his poetry's power. For his poetry proceeds to dedicate itself to the exploration of this reality; that is, this image, free of the accidents and chances of history or the everyday world, and existing in spite of them rather than because of them.

The nature of this image then is the subject of the third period of Yeats' work. In the poem just considered it is the moon; and this too is an image of the non-social, the night not the daytime, a different, unusual means of seeing. The contemplative whom Yeats rejected, and the poor poet, sits in his tower at night with a lamp; that is, when the moon is full, the incompetent thinker persists in straining to use a feeble replica (a lamp) of the sun. But even so the moon is not the final Yeatsian poetic image, which is that of the hammered artifice of beaten gold. The moon is a visionary, occult image of the final *way* reality is seen; it is not the poet's image itself. The poet's image is the image *made* by the poet to capture what cannot be expressed and is not available in ordinary discourse. The work of hammered, beaten gold is the work by which opposites are forced into unity by the poet's power. It is hammered, a matter of sweat and difficulty, the more so because the sociological world is antipathetic to poetry, is surprised and bewildered when it encounters poetry interrupting its unexceptional communicative processes, and therefore forces poetry back on to such overconscious and insistent method; an insistence which, however, Yeats recognizes and capitalizes on. Yeats' golden bird, pure and isolated ('on a bough') is the result; and it is idle to state that Yeats is all along coping with either an authoritarian father, or two sides to his own self, for these are merely the occasions in our time of the sociological idea's particular embodiments. Such is the theme of the two Byzantium poems and, in a different way, 'Among School Children'.

In the Byzantium poems and elsewhere we see what happens when the idea of image itself, and the idea of the hammered gold as the central image required, come together. The unpurged images of day, all the mess and the undifferentiated matter of everyday life, recede, and before the poet floats another image, that of the 'bird or golden handiwork'. The act of imagining, with one's whole being and neither body nor mind separately conceived, is the poet's task. It is not affected by 'psychology' or 'personality'; on the contrary, those things must be removed for the image to emerge in safety. The vocabulary in which Yeats describes his approach to the image is curiously unpsychological; always to do with summoning, calling, hailing, declaring. This non-sociological, non-psychological base is parallelled in Yeats' occult or magical views, as when he says that what we call emotions are in fact 'disembodied powers, pressing their footsteps across our hearts'.

The extraordinary result is that, by finding this pure image of reality, Yeats is set free in his own imagination and indeed unified being, simply to exist as a pure soul despite what he must now feel as bodily decline in old age. And old age is the subject of Yeats' later work. For sociality, which could be defined as the power with which the sociological idea holds sway, diminishes as old age is encountered. The world of the sociological idea, as opposed to the world of tradition, does not know how to use old people. For the old in the secular world this is often extremely distressing. But the poet can turn it to good account, as Yeats did. At the end of 'The Tower', having asked what he is to do with 'this absurdity.... Decrepit age that has been tied to me/As to a dog's tail'?, he declares his answer:

> Now shall I make my soul,
> Compelling it to study
> In a learned school
> Till the wreck of body,
> Slow decay of blood,
> Testy delirium
> Or dull decrepitude,
> Or what worse evil come

Having discovered an image for the unity between what, when younger, he wretchedly experienced as manifold psychological and social pressures, Yeats can use his soul direct and unmediated despite old age. In 'Sailing to Byzantium' the artifice has become the artifice of eternity. The declaration is that such bodily form as eternity holds for him will be in the image of hammered gold and gold enamelling. Nor is it simply chance that led Yeats to this position at just the point when old age would lead him to reflect on the soul's nature in any case. Rather it is all of a piece, for it is at exactly that period, in the whole life of one dedicated to the search for such unity, that the discordances of earthly circumstance ('all complexities of mire or blood') begin to decline in importance, shrink, and lift their burden off one's vision.

Yeats' great topical poems, such as 'Easter 1916', are not discounted by this discussion. But they must be seen in the light of this context and the central corpus. When 'a terrible beauty is born' in the year 1916, that is itself a poetic transmutation of Yeats, a reconciliation of antinomies, terrible and beautiful, used in the location of a historical event in which, even so, all is 'changed, changed utterly'. That description, taken literally, is more than mere 'revolution' for it again lifts us out of the ordinary progress of history and everyday events. Major Robert Gregory is seen as the model of Yeats' own Renaissance-man ideals, the uniting of several talents;[9] and I believe too that the success of the poem, which is undoubted, lies in the change within it from a celebration of many friends to that of one, Robert Gregory, as a result of the poet's own experience in writing it. It is from this that the resonant refrain 'soldier, scholar, horseman he' results. The arrest of the change itself, that sudden moment of awareness, is what lasts. Similarly, 'The Municipal Gallery Revisited' gathers Yeats' own friends, at the end of a long life, into eternity's artifice.

CHAPTER 10

THE POEM AND SOCIETY – ELIOT, POUND, THE COMMUNIST POETS

Unlike the poets just considered, the group which includes Eliot, Pound, MacDiarmid and others is much more concerned with what is called society by sociologists (and now many other people too) although the poets would call it civilization or history. Instead of claiming autonomy for self or poem they want to suppress their 'personalities' altogether. The passages about personality in Eliot's article 'Tradition And The Individual Talent' are too well known to need quoting, and Pound himself made the point repeatedly. MacDiarmid wrote, 'One must die to life in order to be/Utterly a creator — refusing to sanction/The irresponsible lyricism in which sense-impressions/Are employed to substitute ecstasy for information'.[1] For this reason the large-scale poems and interests of these poets offer themselves for contrast with the equally macroscopic large-scale area of sociology, the area concerned with overall social coherence. Social organization, stratification, work, culture, bureaucracy, polity and economy are the sociological abstractions drawn from the original things this group of poets addresses. The large scope and complexity of the matter makes it seem best to give a fuller discussion to one poet. So I will say something briefly on Pound and the communist poets later in the chapter, but the poet I shall concentrate on is Eliot.

It is important first to recognize how much of the material of Eliot's writing, particularly in *The Waste Land* but also in 'Prufrock', the *Four Quartets* and elsewhere, is historical. It refers to individual or past events and phenomena which are then subject to hermeneutic attentiveness. That is to say, they are then interpreted in terms of their actual, contingent meanings on their separate occasions. Eliot certainly generalizes outward to the idea 'history', most of all in its relation in the *Four Quartets* to timelessness; but the material which weighs on him before that is the detritus of past civilizations. There is no generalizing historical 'process', but simply examples remaining themselves in the richness of a culture. These may be imaginary, and many are literary rather than political, but they are unique and individual. The poems are thus saturated with this material in its original form as near as possible.

Let us consider for example *The Waste Land*. At the start of that poem we have someone 'staying at the arch-duke's', who took Marie out on a sled; we have the Tarot pack, King William Street, and then the call across historical time to the contemporary, although imaginery, person Stetson who fought at the actual battle of Mylae in the Punic War. There is then strained altercation between a man and a woman ('My nerves are bad tonight'); pub talk about Lil and Albert, and a snatch of song; and the affair of Elizabeth and Leicester and the actual place, the Isle of Dogs. This again is interspersed with the past in the form of actual lines of past poems and present jazz or light-music songs. The generalized voice (supposedly Tiresias, although Eliot's note on him has always seemed to me one of literature's larger red herrings) has a guarded, fatigued relationship with this historical material it nevertheless itself cites. This characteristic of Eliot's is not merely the necessary particularity of art. Its historical quality is a matter of events which are unique and contingent yet not just part of the physical world of nature. They therefore require an interpretation (not just in the poem) of their meaning. Thus the past is invoked as a matter of examples which considerably emphasize the separateness of civilizations, so that what value they have is peculiar to each.[2] They are thus united not by an underlying metaphysic of their unity but by an actual act of bringing them together; of absorbing 'the mind of Europe' in one's mind.

So Eliot's materials are seen historically. We need next to see how a historical attitude turns into a sociological one. When historical consciousness is so saturated by the extent of its past the question arises of how this can be apprehended so that the burden is alleviated. It is not simply a sense of the past being 'over'; the theme of the decay of Western civilization is a common one, but it may have deeper origins in this very malaise at the sense of the past's size and cultural oppressiveness. But it is by elaborating a method of using the past no longer so much as a living heritage but rather as material for a general investigation of our own nature, that one central tradition of sociology developed. This is the historical and interpretative sociology of Weber.

Weber's response to history needs to be summarized a little further than it was in Chapter 2, for the sake of the contrast it gives with Eliot's response to history. Weber has certain tenets, the first being that people nearly always act on the basis of generalizations from all prior social action. We typify from past experience and act on that with a view to future experience. What for Eliot might seem merely more of the 'drifting wreckage' that we are, affords for Weber a basis for a general account of social reality. But Weber's central point is that it is rationality that must be used to examine historical events to find these recurring sociological features. Only rationality is free of the particular characteristics of the several typifications considered. Rationality, rather than 'affect', tradition or other attitudes, is the mode of examination of social purposeful action, and it is the only means of interpreting historical phenomena to see what society generally consists of. And Weber proceeds to embark on his studies of religion, the economy, the city, Protestantism and other subjects from his collections of historical sources.

But what Weber then begins to find by rationalistic analyses is that *rationality is itself* the necessary principle of modern societies after the earlier stages of traditional and charismatic authority. After a charismatic stage (typified for Weber by Luther or Napoleon) authority is necessarily rational. That is to say, it is bureaucratic, because bureaucracy is the palpable embodiment of a public rational structure. But it turns out also that this is not merely a sociological method, but a claim for the importance of the sociological idea itself. Weber's profound history-based interest in meaningful social action — in how individual historical actions social in import have in them purpose and meaning — has changed, not merely into the idea that this 'meaning' is general, permeated through the society, embodied by it generally rather than in unique actions, but that *the sociological idea is itself that general meaning*: that, after the traditional has ceased to be a viable basis for authority, only a rationality that itself becomes sociological can perform that function. He furthermore holds that bureaucratic organizations are not merely the utilitarian agents but the embodiment of rational authority, and that the sociological idea which so understands that legitimation, is that legitimation itself. This seems to me the undeniable outcome of Weber's own position, and while in some ways it simply suggests the general sociolocial idea of our second chapter, it is important that this derives from the earlier step of generalizing from the many meanings, hermeneutically grasped, of history's several acts, rather than from Durkheim's more scientific notion. Durkheim's method was the collection of evidence about an entity (society) already seen as not plural but homogeneous, evolutionary in its one self, organic.

We can now come back to Eliot. For his response to the same historical phenomena is entirely different, leading to his ironic, fatigued, poetical, non-sociological voice. This is even stronger in *Four Quartets*. Far from thinking we can generalize out of the weight of our heritage, Eliot finds that we aren't the people we were a moment ago, and that the more do we arrive at new places (and so new knowledge) the more is old knowledge and place left behind us. For the place we arrive at is not the place to which we set out:

> And what you thought you came for
> Is only a shell, a husk of meaning
> From which the purpose breaks only when it is fulfilled
> If at all. Either you had no purpose
> Or the purpose is beyond the end you figured
> And is altered in fulfilment . . .
>   If you came this way,
> Taking any route, starting from anywhere,
> At any time or at any season,
> It would always be the same: you would have to put off
> Sense and notion. You are not here to verify,
> Instruct yourself, or inform curiosity
> Or carry report . . .
>
>   (*Little Gidding*, 30–5, 39–45)

In short, if Weber's *verstehen* (understanding) can yield only a society seen necessarily to have to organize itself in bureaucratic, rationalistically-embodied terms, then the problem of the 'meaning' of it all is not, Eliot would say, answered; indeed it is not even considered. This is despite Weber's avowed aim to understand 'meaningful social action'. What we might see as Eliot's response to such an 'understanding' of the world which looks back at its own several civilizations and their traces, and then tries to wrest an order (bureaucratic) from them, is as follows:

> O dark dark dark. They all go into the dark,
> The vacant interstellar spaces, the vacant into the vacant,
> The captains, merchant bankers, eminent men of letters,
> The generous patrons of art, the statesmen and the rulers,
> Distinguished civil servants, chairmen of many committees,
> Industrial lords and petty contractors, all go into the dark,
> And dark the Sun and Moon, and the Almanach de Gotha
> And the Stock Exchange Gazette, the Directory of Directors
> . . .
>
> (*East Coker*, 101–8)

The rational bureaucrats merely go into the dark, and it is the dark already known to Sampson and Milton; it is a repeat now of the human condition which we cannot avoid experiencing through the tradition of the words and indeed the traces of civilization with which we are left. Although we may achieve a desired 'understanding' at something like the Weberian level, and in some sense analyse rationally our world and society, nevertheless we cannot *understand* that understanding; we can see no ultimate meaning in those more superficial meanings which may, perhaps, serve passably to account for our everyday affairs. And this is because whatever we do, it is all in an instantaneous moment we can never catch, simply because our very action, our 'purposeful action', distracts us from the true, existential grasp of ourselves in time, by which consciousness of that very fact we defeat time. 'For most of us' — except the saint, says Eliot — 'there is only the unattended moment', and therefore, in even our analysis itself, our attempts to understand at the immediate level, we, hopelessly, 'are the music while the music lasts'.

I think Eliot's mode has been so important in our day, and is so to this discussion, that it needs a rather closer analysis than we have given to some poets. The question is of how the idea of generalization from history is rejected as any final statement or position. And I would like to argue that its nature as poetry, its 'poeticality', is inseparable from that rejection. In *The Waste Land* Eliot uses a collage method by which the poem, though unified, is made of fragments of all kinds. *Four Quartets* also uses this technique to some extent; here it is more a matter of the five different kinds of voice (which internally carry variations on themselves too) corresponding to the five sections each quartet contains.[3] What effect do these juxtapositions have? It is not collage alone, for Eliot himself writes intermediary passages as we have said, and alters those he borrows with clearly ironic or more deeply tragic effect. Nor, however, can we go to the other extreme and make the 'Eliot' voice so central as to subordinate the borrowed passages to mere illustrative quotation. For that would defeat the very point of leaving the passages, and so many of them, in their original form. (The implication that the poet's message is just 'It's all been said before' is as banal as the idea that everything once had a meaning but the modern world has none.) We thus cannot answer the question without considering closely our own response when we read one such juxtaposition. Surely the answer is that we are thrown on to a different *type* of understanding of the connection, on each occasion. Let us take for example Section III of *The Waste Land*:

The river's tent is broken; the last fingers of leaf
Clutch and sink into the wet bank. The wind
Crosses the brown land, unheard. The nymphs are departed.
Sweet Thames, run softly, till I end my song.
The river bears no empty bottles, sandwich papers,
Silk handkerchiefs, cardboard boxes, cigarette ends
Or other testimony of summer nights. The nymphs are departed.
And their friends, the loitering heirs of city directors;
Departed, have left no addresses.
By the waters of Leman I sat down and wept . . .
Sweet Thames, run softly till I end my song,

Sweet Thames, run softly, for I speak not loud or long.
But at my back in a cold blast I hear
The rattle of the bones, and chuckle spread from ear to ear.

A rat crept softly through the vegetation
Dragging its slimy belly on the bank
While I was fishing in the dull canal
On a winter evening round behind the gashouse
Musing upon the king my brother's wreck
And on the king my father's death before him.
White bodies naked on the low damp ground
And bones cast in a little low dry garret,
Rattled by the rat's foot only, year to year.
But at my back from time to time I hear
The sound of horns and motors, which shall bring
Sweeney to Mrs. Porter in the spring.
O the moon shone bright on Mrs. Porter
And on her daughter
They wash their feet in soda water
Et O ces voix d'enfants, chantant dans le coupole!

(*The Waste Land*, 173–202)

In these thirty lines we have Spenser, the Bible, Marvell, Day, Australian ragtime, Verlaine, and Eliot's own lines between and linking these. And reading there 'Sweet Thames run softly . . .' we may think, 'How sad, if Spenser were to see the Thames today', or quite differently, 'How beautiful a line; it is the line that counts'; and the quickly following 'By the waters of Leman I sat down and wept' may invoke in us 'This must be as profound, as universally significant, as can be, since only a Biblical echo can give us it'. And then that echo is itself doubled in power by the switch to 'Leman', the lake by which Eliot himself was staying when he wrote much of the poem. There is the further connection between the two allusions by virtue of their both referring to water (in the second case also the water of tears, which ease the weeping one in that they merge back into the wider water or lake or sea). This simply postulates more and more layers of meaning and feeling, such that we cannot make any one line the anchor by which any other is explained. In this light the key passages are those about writing itself. For example there is in *Four Quartets* the renowned line 'That was a way of putting it — not very satisfactory. . . .' What is being parodied, if parody it be? Is Eliot the poet looking askance at his own writing in the previous passage, or is he parodying a schoolmasterly comment which might have come from an external source? Here we come to the important conclusion; for what seems to happen in that and the other *Four Quartets* passages which raises the problem of writing itself, the 'raid on the inarticulate' and 'the intolerable wrestle with words and meanings', is that, by raising the question of language in a poem which itself so varies its language-sources, we see those references to language as *themselves* also one more set of lines which may play off against other passages allusively, ironically, or in any other way. Even lines on literature itself, writing itself, have to be seen as just one more piece of language which we may shortly be asked to compare— and to hear accompanying echoes to— with others from virtually anywhere.

This is the 'music' in the poetry of *The Waste Land* and *Four Quartets* — the way that material left historically as it is, is not then subjected to rational generalization (which becomes sociology) but floats, drifts, 'is the music while the music lasts'. Eliot's answer to the Weberian position is, roughly, as follows: There is no end and no beginning. You know and you do not know; there is neither here nor there; all are going into the dark, and the trains stop too long between stations. Where you are is where you are not: you learn to get the better of words for the thing you no longer need to say; you must go by the way of ignorance, and we must be still and still moving; you are not the same people who left the station earlier; the way up is the way down; and where is an end of it, the soundless wailing and the drifting wreckage? Eliot has his own spiritual and metaphysical answers, of course (present in 'Little Gidding'), but I suggest that we have in his poetry a set of profound extensive ironies emerging from the very existence and nature of meaning and language in the modern world. This is because no expression can ever be an ultimately complete *logos* or account of its subject, for each expression has only the particular echoes, resonances, references and experiencing speaker that it does contingently have. No expression, equally, can ultimately know what it is saying. More sobering still, and more Sophoclean in its recall of Oedipus' predicament; it does not know that what it says is true, or indeed if, or how it is true.[4] Thus the collecting of several echoes of meaning from past and present, the line of Dante, the parodied line of Bible or ragtime, the voice heard in the pub, serves merely to set up endless chains of more and more irony; not the superficial irony of the oblique remark but the deeper Sophoclean irony (where Oedipus talks to his mother not knowing it is she, and puts out his eyes without seeing he was already blind). These meaning-carrying quotations and references can never amount to more knowledge, only to the increased reverberations of their own echoes. The use of copious material is practised by Pound and David Jones too, of course, but in quite different ways (Jones for example 'made a heap of all I could find', in *The Anathemata*). This is Eliot's use.

The implication is that we cannot take such sayings and moments (as Weberian sociology does take them) as data for sociological research, because these sayings will at no point suddenly stop and rest, simply to be meek, inert data. They will go on and on reverberating; there is always one more 'word', remark, image, echo, or quotation against which they will set up further reverberation; all, with deeper and deeper irony, revealing more and more layers of meaning, 'true' in a sense, but logically more and more unknown to the speaker as one who has those feelings. It is not too whimsical to say that the sociologist of this persuasion may turn out to seem equally ignorant, in the literal sense, of these implications, for otherwise his investigations would not have been allowed to proceed. The sociological enterprise is legitimate enough if, as we said earlier, it limits its aim to finding passably workable accounts of our local life, and the larger social institutions.

Eliot's consciousness of poetry's new consideration of itself is permeated through his poetic criticism in his concern with what poetry can be expected to do in any particular age, as though Poetry exists in some obdurate and irreducible form, then being put to work by successive generations.[5] He feels (as does Pound even more angrily) that poetry now needs very special consideration. Yet it seems that this new consciousness in poetry is expressed as deeply in Eliot's poetry itself, where the fatigued tone (apart from the end of 'Little Gidding') is pervasive. The gathering into poetry of voices heard from near and distant past (where 'Footfalls echo in the memory/Down the passage which we did not take') seems to be poetry's own weariness, perhaps, at the end of its long journey and its pilgrimage. The weariness grows, making poetry more and more a mug's game, if civilization is increasingly felt to be merely an accretion of attempts by man to bear his time-bound condition. As time goes by, the more the civilization's memory has to hold, so that as Kenner puts it (writing of Eliot) ' [Europe is] exhausted by the effort to stay interested in its own contents'.[6] This is what Eliot faces ironically, Pound by 'programming a decade', David Jones by, seemingly, almost loving a civilization back into existence, the communist poets by longing for an ideal state of the future. The sociological idea, on the other hand, would take that diverse historical material and generalize to a new description of our condition as predominantly a social thing, a matter of sociality. In that case we would not need poetry, for sociology would be our 'Word' and poetry decline to certain psychological manifestations of disturbance, or linguistic experiments.

As C.H. Sisson, an Augustan poet of our period, has put it:

We have only to live and see what happens
— Nothing, perhaps; for it may be that history,
As Mairet remarked, is coming to an end
And we shall wander around without meaning.
That is what most of us would like, and it is death . . .

*

One could argue that Pound copes with the sociologizing of historical uniqueness in just the way Eliot evaded; that he took positive action, as one might say, rather than letting the stubborn plural body of voices of the past run through him. ('Say this to the Possum: a bang, not a whimper,/With a bang not with a whimper' — Canto LXXIV.) In the poems in *Personae* Pound is casting about for a subject, and for a way to fight through the out-worn Edwardian conventions, in a way far beyond that of most young writers simply looking for a voice. His exasperated damn-this-nonsense energy is clear, but can only long for 'some breath for beauty and the arts'. The project of remaking poetry is latent, however deeply, in Pound from very early.

The poems in *Lustra* are extremely interesting for our argument. This largely because of the *envoi* poems, of which there are at least a dozen in that volume. When a poet writes many poems, accompanies them with a few rather self-consciously on the act of writing, but then finds that those few turn out to be the most important, it seems likely that the question of how actually to write poetry is pressing him very near the surface. But it seems to be explicitly a matter of actively sending the poems out, as a 'communication', in our sociological world. And it cannot work. It is curious that even a public poet, a poet concerned with the outward social structures, history, economy, politics or war, can wistfully address his poems themselves when they go wrong or do not have the effect he wants for them. 'You are idle, my songs. I fear you will come to a bad end'. The poet is singing the very fact that if the *persona* motif is not adopted successfully, that is poetically, then it is merely an intrusive example in the social arena of one more person speaking: that is to say, it itself becomes an attempt at a social interaction, something a poem can never be. It is too direct, and the public world, let alone the explicitly sociological world, is offended. There is no way for Pound along that road. The *envoi* songs are successful, in fact they are wonderful, but precisely because of their wistfulness, and because they do not meet some waiting audience but record their sad antipathy to an audience.

As a result Pound turns to the task of remaking poetry from history's materials in more direct and programmatic fashion; and this produces, finally, the *Cantos*. Here we encounter the culmination of the poetry's compulsion to *insist* in the twentieth-century world; a compulsion that appears in the face of history's new self-consciousness, and the backward-looking awareness that occurs without that older unifying vitality stemming from a particular origin; the Hellenic or the Hebraic. Pound in fact is the high point of twentieth-century

The Poem and Society 175

programmatic activity. I think a straight reading of the *Cantos* right through at one sitting (as far as this is possible!) demonstrates this insistence in profound fashion; the bass tone, unless I am completely wrong, of a deep strain to keep it going, an act of empowered will which necessarily exhausts itself before the end. It is as though a strong man held together a row of bricks horizontally, without cement and solely with the pressure of his hands. One can quote from almost anywhere:

It is said also that Homer was a medic
who followed the greek armies to Troas
so in Holland Park they rolled out to beat up Mr Leber
(restaurantier) to Monseiur Dulac's disgust
and a navvy rolls up to me in Church St. (Kensington End)
with:
    Yurra Jurrmun!
To which I replied: I am *not*.
'Well yurr szum kind ov a furriner.'
    ne povans desraciner
But Tosch the great ex-greyhound
    used to get wildly excited
        at being given large beefsteaks
in Tolosa
    and leapt one day finally
right into the centre of the large dining table
and lay there as a centre piece . . .

                                          (*Canto* LXXX)

And so after about Canto XC the repetitions ($κάδμου$ $θύγατωρ$, law rules the sea/Lex Rhodi/leave the duke, go for gold/bischniz, etc. etc.) seem to be just rounding the thing off and down rather than acting as the sonorous litany they had been earlier. After about the hundredth it too often sounds last-resortish and weary. Yet it is part of the poem's immense force that this strain one detects, occurring not solely at the end but all through, is like the tension in a massive cantilevered bridge, so that the weakening end is merely a slight slackening, rather than an embarrassing strain toward the wholly impossible.

    This brings us to the main point. The ideogrammatic

method Pound elaborated is a use of historical materials in poetry in a way exactly opposite to and incompatible with that of the sociological idea. The sociological idea, of Weber, Parsons and indeed all the grand theorists such as Pareto and Comte (though not all sociologists) is that sociological truths generalize from historical examples. But Pound's dictum was that we should set out to discover the literary heritage by 'detailed examination of actual specimens', and he believed furthermore that we should not merely consult the originals but also preserve them in their original state. This differs from Eliot in being not a self-subjection to their drifting rhythm of time, but a conscious programme. The avoidance of deliberate exoticism and the showing-up of politically-biased descriptions of history found elsewhere is part of the aim. The precept 'consult the originals yourself' is the only way to prevent the acceptance of civilization's already rubbed-smooth arrangements.[7] The question of the poem's structure (i.e. the *Cantos*) is therefore a 'literary' question, a non-question; for the assemblage, as with Eliot and David Jones, of material often in exactly its original state is a way of ensuring the success of such aims.

But is this not what historians do anyway; that is, attempt to establish exactly and in detail empirical fact, not rubbed-smooth generalization? If there is a quarrel, is it not between sociologists and historians? But, the poet would say, it is only poetry that can render such exactitude. That is, it is only poetry remade along the incisive and scrupulously clear lines Pound and the imagists sought. What Pound said about style being simply 'language which renders its object accurately', the idea that every phrase must find its own unique shape to render 'the exact curve of the thing' (Hulme), the 'sharp cutting-edge' of each word, and Pound's remark about poetry needing to aspire to at least the condition of prose, are all part of the same insistence. The rendering of these things exact *is* the poetry. And it cannot be exactitude in terms of the historian's accuracy, for there is no such thing, since past history is only renderable in the exactitude of words. It is the poet's capacity, no one else's, to render words usable in historical reference that is exact. Again there is no 'essence' of poetry: the poetry, for Pound, simply *is* the language in such condition that one cannot extrapolate from it in vague generalization or 'a terminology of indefinable middles',[8] a phrase that most sociologists today would surely agree warns us of the pitfalls to be avoided.

This finally is why we have in Pound yet another variation on twentieth-century poetry; namely, the ideogrammatic idea for epic-historical purposes. What matters is Pound's own statement that the epic is a poem that 'includes history', that is, is larger than history in some sense, and projects it. Its deliberate and insistent projection of history is parallel to Milton's stated purpose for his poem, to 'justifie the wayes of God to man'. If our earlier suggestion that grand sociology itself aspires to be our 'Word' is not wholly fanciful then here we have the largest incompatibility between sociology and poetry that we have yet found. For grand sociology also tries to 'justifie' society (and the radical sociologists' criticism of Parsons is that he did not just analyse society but implied the superior stability of his own model), whereas a poetic justification of history is a capturing, a seizing, of history in words which, if successful, cannot then be changed. Pound's poem is epic because his ideogrammatic method of juxtaposing words to yield historic resonances is powerfully cumulative over so many amazing passages and pages.

*

No one needs reminding of the politics of Eliot and Pound. But while this is inseparable from their poetry from some points of view, it is not the poetry itself. Briefly we must refer to the poets of the Left — MacDiarmid, Brecht, Neruda — since if the argument about poetry's evasion of the sociological idea is to hold it must do so regardless of political allegiance. If the poets of the Left are also focussed on the wider world rather than the self or the poem, then that must take some recognizable form in their work.

We might on the face of it have expected the eulogizing of a certain set of social arrangements in their poetry or descriptions of activities in a utopian and sociologically-angled world of the future. It does not emerge that way at all, and it is the physical world, loved and seen as wonderful, longed for when absent, that comes through in all three, more expansively and luxuriantly in the two poets — MacDiarmid and Neruda — who are not experiencing actual exile or privation and suffering, at least not immediately to themselves, at the moment of writing. This might seem a contestable remark. But the collective constraining force on humans is never once seen in their poetry as itself a metaphysical social reality, a Durkheimian social 'thing', or as something worth investigation, or even linking to its physical, natural emanations. The force when it constrains is always by its nature evil, stupid, bad: Fascism, imperialism, capitalism, private property, the sickening bourgeoisie (whose poems are 'the pale maggots in the cheese of capitalism'— Neruda), and there is not the remotest suggestion in these poets that an analysis of human behaviour collectively would explain away these defects, or help toward a more desirable society. The future itself has a halo and is utopian. It is simply one in which men are open to each other, free, equal, and enriched in experiencing the natural world in the light of a serenity born of knowledge (MacDiarmid) or an anthropological understanding of their own roots and history (Neruda).

MacDiarmid for example has Fascism (and the English) always present for contemptuous dismissal, in a single line, or poem. 'Out of the perilous night of English stupidity' says MacDiarmid in the quickest of throw-aways in 'Direadh III', his wonderful poem in which he rests after walking on the mountain Sgurr Alasdair, and sees a bird fly back up to a rock, symbolizing what really matters to him: 'So every loveliness Scotland has ever known/Or will know, flies into me now'. The tension in MacDiarmid between left and right, Leninism and Scottish Nationalism, is that between his sense of historical humanity and his sense of the necessary experience of that in an actual, loved place. MacDiarmid's detestation of all that is individual seems paradoxically to account for what so often seems his arrogance. In a curious sense there is peace in MacDiarmid; the exuberant, contemptuous peace of a man who has located to his satisfaction the source of what is wrong in the world, and so can throw it down fearlessly without spite or neurosis. The root of it is the physical quality of reality located, and it is tensed against what defiles it. The natural rhythm that expresses this is the movement of feeling in ordered language, in the freed person who says it: that is, it is poetry. His *ars poetica*, 'The Kind Of Poetry I want', has a confident finality about it; it is not prescriptive or didactic but a proud statement of what will be. His hymns to Lenin achieve the same kind of finality by merging the same confidence with a complex and regular rhythm so that, since there even Glasgow's appalling poverty and ugliness seem beautiful ('Third Hymn To Lenin'), the tension lies between that and what we know to be the true case.

Neruda, even more than Brecht or MacDiarmid, illustrates how the utopian poet of the socially collective world order is rooted. After his central period, of the *Canto General* and poems like 'We Are Many', he returns to an even more exclusive preoccupation with the natural world. As with MacDiarmid's, his poetry seems to shine and to be utopian — 'of no place' — in the sense that it deals not with the impossible but with nature as that might be experienced in a better world. In that central period Neruda experimented with colloquial, deliberately simplified language as did Wordsworth, on the argument that this would produce a poetry of the proletariat more truly. But he himself came to reject this, and said so,[9] for he realized that poetry simply cannot have that sort of obligation; it is not subservient to any class, institution or collectivity any more than any other, and if it should seem to be then it has been either appropriated or limited.

Since Brecht was privatized by circumstances in a way the other two were not, his poetry has different emphases from theirs, his response to nature being sadder and his political entanglement more poetically transfigured. But the natural world, and the transfiguration of the political world, is still there. The natural symbols to which he returns are predominantly trees and birds, taken generically. As Brecht says, 'The coldness of the forests/Will be inside me till my dying day', a theme which repeatedly occurs and which is the more resilient because it seems to survive the privation. The natural world also mourns the dreadful events of the political: 'At that all the birds/Fell asleep among the trees' is the refrain of one poem about atrocities in the war. But his method of writing poems on the urban, political situation itself is more interesting still.

This method, avowedly political and propagandist in purpose, works precisely by *not* directly engaging with the envisaged opponent but by catching him and us off-guard; such is his alienating, shock-tactics method. The form of the poems is not ever, 'You shouldn't be doing that. . . . You will be overthrown . . . . Workers unite'! or any similar position. Rather he writes an ironic poem called 'Ballad on Approving of The World', or one on an author who, hearing of the burning-of-the-books activities of the Nazis, is annoyed his own books weren't burnt. A foreigner returning to Germany asks who is ruling the Third Reich now. Answer: Fear. Because of the question 'Who'? rather than 'What'? we expected a name. Thus to show the dialectical process in terms of actual interactions entails not poetry but drama, and Brecht's drama is a demonstration of the taking of quite different literary-political risks. Brecht's poetic tactics are poetry because the result does not merely shock; it haunts. The sociality is arrested.

The world in which the communist poets' work has its roots is a world of the future. As such it can be idealized and is open to the play of the verbal imagination; as such also it contrasts with the world of the past in which Eliot and Pound and poets of opposed political persuasion are rooted. But both kinds have in common, then, that their ideal eschews the present: they share the aspiration away from the secularized world and its sociological description. The Left poets differ in tone from those of the Right, naturally, since if the future is not yet here its traces are not available for the *collage* poetry of Eliot, Jones and Pound. Instead a diffused longing is expressed, commonly in terms of the natural world, but one as it might be rather than as it is now. Perhaps MacDiarmid captures it best: 'Materialism promises something/Hardly to be distinguished/From eternal life'.

CHAPTER 11

THE POET IN THE SOCIOLOGICAL WORLD: HARDY, BERRYMAN

I have so far suggested two of the three ways in which poetry has had to cope explicitly with the sociological idea in the century in which that idea has become explicit. These were in terms of the poem itself, and society itself, and we now have to deal with the poetic orientation round the poet himself or herself. But the case of 'the poet himself' is a little more complex, for reasons I will suggest, and so I want first to elaborate a little further again what I mean by this tripartite emphasis on poem, society and poet.

The twentieth-century poetic response to the sociological idea is a negative one. This can be put more specifically than we have done hitherto. In the case of the poets who aspire to produce 'the poem itself', the emphasis is that the poem is unable to be seen sociologically. In the second case, of poets like Eliot, Pound and Neruda, we see that it is society that they render non-sociological — or, if that sounds too perverse to be useful, let us say that according to these poets the nullity of the sociological idea is demonstrated by the history of civilizations or by the teleological pull to their ideal version in the future. But, thirdly, there is the response that it is the poet who is, as it were, not sociological; that is to say, the necessary response (if my argument is true) that the poet has no place in the sociological world. In this case the poet has nothing to do but express that very fact; not merely state it, but make poetry which simply is the poet's self-abnegation in that situation. Here the poet is not trying to make an autonomous object out of language, nor trying to show the very poeticality of civilization itself, but trying poetically to express the pointlessness of his own poetic existence. As is clear from the poets who fall mainly into this category, this raises, quite literally, the question of death. There seem to be various kinds of poets concerned with this matter. First there is Hardy, who wrote what I would call a poetry of the espousal of death. Then there are the confessional poets such as Berryman and Plath who went to the end of this road and took their own lives. Thirdly there is a very mixed group of such as Edward Thomas, Lowell, and some others still living, who have not needed to do that, yet nevertheless seem to have the same pressures on them from the same direction, which they resolve in certain ways. Apart from Hardy and Berryman I will keep my remarks brief on these poets.

This third orientation, then, is complex to discuss because if the poet, not the poem or that nebulous thing the 'society' is what is at issue, then the poet is putting himself— herself— at risk, and playing dice with himself rather than just his work alone. And the ultimate risk is death. Yet it soon becomes clear that although the poet, rather than poem or society, is the important force, it is not simply a matter of poetic concentration on that poet's personality or psychological troubles. Those matters inevitably arise but, if we can put it like this without seeming mechanistic and insensitive, they are for the reader a means to the end, not the end itself. It is said of the confessional group of poets that they make their own poetry inseparably from their own life-circumstances, so that to understand their poetry is impossible without knowing something of those circumstances. That is true, but it is not the *raison d'être* of the poet's work. That involvement of life-circumstance with the poetry has to be present, but that is in order to achieve authenticity. It is the fact of the extremity, not its psychoanalytical interest, that is ultimately important; and yet to be convinced, and to believe that this poet actually has made the total sacrifice, we do need to feel and know those circumstances. Our knowledge of the final step the poet took does admittedly, in fact certainly, intensify for us the poetry that poet leaves and which we then read. It is by the nature of the case impossible to know the effect on us of Plath's 'Daddy' or Berryman's 'Dream Song No 324' if those two poets had lived, and one has to presume it might be different. But the fact of the death does not change the words which the poet had written. The sad outcome, if it should occur, intensifies the meaning but can scarcely alter it. To deny that would be to deny the possibility that some poets experience the same extremity but somehow survive it. We can summarize these introductory remarks with Gabriel Pearson's comment on Lowell's *Life Studies*: 'Perhaps this is what the poetry is really about: the astonishing fact of its own existence'.[1] Let us now first consider this question of death and its relation to the sociological idea.

To put it I hope not too fancifully: it is part of the sociological idea that death does not exist. Not that there is necessarily a belief in after-life for the individual but that society survives the individual and therefore does not take much account of him. A biological or even psychological account of the individual cannot avoid facing the finitude of the process; death comes as the end. The social order very rarely ends. Societies may conceivably be exterminated but it is much more likely that they will evolve or be absorbed in others. It is a commonplace that our everyday symbolic description of ourselves in the modern world attempts to suppress the facing of our deaths. The word itself is taboo, and we speak of the 'terminal ward' and 'passing on'.[2] The increasing display of death on the television screen is so often the emergency, the car crash or airport guerrilla attack. This subject occupies our consciousnesses very much as a result of actions that have certainly not held individual life dear. So much has commonly been stated.

But if death and the sociological idea mutually exclude each other, if not indeed denying each other, then according to our argument about poetry we might expect to find poetry that takes death for its subject or, in some sense to be examined, uses a death-inspired language. The elegiac tradition has usually done exactly that. To revere or honour a dead person, or mourn grievously a loved person who has died, cannot be done in ordinary language; it cannot be merely a matter of statement and answer, nor can it be simply an exaggeration of those (as in 'He was *such* a wonderful man, his friends loved him *so* much'), for such expressions seem all the more poverty-stricken in the face of the loss. That is because they attempt to use for death the most inappropriate language; namely, the language of ordinary life. It is well known that thousands of people, no matter how unliterary, will want a rhyme or verse to mark a gravestone of a loved relative, or to have on a card that sends sympathy. And the reason why poetry does what ordinary language cannot is that the death of honoured or loved people has to be marked irreversibly and with finality. Since death is irreversible and final, so must the words be that mark it, otherwise it cannot be felt that we have matched up to the event of the death itself. The consolation attained by the elegiac poem may never replace the person missed, but it must at least stand the test of time, otherwise it is worse than nothing, a mockery.

Clearly therefore two apparently contradictory things have to be achieved at once. The dead person has to be mourned, and it has to be clear that the chief result of death is profound grief; yet equally Death itself must not be allowed to be a permanent victor; the grave must have no victory. The achievement of a permanent reconciliation of such contraries so that both are present as one and thereby compel us with their united power, *is* elegiac poetry. Again there is no deeper 'essence' of such poetry we find and compose into poems. When composition is done, the poetic effect is there. And so we have the tradition in which the dead person is in some way transfigured, as in 'Pearl', or the dead person himself is felt to be the inspiration for the poet's thought of new hope, as in *In Memoriam*.[3] Donne's 'Death be not proud . . .' is itself proud, and Shelley's 'he is not dead, he doth not sleep/He hath awakened . . .' is an exultant, more immediately impulsive expression of the same duality in the one image. By inverting life and death to dream and reality, it is death's sting that is drawn.

This brings us to Hardy. For all that I have just said refers to the elegiac traditions of mourning. That tradition exists before society becomes conscious of itself in the sociological idea. But when that idea appears something happens to the elegiac tradition which is very clearly illustrated in Hardy. For if poetry in the sociological world has not merely to go on being 'non-social' but actually to fight against that concept, then death, that most non-social thing, begins to be seen by the poet as something which cannot be dodged — and this occurs quite aside from occasions when a loved individual or honoured person is mourned. Death itself, omitted by the sociological idea, has to be recovered by the poet, and the poet's own death, not that of a loved person, has to be faced.

Some of Hardy's poems are mournful, though at a distance, in the old sense. But in the majority mourning's positive side — as Freud says, the attempt to set the lost object up in one's own ego— is missing. It is as though Hardy himself is dead, or is adopting that stance. (Hardy once said that he was himself a dead man long before his death.) The most explicit cases of this occur in the quite large group of very disturbing poems in which dead people speak from the grave.[4] Among others is 'Not Only I', worth quoting in full because it illustrates many features of this sort of poem, and indeed of Hardy's poetry more generally:

>   Not only I
>   Am doomed awhile to lie
>   In this close bin with earthen sides;
>   But the things I thought, and the songs I sang,
>   And the hopes I had, and the passioned pang
>   For people I knew
>   Who passed before me,
>   Whose memory barely abides;
>   And the visions I drew
>   That daily upbore me!
>
>   And the joyous springs and summers,
>   And the jaunts with blithe newcomers,
>   And my plans and appearances; drives and rides
>   That fanned my face to a lively red;
>   And the grays and blues
>   Of the far-off views,
>   That nobody else discerned outspread;
>   And little achievements for blame or praise;
>   Things left undone; things left unsaid;
>   In brief, my days!
>
>   Compressed here in six feet by two,
>   In secrecy
>   To lie with me
>   Till the Call shall be,

> Are all these things I knew,
>   Which cannot be handed on;
> Strange happenings quite unrecorded,
> Lost to the world and disregarded,
> That only thinks: 'Here moulders till Doom's-dawn
>   A woman's skeleton.'

Who is being addressed? The poem presents a disembodied voice, recounting all the parts of sociality which simply no longer exist after death. The feeling is surely not so much of loss as simply absence; it is too general for loss. Then there is the extraordinary 'Voices From Things Growing In A Churchyard': ('these flowers are I, poor Fanny Hurd'), 'The Graveyard Of Dead Creeds' and, probably best-known of all, 'Channel Firing', in which the 'gunnery practice out at sea' wakes all the skeletons in the churchyard. They talk to each other, bemoaning the fact that man will, seemingly for ever, practise enmity and strife. In this poem's first two lines we learn 'That night your great guns, unawares,/Shook all our coffins as we lay'. The important word is 'our'; it is the poet himself who impersonates a dead man.

In another group of Hardy's poems the event described is over and finished before the poem is written. The time gap may be hours or decades, but the sense of finality is always total. An excellent example is 'A Hurried Meeting'. A highborn woman goes to meet a lover in the woods, not to make love but to tell him about her pregnancy by him. What is curious is the dry way the end of the affair is mutually assumed; but equally curious is that there is no social problem whatever. The lovers cannot conceivably marry, but all is well, the woman will go to a distant spot where her mother lives, have the child and return. The baby can easily be brought up as though it were born of the woman's mother, for as Hardy disarmingly tells us, 'She's forty-one/When many a woman's bearing is not done'. The drama is taken right out of the story. There is no excitement of that kind. Not a syllable depicts the man, his bearing or his character; only 'inferior clearly he', but that is merely why they cannot marry. Their meeting is haughty; not hostile but cold. The poem's point is solely that 'Love is a terrible thing; sweet for a space, and then all mourning, mourning!' Thus the event itself, the actual meeting, is 'social' in a wholly insulated way; the interaction is metaphysical. Other examples of this finality are 'Throwing a Tree', in which because a great tree is chopped down 'two hundred years' steady growth has been ended in less than two hours'. And that is the last line; no comment, just end and removal. In 'A Thunderstorm in Town' the poet reflects that if the rain had lasted two more minutes a desired lady would not have got out of the carriage, and he would have kissed her. Here we have an aesthetic not merely of what is long over but of what, still in the past, did not occur at all. 'The Dawn after the Dance' and 'Where the Picnic Was' are also of this kind.

The poet's presentation of himself as figuratively dead is itself a quality of Hardy's language in these poems. It is not only the linguistic tone but also the poet's stance that achieves this effect, and this is true in the many cases where the poem is a piece of very physical perception, so that a small scene is captured as by a camera. This of course has often been noted of Hardy.[5] The obvious example is 'On the Departure Platform', where the loved woman walks away down the platform to the train;

> We kissed at the barrier; and passing through
> She left me, and moment by moment got
> Smaller and smaller, until to my view
>   She was but a spot;

In 'The Photograph' the poet sets fire to a photo of a loved woman, long dead. An even more striking example of Hardy's espousal of death is the irony of refrain in so many poems. This has surely a most weird effect. In poem after poem each stanza has the same form and only a modified version of the same content. In many the refrain is orthodox; with repetition of a line or two at the end. For instance in 'The Ruined Maid' a girl is complimented in a number of ways — one for each stanza — on her material prosperity. The answer is always the same: ' "That's what its like when you're ruined" said she'. Another example is 'At Lulworth Cove'. Finally, 'The Wind's Prophecies' shows the wind relentlessly reversing the poet's expectations of the result of his journey — again one prophecy for each symmetrically identical stanza. In these poems the refrain effect, the essential repetition of each stanza, renders the poem static and unprogressive. There can be no envisaged hearer or answerer, and the poet is bleakly addressing air. The stanzas simply replay the idea in a timeless setting like a stuck gramophone. But the point is more than that. The ordinary refrain or repeated stanza in the folk-mode like the rousing camp-fire song, rugby song or similar example is common enough. Its effect there is precisely to enable all comers to join the shared and roistering event. It is not unsocial at all. But Hardy's ironic stance reverses that. Because the poem ends where it began, repeating itself all the way, it seems to do something to the individual and lonely voice we hear speaking it. If the voice speaking does not develop an image or argument, it withdraws language from any possibility of social function. The poems seem to be saying, 'No matter how I say this, it's still the same; we bear it and that is all'. That is what the underlying echo seems to be achieving. And in now suggesting such a duality of voice levels, the immediate repeated voice and the echo beneath, always adding 'I know I am saying this, simply saying it, inescapably' we touch on the deepest irony, the *eiron* as the Greeks called it and which as Northrop Frye has suggested is the archetype of winter, the dead season where there is no growth. This is not elegy or tragedy, for no alternative was available which was then tragically missed. And again, what constitutes it as poetry is exactly that encapsulation of the two ironic voices in their refrain, separated from all social function or intercourse, and ending where they started.

By taking the death stance himself, Hardy has defused the sense of loss and the mourning that elegy normally presents. So much is *a priori* lost in the world where faith, animism in nature, and such earlier realities, have disappeared, that no more 'loss' can be experienced. I think that because Hardy took this step he has far greater appeal to the contemporary world than does Tennyson, whose ruminations on the same subjects are so often, as Eliot says, 'almost totally encrusted by opinion'. Tennyson fights vainly by means of the very thing he also says in vain. Hardy's heart-felt stance makes language's very possibility, from the start, a poetic one.

We can now, although briefly, put this into a wider perspective for our purposes. Donald Davie has argued[6] that Hardy was a genuine Victorian, an 'engineer', and that his poems were thus works of engineering, so that in them he expressed a faith which we all necessarily now hold, that of scientific humanism. By a process of reasoning too long to summarize here, Davie connects this with social and class considerations of Hardy's time — with, in my view, some curious results. Davie argues that 'The Wind's Prophecy' is a poem about class-guilt because Hardy is transferring loyalty from a lower-class woman to a higher-class one. Whatever the background in Hardy's life, there is surely not a syllable in the poem to justify such a reading. The poem itself suggests a much more haunting and universal feeling, that of believing one is thinking one thing, only to find that an opposite thought or emotion keeps presenting itself. And that is all. Hardy's espousal of death, which I believe the poems clearly express, is not accounted for in this scientific-humanist view, a position Hardy the man no doubt held but which is related to his poetry in altogether more profound and complex fashion.

This brings us to the question of death as espoused with grimmer result by many poets of our century. They had direct concern not with technology as such but with the poet's position in the modern world. Hardy was the first and therefore unique and only possible instance of the poet who could take simply the stance of death and who could 'affect' death, if that word does not seem to make light of it; and then from that affectation make the detached observations, voyeuristically at times, of what he wrote about. But equally because Hardy did it the later writers, many of whom in the American world have been much influenced by Hardy,[7] no longer had that option. They had to face the implication of poetic death, so to call it, directly.

Before going on to discuss poetry's orientation toward the poet himself in the twentieth century, we need to consider the relation between suicide and the sociological idea. The first sociologist of suicide was Durkheim, whose conclusion was that suicide is a product of certain general social conditions.[8] Although this or that suicide may seem to have different causes, these are really only occasions, and the individuals most prone to suicide are merely those who most feel those general pressures. According to Durkheim there are three sorts of suicide, the egotistical, altruistic and anomic, and he analyses them. But he makes clear his view that in all these cases it is society — even that as apparently distant from the individual — that brings on the suicide. It is not material poverty, insanity, fear, or any other such category.[9] Now Durkheim claims to have proved this scientifically. He is not merely defining suicide in those terms. Yet even so, the fact that such a theory can be presented is itself symptomatic of the sociological orientation of our time. Our world and our perception of our world are close. Even if there is some objective truth in Durkheim's findings, or those of more up to date researchers, it remains true that to take one's life becomes deeply embedded in our consciousnesses as something that is, so to speak, at the opposite end of the continuum of total social acceptance.

Next we have to consider the relation of this to death more generally. A. Alvarez[10] argues that artists' suicide in our time is related to what he calls 'absurd death', death which has no context in a religious or other wider world view, and which is also product of the apparent fact that in our world the taking of others' lives as policy has become too easy. This is because individual life matters less where it is society, not the individual, that is most seen as constituting human reality. The First World War, Auschwitz, Vietnam, the perennial road-accident — all these familiar cases of mass death may not be greater than in the past (consider the Black Death, or the wholesale sacking of cities) but their meaninglessness seems for the individual suddenly very evident. It seems that the sombre realities of mass extermination and death by one's own hand have at least some conceptual connection.

How does the artist himself see that connection? Alvarez' argument is that the ominous, black presence of pointless death weighs in on the sensitive antennae of the artist who then must face it 'straight' if an expression of integrity is to be achieved by which death can be faced and overcome. The artist becomes a scapegoat, for if death is an immediate presence, it cannot be imaginatively understood except by at least close experience. The poet is faced with this reality of absurd death, and there is no recourse to religion, nature, chivalry or anything else. It is incumbent on the poet therefore to cope with this absurdity by, as Alvarez puts it, ' [forging] a language which will somehow absolve from or validate absurd death, and to accept the existential risks in doing so'. (As he puts it in the context of Plath; 'It is as though she decided that, for her poetry to be valid, it must tackle head-on nothing less serious than her own death'). This seems a reasonable statement of the position, for it is not contradicted by a feature of suicide commonly noted (certainly true of Hemingway, Plath and Berryman) that the writer's father was also a suicide or died when the poet was very young. For this merely means that the poet was confronted much more poignantly with the circumstances of our time with which, in more diluted fashion, everyone is confronted. It is in fact the most obvious of Durkheim's 'occasions'. It is not that the poet of the espousal of death is somehow the prototype modern poet, the extreme and authentic case, leaving the poets of imagism or communism as only halfway examples. Rather his is a highly special case, perfectly valid (to use so feeble a word in such a context), and heroic we may well think; but a kind of cul-de-sac of human effort except insofar as it redeems itself by the poetry it produces. The poetic espousal of death is but one way of facing the consciously sociological world of our time. The shadow of a dark bird of extreme particularity is always over Berryman's shoulder in 'The Dream Songs':

> freezing my helpless mother
> he only, very early in the morning
> rose with his gun and went outdoors by my window
> and did what was needed.
>
> I cannot read that wretched mind, so strong
> & so undone . . .

*

Early on, Berryman produced a remarkable collection of sonnets in which the congestion of highly-tensed words for their own sake seems to have been his motive and interest. These seem a very direct product of his formal and conscious interest in literature. Later he wrote *Homage to Mistress Bradstreet*, a work which, although it has a far more broken-up texture and more wiry vocabulary than the sonnets, is nevertheless still external to himself (in contrast to 'The Dream Songs') by virtue of its organizing framework, the historical material about 'this boring high-minded Puritan woman who may have been our first poet but is not a good one'.[11] Berryman testifies to the research he did for this work, which seems parallel to Lowell's *Imitations* and Anne Sexton's *Transformations* in being a deliberately bracketed event, with an external subject, allowing a hiatus in the extremity or self-abnegation of their more usual preoccupations. Later still, and over a long period, Berryman wrote 'The Dream Songs', but these are quite different. Virtually all are of three stanzas each, totalling eighteen lines, and nearly all have rhyme schemes although the nature of these varies. Relationships in a full human sense are almost never referred to, with two important exceptions. The first exception is with 'ladies', and the two-dimensional nature of the sexual element seems marked, although one intuits also a level of cerebral intercourse, though not more than that, along with the sexuality. The second exception is of relationships with people who have died. The loss of these he feels most deeply, and accords them a near-reverent feeling of affection and adulation of their graciousness. Thus he speaks of William Carlos Williams 'the lovely man', and of Delmore Schwartz who was 'alive with surplus love'. But not even the dead are always praised in this way. The concern is different elsewhere, particularly in the reference to his father and Sylvia Plath, both of whom committed suicide. The only other *persona* in the sequence is the minstrel voice who calls him 'Mr Bones' in negro vernacular; 'Thass a funny title Mr Bones'. There is concern with God and the soul, and fear of that subject ('Am I a bad one —? I'm thinking of them fires . . .'), his father whom he would 'join', the 'horror of unlove', and the declaration that 'Henry's mind grew blacker the more he thought'. The high-pitched writing is harsh and deliberately nervous and inelegant, it eschews straight 'imagery' in an ordinary literary sense, and says of

Yeats that he knew nothing of life but was 'all symbols', a device Berryman does not use. There are odd inversions like 'We must be sad/And feel by the weather had' on several occasions, and there is the very strange, frequently used filler-syllable 'O' (or 'oh') almost brazenly or mockingly sounded.

At the same time two things contrast with this highly-strung and uncompromisingly black mode. First there are the sudden patches, usually whole songs, of writing in a deliberately older tradition, sometimes in echo of Donne, but more particularly the elegy to William Carlos Williams already mentioned, and the beautiful and extremely wistful Wallerian 'Go ill-sped book...', picking up Pound's 'Go dumb-born book...' as though poetry alone was important. Second there is the sudden occasional reference, indicative surely of some profound desire, to Song: 'High in the summer branches the poet sang./His throat ached, and he could sing no more'. And again, also the bird in the treetop: 'Once in a sycamore I was glad/All at the top, and I sang' (which to me at least echoes Dylan Thomas' 'Fern Hill'). In the three-hundred-and-eighty-fourth poem, almost the end, the poet, or Henry, goes to his father's grave and with savage desperation demands 'ha to see/just how he's taking it....' For me, though some will disagree, it ends there.

Briefly to suggest inferences from all this I would use Robert Pinsky's word 'attribution'[12] to describe a basic stance throughout the sequence and indeed in the writing of other extremist poets. In writing attributively the poet uses phrases sadly or ironically, to suggest what might be said in a certain vernacular or slang, or indeed more general mode of language, if a potential speaker were present. When done shallowly this is what it seems Jonathan Raban refers to in his phrase 'Talking Heads'[13] (or C.H. Sisson calls 'chatter-poetry'); the poet that rattles on in affected adman or oh-so-sincere or fiery-eyed-protest style. Raban's inference, with which I agree, is that this is too often phoney, but 'attribution' is subtler and deeper, for it may proliferate in many different modes in one poem, these modes interplaying to suggest a multitude of stances to the matter in hand, and a range of possible emotions. This is not at all phoney, but equally it is not the other extreme of total detachment or 'throw-away', for that in a different way would be as homogeneous an effect (though more genuine) as the talking-head mode. Very often Berryman himself detachedly brings in a line from street-talk or journalism, but often it is more subtle, even understated, as in Song Number 153: 'I'm cross with God who has wrecked this generation', followed by a list of Berryman's dead and dear friends. 'I'm cross with . . .' is a phrase of the nursery or coyly affectionate reprimand. Berryman is trying it on, seeing how it sounds:

> I'm cross with god who has wrecked this generation.
> First he seized Ted, then Richard, Randall, and now
>   Delmore.
> In between he gorged on Sylvia Plath.
> That was a first-rate haul. He left alive
> fools I could number like a kitchen knife
> but Lowell he did not touch.

How different that is from:

> Go, ill-sped book, and whisper to her or
> storm out the message for her only ear
> that she is beautiful.
> Mention sunsets, be not silent of her eyes
> and mouth and other prospects, praise her size,
> say her figure is full . . .

Most of Berryman's attributive language echoes some aspect of contemporary talk — the street, the black, the sophisticated student, or the snatch of old parodied tale ('Lo, he went away/to Dublin's fair city', etc.) — but in a number of cases cited by Pinsky, such as Songs 29 and 75, a recognizably literary language is used. This time the colloquial language accompanying it is there to allow the poet also to use the more traditional language which he actually prefers. A merely traditional poem in the formal language of Georgianism or the seventeenth century would be impossible in our time, because of the battery of vernaculars which a democratic and egalitarian world gives us; yet the poet longs to write in some way at least comparable to that earlier time. He therefore works out a way of doing so legitimately (to the twentieth-century ear) in that it often seems self-parody as well. It seems important (a point that Pinsky does not mention) that in the deliberate elegies, to Williams and others, traditional language is used very thankfully and directly.

In these observations I think we have the clue to what occurs in John Berryman's dream songs and how they relate to our main theme. Today's language, in at least some cases, is pluralized, attaching to classes, jobs and professions, as those have been linguistically propagated by media and particularly television. Much of our present language is therefore already pre-cast in the modes by which it is spoken publicly in some prototype or role. The person sensitive to language cannot but be aware of this. And of course in a sense it is common knowledge; but the almost over-intelligent writer, as Berryman was, cannot resort to some single language of his own in which to write his poetry. His sensitivities cannot avoid being open to all the possibilities. The universality of a traditional bardic 'Voice' or Word has broken open to the new and parallel universality implied by the totality, no less, of all the vernaculars. But this leads to another suggestion. For if language is thus pluralized, and if also we may not legitimately make a form-content distinction for poetry, then it follows that the poet sensitive to these things has — and I hope not to be misunderstood — nothing to say; he has no subject. There is a curious sense in which both Berryman and Plath seem to arrive at the discovery that they do indeed have no subject. (This is why *Homage to Mistress Bradstreet* and other extremist poems were an attempt to bring in a subject externally.) When I say this sort of poet has no subject I do not mean that he is empty-headed but that, especially sensitive to and therefore using the myriad of voices which is synonymous with language in our time, he necessarily encounters the cognitive implication of such language humanly; it is all corners and no centre. There is no nub reality being expressed, or offering itself for expression. Of course this is analogous to what we said of T.S. Eliot, that he drew from diverse cultures in our history, so showing that no one idea (in our case the sociological idea) could embody reality adequately. But Eliot selected from separate whole cultures, all of which had their own richness and autonomy. That is to say, his inference was outward and positive (his 'fatigued' tone came only from the implications of that for our own present, brief period). But Berryman's attributed voices are largely of the same culture.

We must ask the reason for this and what it has to do with the sociological idea. Although the several voices in amalgam are a chaos and have 'nothing to say', as I have put it, they do in another sense say something very important. They are the expression of our relationships and interaction. Language as seen through the eyes of the sociological idea does not convey or state this or that, but is based on and woven into an acknowledgement of each other as we talk. So much was said when in Chapter 2 we discussed social interactionism and ethnomethodology. But if that is so, and it is language's use in interaction and its power to cement our relationships that makes it important, then the mode of its use in literature would tend not to be poetic at all. It is the relating power of language-acts, not their tangibility or embodiment of truth, that offers itself. It is as though through such media as television the sociological idea, the interactive act, is visibly presented before us every time an interaction through such media occurs. Many of Berryman's voices are TV voices, committee voices, salesman's voices, recognizable as the interactive fabric of the sociological world:

— Are you radioactive, pal? — Pal, radioactive.
— Has you the night sweats & the day sweats, pal?
— Pal, I do.
— Did your gal leave you? — What do *you* think, pal?
— Is that thing on the front of your head what it seems to be, pal?
— Yes, pal.

In the extremity caused by this, it is not isolation but precisely neurotic over-interaction, the double-bind that breaks marriages, and brings violent reaction, that results; and the artform for that is drama. But Berryman and others would make their extremity poetic. Therefore they must draw on the language of voices but then find that the attribution, the distancing and plurality, indicate a hole, a void in the middle and at the heart. Nothing is being said, no assertion is being made, yet equally interaction is not being cemented, for the poet is and must be alone. This I take it is why when Berryman confronts an actual death, as of Schwartz or Blackmur,[14] he returns almost with relief to the language of traditional elegy, as though to say 'At least one can write like this in *this* case, for the friend I here mourn has entered and so rejoins the past'.

If most language is interactive, as at least two versions of the sociological idea assert, what can the poet, sensitive to this fact, do? What can he do, when poems are clearly things insulated from interaction on the page, asserting nothing but themselves? Of course many poets, such as Eliot and Wallace Stevens, simply do not accept that language is merely interactive, and so are able to make solid language-objects or cultural expressions of value. But the poet who feels otherwise has to make a positive thing of poetry's own lonely and socially undervalued, separation. The one to do this will be the poet already gripped by his or her isolation, or with the shadow of death already across him.

PART IV
CONCLUSION

CHAPTER 12

CONCLUSION

If what we normally call the richness of poetry is nothing to do with our conceptions of the social, and even defies those conceptions, then we must do without that richness or modify the dominance of the sociological conception. This is not a matter of merely intellectual or academic curiosity. We are so often told that 'language', that projected commodity, is extremely important; yet most people seem to be happy without poetry, and it often seems that the very thoroughness of our linguistic and literary research enervates the object of its attention. Perhaps science always dissolves, rather than constitutes, its object. If that is so, then poetry and possibly language too are being dispatched.

The foregoing examination of several poets in terms of their relation to the sociological idea has, I hope, convincingly established the nature of that relation. If we are now usefully to generalize, it seems we must first try to suggest what poetry always has been and is; we must rewrite the traditional descriptions of poetry in the light of the incompatibility we see between poetry and the sociological idea. This will be emphasized if we also show how, on the other hand, sociological thought seems to press not merely sociologists but also ordinary people into a language which is the very reverse of poetic richness. We need to suggest also how criticism, in the sociological age, seems to further the effects on poetry of that apparent debilitation. The pessimistic conclusion, and the facing of its implications, seem the position from which any new defence of poetry might now come.

The question 'What is poetry'? feels too essentialist for our time. Perhaps we should rather ask what makes us say something is poetry. During this book I have often found myself saying that such-and-such tension or relation between two aspects of language *is* the poetry; that is to say, there is no underlying 'essence' but rather a certain deflection of language from what we expected, or the capacity of a word-arrangement to hold compelling meaning without the normal everyday reference. In every poem, language is arranged *not* to address a listener or to support a social configuration such as a group or institution, and yet also that language thereby becomes arresting and intelligible. The tension this entails comes from a tripartite paradox; namely, a) language is social, b) poetry is language, c) yet poetry is not social, not accountable by the sociological idea. The act of finding the words we need for social intercourse, or to take a role or affirm an institutional process (or indeed to deal with these fictionally or imitate others so doing, as in drama) is radically different, different in kind, from finding the words we want for the poem, because our poem, prior to writing, has no demands other than our ineffable sense of it. The actual tension between what we are expecting and what we get; that is, between what is supposed to be discursive or directive as in formal prose, and yet turns out not to be: that is what makes us call something poetry. Such language would be impossible in ordinary discourse or social processes, because the huge congestion of contrivance and art in the poem could not conceivably occur in them. (Nor of course could a piece of prose writing, for example an industrial report, but in those cases every single word serves the social cause for which the document is written.) This would be the 'Monty Python effect', as I have elsewhere suggested one might call it.[1] Amazement and anger would occur if a speaker appropriated to himself the right, in discourse or other social negotiation, to hold up such processes in order to give his own narcissistic imagery or rhythm. Poetry truncates the very thing that in all other cases language strives to achieve.

The idea of poetry's tension between language as social and as self-referring can illuminate some of the traditional descriptions of language mentioned in Chapter 1. It is important first that language is, then, not self-referring alone, but is that in tension with the discursive or social use we might have expected to find. Having said this we can consider the traditional designations of poetry as aspiring to music or silence, as being the work of a 'maker', and as being object or icon rather than a piece of dialogue. We can first ask what it is about such poetic self-referrings that makes us want to read them. If they do not convey information or further social processes, then their interest and compelling power must have some other nature. It seems that this lies with a quality normally thought essential to the good poem; that it seems inevitable. The writing seems unable to have been other than it is, it seems not too considered or chosen, although of course much poetic pleasure comes from our appreciation of the craftsmanship which led to exactly that inevitability. It is the emphasis Yeats made, in 'Adam's Curse', that immense labour may be needed in writing a poem but that unless the result seem the work of a moment all the labour will have been in vain.

All the other traditionally-suggested features of poetry, for example that it aspires to music or silence, seem to square with this idea that poetry is the state of language in tension with the normal states in which it assists the constitution of that which is social. If the poem is self-referring it cannot be 'said' as discourse and so has some origin other than saying. This origin has normally been called 'making'; the poet is a maker. It is the ordering or arranging source, not the source of personal emotion or consideration to interpret a social role or fulfil social expectations, that controls the language and the idea of what the language is for. (The emotion is itself one of the things to be controlled.) But one cannot 'make' a verbal interaction, for one is dependent there on the signals and attitudes of the other party, and similarly one does not make a business letter or report out of words in that sense; rather, words are chosen as a result of the already decided material.

Equally, if the poem is not 'said', it may not necessarily sound like talking, and is perhaps musical. But if the words are themselves musical (not merely 'set to music') then the power of that quality on our minds must itself be integral to the verbal expression, whereas ordinary speech cannot wait for any musical ordering, so that the speech is constituted as discourse by quite other characteristics. Of course passages and sentences occur in discourse that are powerfully rhythmical, and one might say on occasion musical, but they are the exception. The importance of rhythm, pure sound, in poetry as opposed to ordinary speech or institutional writing is central to our argument.

It has often been pointed out that, in infancy, the child will necessarily hear sound-patterns prior to developing the general understanding of what they indicate socially or semantically. That being so, the random, if certainly rhythmical, patterns of all ordinary speech will be remembered as, at most, a general tendency, and it is the more patterned and more powerful ones that will be remembered more deeply. With that, the capacity of language to be more memorable when in that condition will itself be internalized. But it is poetry that uses this very rhythm as its medium, whereas the language of both ordinary discourse and institutional writing increasingly plays down such components by eliding and standardizing our rhythmic responses, according to the demands of wider normative (sociological) structure. It is no answer to say that any piece of talk or writing necessarily has *some* rhythm; for, equally, any physical object has some shape, yet that does not stop us from legitimately calling some things 'shapeless'.

Again the poem has been described as an 'object'. The symbolists, among others, held this view. Because of the belief that poems are communications (true enough if rightly understood, or if defined as true) much criticism has played round this matter, but debates about the 'autonomy of art' or the metaphysical dispute over what counts as an object (is a joke an object?) are not the question. There are several features of poems that make 'object' a reasonable, common-sense description of them, not least the fact of the sociological idea's emergence in the modern world. If the poem does not emerge in discourse or interaction as integral to those things, then on that sociological argument itself the poem is an object. But more compelling is the way the poem feels like an object; its co-ordination of imagery, rhythm and word have a sensuousness and tangible quality even when the poem's tendency is abstract and metaphysical, as in much of Vaughan, Wallace Stevens or Roethke.

The poem is also rendered an object in the sense that its actual words, and only those, constitute it. It is not a set of ideas or images that various words might recapture for us, some at one time, some at another. Remembering an admired poem often provides the incentive to check the exact words for the original experience. Equally the poem's objective status, insofar as it has that, comes with its ability to survive its own origins, such that we do not know or need to know the germ of its writing. Much ordinary and institutional discourse on the other hand requires such knowledge for its comprehension; we need the motives and assumptions behind an acquaintance's words. Finally in highly regular and rhymed poems the tangibility of the poem is affirmed almost mathematically, so that the regularity of syllables along the line and the regularity of numbers of lines and matching of rhyme going downwards, feel as though they create something almost four-square. The poem offers itself as one unit, and when we read it we go back, or are taken back, to its beginning, outside its temporal progression; we can see its organization and stand outside it as an entirety. All ordinary discourse is time-ordered, and progresses in largely linear fashion.

Similarly the poem has been described as aspiring to silence. Needless to say, this is nothing to do with silent reading in the head, and in fact the question of reading aloud hardly arises, for the power of the poem to be silent is not a matter of verbal enunciation, but of the poem's removal from the unceasing flow of ordinary language. The successful poem seems to say everything there could be said on a subject, not in amassing amounts of comment or evidence, but in clearing all remaining question away from us, or leaving it in equilibrium. From another point of view the poem's silence is suggested by our inability, commonly, to pick up and read a poem 'in passing' as one may with a joke or story; one must slow down, reduce back to the visceral rhythms which quietly tick over, and thus receive the poem at the opposite extreme from that in ordinary discourse where we are already engaged in an interaction, or wider social or occupational function, to which we may well have to contribute.

The notorious battle between regular form and *vers libre* can be seen in the same light. It is intriguing how, like Pound's refutation of the Romantics, so also the battle between regular form and free verse, in the face of the sociological idea, turns out to be not a battle at all but rather two ways of coping with a common foe; a squabble between two generals over a battle's tactics, rather than the conflict itself. In regular form the insulation of the poem from the sociologically-understood use of language is very explicit. This is why we call regular forms arbitrary (which does not make them purposeless or devoid of origin); and the arbitrariness is that the form's characteristics are laid out before the poem (and any 'social occasion' of it) exists. Thus the form 'sonnet', and this particular sonnet before us, remain distinct entities, and the poem's success lies simply in its ability to make us forget that very fact. In free form, on the other hand, the search is for 'the exact curve of the thing', the unique words for what the poet has ineffably experienced. Here the distance from discourse or institutional language is at first sight invisible, and the poem's self-referring quality stands in splendid isolation rather than having a regular form to declare it. Yet though its non-sociality is hidden at first, this unique and autonomous ineffability in the 'free-verse' poem are what distinguish it from ordinary language the more sharply. Much free verse is, certainly, merely secondhand from what has been done earlier, but even there some originality must be present for the poem to command attention. The free-verse poem has therefore to carry its own criteria for assessment within it as an even more original matter than the quatrain or sonnet, which use their forms like marksmen use targets. The purpose of hitting the target is not to do something to the target but to have it as a measure of one's skill. The analogy is not perfect, but at least to some extent the regular form is an arbitrary measurement against which the poem works itself out.

Through these means, if at all, we are able to address and probe the mysterious qualities of the non-social thing, the things we are not; nature, ideas, God, myths, ancient heroes, works of art themselves, and what is in our subconsciousnesses. What seems certain is that when our sociality itself dominates our use and idea of language, these probes are endangered and perhaps lost. We do not even have the option of them. This is because of the way that this sociality affects our ordinary language.

*

Our ordinary language can be considered by means of the division of the sociological orientation itself into the five main examples of it we gave in the second chapter. Let us take first the oldest and most established mode of sociological thinking, that of 'grand theory'. If we accept and are most dominated by the grand theories of sociology, the universalities of large-scale formal organizations if not whole societies, our communication will be premised on such assumptions. But for that very reason (unless we are ourselves formal sociologists) our talk will approach the ridiculous, for we shall always be talking for others and about others. Personal eccentricity and insensitivity aside, I can usefully talk about God, nature, or my own inner secrets and psyche to others, for they may not have come across those things. But those to whom I speak must in some way, even if not through formal sociology, have come across their membership of social organization and society, for that, *ex hypothesi*, is the dominant truth about ourselves in our time. We cannot therefore forever assert that 'we belong to institutions' or 'we have a class system', without tedium, for others know this. Certainly, we can assert a unique, particular 'society' we belong to, by for example, ritualizing our public speakings to a monarch or deity, or by formalizing our conversation in a slightly elevated society, such as that of the eighteenth century. For there an assertion by contrast, about its advanced state of civilization, is always subliminally present. But our own society is, existentially, simply the total of us, with no mysterious dimension; that at least is the view sociological man holds. The same is true if we feel most strongly the social-interactive view of social reality. Again we cannot, without tedium, forever tell each other that we are interacting, have a relationship, or are taking roles to each other as husband, lover, old-fashioned father or rebellious son. A full discourse based on a belief in a simplified 'interaction' at reality's heart would make for endless repetitiveness, at best an awkwardness, at worst a neurotic condition. Our language cannot endure on the basis simply of analysing our interaction itself and monitoring it as we go. The ethnomethodological school, who tried such monitoring, quickly found that they were taking positions of deviance. They could only expose the taken-for-granted quality of our relationships by not taking them for granted themselves, and doing experiments which, deliberately (for research purposes) risked giving others embarrassment, anger and distress.

Similarly, if we are at heart 'social anthropologists', and look albeit empirically at the communities we study or live in, we shall again return our findings under that influence, and make the tangible and particular, general; we will say 'in this industrial community . . .', 'in this family structure . . .', 'the social problems round here are . . .', and so on. We shall return what was indeed particular to that actual place — an estate near Liverpool or a divorced couple in a Waites house in Basildon — to their general sociological description. And again, we cannot continue with it, for those we address will either cry out that *their* case is different, or that they know already. The response to Marxism is necessarily a little different, for Marxism is a historical description of events rather than a conceptual theory; but it still concludes, at least, in repeatedly talking about only our own position. Therefore when in its strong formulation it recites doctrines about man to men, the strong response will be that men are already able to see their position, so that having heard Marxism once, they may accept or reject Marxism accordingly.

None of this undermines the validity of the sociological enterprise, which has formulated in great detail these things for us. The question is what happens to language when these ideas centrally organize our ways of seeing the world. What happens, it seems, is that phenomenon so commonly noted in our century, that of language's debilitation and truncation. That enterprise which most convincingly, apparently, describes ourselves to ourselves, is that which most of all stops us from forever saying it. In one respect, for better or worse, this means a cutting-off at root of all the possibilities, tensive qualities, economy, rhythm, undying metaphor and other things we have just suggested are the domain of poetry. But the effect on everyday discourse as well is curious and far-reaching. The elision characteristic of modern speech comes from assuming that the other person knows half of what is to be said already. There is a difference, a throw-away casualness, in how we speak; a feeling perhaps of 'you know . . . you know, all that about . . . we don't need to say . . .'; it is that tone. It has been excellently described by Laura Riding Jackson, who sees ordinary language as always referring, in our time, to 'an instinctively immediate objective continually deferred as not immediately convenient'.[2] Normally in societies there is present 'language with a perfect distinctness of meaning-force and a full expressiveness of sense' — a language which, to our ears, would seem either formal or quaint. Laura Riding Jackson spells out trenchantly what she thinks this prevalent quality of language has done for poetry in our time, but her emphasis is on the language itself. I suggest that the continual deferring is itself what cements more tightly the interactions by which we live. We have a bond with another person if we can feel that we mutually understand each other's implicit references. There may be nothing wrong with this, but it has been achieved differently at other stages of human society and culture. There, it may not be elision but convention of phrase that achieves this social cohesion; the use of old sayings, proverbs, and what are by our standards elaborately formal greetings and farewells, enquiries and praises. What someone else is fully and formally saying is gladly allowed. In our time, for the reasons given, it works another way.

The remarkable accompanying paradox is that, despite elision, articulation has increased. Under the dominance of sociological thought, language becomes increasingly important in social cohesion (for other cohesions like patriotism or a central Church are lacking) and yet that same language is characterized by elision. It is as though all we have is this one metaphysic of sociality, a blank cheque or a conception like the similarly irreducible 'all', 'thing', 'Being' or 'reality', so simply that it approaches nothingness (or, in the terms of symbolic logic, the first-premise assertion that '$a = a$'); but that precisely because we have therefore no obdurate outside authority such as God, kings or nature to guide us, we must always articulate this thing, 'society', to ourselves as best we can in order to remain close to one another. It is no doubt an oversimplification to suggest that we say less and less but on more and more occasions. Our society thinks itself aloud; that is our talk and social discourse. We tell each other that we are social; but we knew that already, and there is nothing else to tell; so elision ensues. This is the very opposite of the use of language for poetry. It is the weakening of language while saying more. Poetry is the enriching of language while saying less. Our ordinary language therefore cannot make poetry, use poetry, or understand poetry at all.

The knot of introversion is pulled to its tightest with one more drastic implication. For it might have been thought that some of what has been said is only a sociological version of the older quarrels between poetry and utilitarianism or poetry and science. But the difference is perhaps now clear enough. For, of those abstractions, the sociological one *is us*; it is not our conception of some outside thing which we must somehow come at knowing that in part at least it is something else. Theology, philosophy and biology all refer to other things. Whether we talk of photosynthesis or binary fission; or thought, idea, reality or the Good, these are not our synonyms. But the 'society' of sociology, even in the strong version of a Durkheim who very nearly believes that this actually exists over and above its members, is supposed to be synonymous with *us* in our plurality. Consequently the relation of sociology to poetry is different, because of the different status of language. But through our self-conscious sociality, this enervated and empty language is, it seems, most necessary to us when, in the twentieth-century mode, we are most being what we most think we are.

*

Some of this might seem ominous for the practice and the institution of criticism. For if by its nature poetry eschews the sociological idea, and if criticism is increasingly influenced by that idea (as we suggested in Chapter 1), then it seems *prima facie* likely that criticism's chance of dealing with poetry will be slight. We are in a period in which the immediate practical analysis of texts has given way to a wider attempt to account for the general phenomenon of literature itself. But, whatever the faults of practical criticism, it was at its best a celebratory way of looking at individual poems. If our aspiration is to a science of literature, the resulting account must be in terms of something more general, some universal theory of art or communication or man. An account of how a particular poem came into existence would not be scientific at all, but historical; in fact, no one but the poet could conceivably give it. Now if, again, the 'science' in question is more or less sociological and the literary art is poetry, then it is clear that no progress can be made if the science attempts to explain actual occasions of the poetry that is written. For the poem's very existence *is*, at least in the sociological era, its own unique tension against exactly what sociality in that mode implies, and what it assumes about language. When that kind of literary science considers poetry, it can only in a general way, like any 'native reader' familiarize itself with poetry itself, and then indicate the gap, so to speak, which poetry would occupy in a full description of man. That science would show only implicitly what language has dealt with or gone through to reach that (poetic) gap. If poetry is a human activity the sociological sciences will, logically, have a legitimate interest in knowing where to place it, in order to aspire to their complete description of man; but their description of poetry can only be an outlining of the area within which the actual poems fall; a piece of anti-matter, a 'black hole' of negation in the described universe. Any closer attempt by the sociologically-influenced disciplines to describe individual poems themselves would appear to be based on a delusion.

If we take Saussurian linguistics, for example, it is surely enough for the person who values poetry to see the inference of such statements as that there is a signifier/signified distinction, or that the linguistic sign is always arbitrary. The inference of the first distinction is a question: what does any poem signify? When we see the answer, namely, that it signifies only itself, we can see the value of this sort of insight of Saussure's for poetic understanding. What a poem signifies — namely, itself — can be found only by looking at the poem. Equally, the insight that the linguistic sign is arbitrary suggests that *poesis*, making by words, is limitless, for there is no bound to the combinations of sonority, meaning, spelling or many other things that poems may employ. Linguistics itself does not comment on those combinations but confirms something the poetry reader will have sensed from a different perspective.

But that is not what happens: these general disciplinary

concerns do not keep their distance from specific poems. Since the question of poetry's sociality is commonly begged, the linguist takes individual poems, rather than poetry's general possibilities, for analysis, and finds his efforts bump up against poetry's intractability. Unabashed, he may still press on to more and more microscopic research. The literary historian often takes it for granted that individual poems reveal the poet's 'social background', and he used quotations to illustrate the poet's real-life sources, such as Keats' interest in Fanny Brawne and Pound's interest in Fascism. But it is surely far more arguable that those interests of Keats and Pound are what should illustrate, and lead us to, the real qualities of their poetry. Millions of people have done the things poets have also done, but that is not, in this context, interesting, nor is it legitimate to assume that the poetry was written to express this material. Rather the poet must be assumed to have used this material to make poetry, which is its own justification and its own end. To revert to linguistics, it seems that the entity of language has been made so paramount by linguistics and socio-linguistics that any poem has simply been taken as an 'example of language'; so that even poetry, which so often seems deliberately to subvert language laws, has had to be seen as dutifully following those laws, if only we could find what, in this case, those laws are.

Aside from linguistics specifically there are those critical theories that stem from a more generally sociological position. I should like briefly to mention some aspects of the structural poetics of Culler; and of Marxism.

Much of what Culler says of poetry is surely true and important; that it insulates itself from discourse; that an attempt to make an inventory of linguistic characteristics of a poem (as Jakobson proposed) is of no use since the patterns we can trace are limitless; and that when a theorist and an ordinary or 'native' reader differ on the reading of a poem it is the native reader we must trust.[3] But Culler then argues that literature is dependent entirely on conventions, and is embodied in an institution made up of schools, universities and Arts Councils. His argument is so emphatic that this freedom of poetry is largely swamped. Culler insists that we cannot read poetry without knowing the conventions on which it is based (in which case we must ask how it ever started or how conventions can change); that by convention we assume a poem always expresses 'an attitude to some problem of the universe', that we know by convention that when words at line-ends rhyme they are meant to be connected; by convention that the poem is supposed to cohere; by convention that poems — and other literary works — are fictions. How are these conventions? When two words sound the same and are matched to bring out that assonance, that is a real connection which we cannot avoid. How much the raw material in Milton or John Betjeman is fictional we cannot, and may not want to, say. As for coherence, one could argue, according to taste, either that a good poem is coherent of necessity, or else that many good poems, for example those in Lowell's *Life Studies*, succeed by virtue of their intentional incoherence. Both have been argued. The general point about conventionality seems to me simply contradicted by experience. When we read a poem we do not need to assume that an attitude to some problem of the universe is being considered (even if that is commonly so) or anything else. We read what the words do in fact say, and we read to find out what they say. Of course repeated practice of this leads to expectations, which are then either fulfilled or confounded, but these derive from language's nature and possibilities. Those conventions and expectations are just what poetry is not. The poem is made of the hard realities of rhythm, the words in the cultural store, and a number of other things. Anyone who has read poetry to a four-year-old child and noted the response can see the true place of convention in understanding the basic possibilities. The conventional aspects of a poem may be useful enough but they do not, in the last analysis, matter.

This belief about convention then leads on to a belief about literature's institutional status. Culler refers mainly to our educational institutions, whereas other exponents of these beliefs think of literature itself as an institution. But this cannot but raise in our minds the tradition of poetics that regards the heritage of poetry as an 'institution' as well. In this sense of the word it is a cultural possession which people explore and love, and to which they may be loyal; and which has its own ages, genres, traditions and high points, constituted however not by the social features of 'institution' but by the poems themselves. This is therefore an institution in the sense of a canon. Apart from traditional critics such as Johnson, those who have most celebrated this idea of a poetic institution or canon have been Eliot, Frye and more recently Harold Bloom. Eliot's famous view, that a major new poet means critical readjustment of all that has gone before, suggests that it is not institutional factors that tell us that a new poet has appeared; it is the unique, new poet who redefines the tradition. Frye's anatomy of genres is universal in its use of terms from which to draw its archetypes. They are not social, but mythical and seasonal. It is the poetic works themselves that draw forth the necessary critical terms. Bloom's theory of the deliberate misreading, by a poet, of the older poet who influences him, is the most dramatic theory of all.[4] According to Bloom there are a number of modes by which the poet can attain 'priority' (that is 'firstness' or originality), and Bloom describes them with deliberate extravagance in terms drawn from areas as diverse as myth, kinetics, Freudian psychoanalysis, and theology. He too allows the material he examines to make its own demands upon him. Among the ways in which Bloom conceives of the poet's struggle is that of sonship with a poetic father; wrestling with the dead; the 'fall' and the 'second change', and such modes as the swerve (*dinamen*), self-emptying (*kenosis*) and daemonization or the counter-sublime. Bloom's theory is germane to our present argument at many levels,[5] but his immediate relevance, and that of Eliot and Frye, lies in their establishing of the poetic tradition as an institution autonomous to, and in fact made by, poetry itself. Its critical terms faithfully follow it, and this criticism is therefore an appreciative rather than analytic mode.

Culler's argument takes institution to mean something quite different. It means social institution, answerable to the sociological laws of all social institutions. There is a curious inference from this. If literary institutions are overridingly important in a mainly sociological sense, then they will be powerful, not only in teaching the conventions Culler lists, or emphasizing them or formulating them. They will also, if unwittingly, decide upon those conventions. The tendency to state, or certainly to imply, what poetry 'should be' is likely to come directly from the sociological nature of institutionalization itself. (To this end Culler can even propose the interest of studying boring poetry, to see where its capacity for boring lies.) This same institutional feature of our lives is the palpable and tangible embodiment of the *zweckrational*, the very sociological principle itself. And the further, extreme view (not Culler's) that poetry comes into existence in order to enable criticism to take place, that poetry is the means and criticism the end is, perhaps, arrogantly comical enough.

The practical outcome of such a tendency could be alarming. The professional and institutionalized critic will get his pay from that source, will be likely to adhere to certain schools of thought to stay in the running for advancement or else be in isolation; moreover he would be constrained always to find a reading for any text because that is his job, and in order to have something to say. By the laws of institutions the critic will in fact exploit literature; such would have to be the straight sociological view. On that view (which I do not hold) the very critic who holds this institutional view encircles on his own practice.

With Marxism the position is a little different in that Marxist materialism implies an appropriate feeling, by Marxist critics, for the tangible and palpable realities of poetry itself. They are less interested in 'convention' or 'institution' than in the individual poem's relation to the ideology of its time. The text, in fact, may respond to the ideology by the very act of deranging or subverting it. But it seems always to work out that Marxism, too, either draws back to a recasting of the truths about poetry to fit the tenets of dialectical materialism, or else that Marxism itself seems almost to derive, in its poetic as 'Word', from what the Marxist critic understands by poetry. There are of course extreme views still, under the heading of Marxism, such as the recent one declaring our duty of *'actively politicizing* the text, of *making its politics for it'* (his italics).[6] More commonly the Marxist critic of poetry seems actually torn between two loyalties. This seems predominant in Terry Eagleton's work. His 'straight' appreciation of literature seems like that of any perceptive critic, but then the reworking of this to fit Marxist tenets can become so tortuous that almost anything is allowable. The poem may affirm the ideology or subvert it, and the reading may be spontaneous but that spontaneity of enjoyment then be refused in the search for the original ideology whence the poem came. The text is so constituted as to 'actively determine its own determinants'. Equally surprising are Eagleton's remarks that 'the text is *in a certain sense* self-determining . . .' (his italics); elsewhere that the poem is 'relatively autonomous', that 'literature belongs *at once* to base and superstructure' (his italics again).[7] Stringing such quotations together out of context is all too easy, but it does seem that a kind of excess of virtue is being practised. Eagleton — and Fredric Jameson — respond wholly to the work as literature, but then rewrite their response to it in terms of the most enlightened historical and dialectical materialism they can muster. Marxism's abolition of philosophy's supremacy in favour of the material (thus reversing Hegel) makes the critical attitude very important, but when the criticism is done its findings are hindsighted, as we might say, into historical dialectic. This, surely, is connected to Jameson's revealing view that Marxism is itself a form moving through history.

As a result this Marxism does not so much sterilize poetry as get it out of the way. Poetry can get an unequivocal response, but whatever that is must then *a posteriori* be subsumed under an ideology. This is the reverse of 'vulgar Marxism' (something which Eagleton frequently condemns) which traces literary works to their ideological origin and its economic base in near-determinist fashion, but the result of the greater enlightenment of these critics is, again, a form of banishment. It is banishment from the central Marxist discussion. This need not matter to those who believe in any degree of autonomy in the poetic canon, but the inference for our discussion is, again, that of how far Marxism is itself a version of the sociological idea. It works out quite simply, that the more the Marxist criticism is sociological in cast, the more is poetry considered to derive from social processes. On the other hand, the more Marxism is true to its uniquely materialist nature, the more does the poem survive, if only as a sort of companion to Marxism's irreversible course. Perhaps we can suggest, fancifully again no doubt, that the Marxist critic's attitude is that of the author of *Paradise Lost*. In stumbling on the sociological idea Milton abolishes his poem; and the Marxist critic may equally abolish the poem precisely by so appreciating it but then recasting it to the purpose of his own dialectical advance.

Criticism then is either appreciative and celebratory, or is not narrowly 'criticism' at all but an acceptance of poetry on poetry's terms, and then a placing of that phenomenon in a wider theory or description of reality. If it misses both, then it does what it is now so often accused of doing; eating up its own origins; becoming a dinosaur and grinding to a halt under its own weight; cutting the roots of its own rose-tree; sterilizing and sucking out literature's life, or at least that of our responses to it; certainly achieving vastly diminishing returns in each new phase of its activity. Since my whole argument suggests that poetry's own nature is its very tension with, so to call it, the sociological imperialism that gives rise to these tendencies, then it seems that, as Eagleton says, a time comes when poetry has to be apologized for, and now might be such a time.

*

The defenders of and apologists for poetry have usually been the poets, or those who would celebrate poetry. I can only draw inferences from the general positions I have hoped to reach. Yet this must presumably look for a defence, for we can scarcely end simply silent on the meaning of poetry's state in the world of 'society', or on poetry's value, or lack of value.

The conventional contemporary defences of poetry do not sound confident; they often sound routine, and sometimes pious. It is said that the function of poetry is to re-vitalize language, and to communicate and intensify our perception of experience. Both these suggestions can only be voiced in the world that sociality dominates. One could not think of re-vitalizing 'language', just like that, had not language itself appeared as a commodity for study within the wider and deeper sociological idea on which it depends. It is not sociologists or orthodox Marxists but students of myth and the subconscious who are willing to see language as more primal and deeper than simply a mechanism or go-between of human communication. But the work of those writers (as different as

Chomsky and Lacan), although it has attracted considerable attention, does not yield an overall account of our human position itself, like that to which sociology aspires. Poetry cannot re-vitalize *our* language; it can only — if we must talk in these terms at all — be a vitalizing of its own; and people will then, or will not, go to it for sustenance. For how does poetry re-vitalize our language? Do we use it to enrich our talk? If we read *Paradise Lost*, or Homer or Hopkins, and our discourse is influenced, people will say 'you sound archaic, you sound like a poet', not because we have used quaint phrases or flowery metaphors but because we have presumed to hold up discourse by giving attention to language for its own sake, an activity that ought to be 'deferred to a time more convenient' (such as a Poetry Evening Class). And how does poetry intensify our experience? By confirming the experiences that the more dominant idea of our time allows to be valid and important; that is, when it is merely a piece of solo 'effective writing', not properly poetry at all. Any true defence of poetry that commanded attention would have to be found elsewhere.

I suggest that such a defence can be found through the quality of the tension we have emphasized. The tension is between the necessarily social (in one sense) quality of the language, and something else, some other quality, not yet defined, and perhaps not susceptible to definition. The dilemma the tension can pose for the modern world was first stated, doubtless unwittingly, in the defence given by Wordsworth. He described the poet as 'a man speaking to men', an extraordinarily modern notion, but in the next breath — literally, in the same phrase continued — this man is 'endowed with more lively sensibility, more enthusiasm and tenderness, who has a greater knowledge of human nature, and a more comprehensive soul, than are supposed to be common among mankind'. Shelley equally was realist enough to temper his ecstatically expressed claims for poetry with the recognition that 'society's vices are . . . the temporary dress in which [the poet's] creations must be portrayed'. The Romantic belief there entailed, that something was brought *in* by the poet to ordinary man, and that the 'planetary music' was 'tempered for mortal ears', is one we might be tempted mechanically to reverse by saying that the poet merely *takes* society's beliefs and words in order to go outward to whatever he might find. But I will argue that it is the tension itself, that quality, that is the key to the liberating experience, and not the substantive content it is supposed to afford us. Intriguingly, it is contemporary theories of metaphor that most support this proposition. Instead of seeing metaphor as simply comparison between two things hitherto regarded as unlike, our idea now is that metaphor compares the obviously incomparable in order to collapse ordinary common-sense meaning in the interests of something further.[8] Metaphor, in stating the manifestly untrue and absurd ('Juliet is the sun', '(the gardener) is trying to grow the Kremlin') forces the two entities together to a point where, however, they will not mingle but encounter; and in the existential gap that is left, we see something, unnamed and unnamable, but something. We need not regard metaphor and poetry as synonymous to find that a fruitful basis for seeing what poetry achieves too.

But what then does this tension lead to, and what is the gap? And if this is a defence, what is the value of the gap? What does the tensive presentation of Donne's mistresses, Hardy's bleak confrontations and Spenser's sweet knights and ladies open the way to? All the traditional defences of poetry have argued that poetry is a matter of enlightenment and knowledge. Sidney, Shelley and Wordsworth say it repeatedly. Yet to our epistemologically-compulsive world this turns out a very odd kind of knowing. It is invariably accompanied, in the same writers, with the notion of delight. Sidney's assertion that the poet does what the historian and philosopher do, but does it better, is so accompanied by the belief that this is delightful, that much of his argument is a defence against the charge that this delightfulness is an abuse or a tissue of lies. Shelley's answer to Peacock, that poetry is in fact useful, is curiously close to the same defence of theology in the epistemologically-fascinated J.H. Newman, yet Shelley's preoccupation with 'pleasure' as poetry's means of effect saturates his argument too. That most truly innocent and truly modern of traditional poets, Wordsworth, seems to have encapsulated the two ideas in one phrase. Poetry is 'the breath and finer spirit of all knowledge'. It seems impossible that we in the positivist or post-positivist world can make much of a 'breath and finer spirit of all knowledge'. Not very promisingly, I have already referred to a 'gap'. We must look into this gap for our defence.

The traditional poets — the 'innocent' poets as Bloom has called them — thought they could teach or instruct, at the same time making such instruction delightful by the use of rhythm, imagination and invention. Spenser consciously used 'allegory or darke conceit' to come at virtue, and Milton, by pleading with his Muse for inspiration, described a wholly unverifiable universe in order to justify the ways of God to man. But the very realities the poets wished to present to us were already imaginatively retrieved; already in the unconscious mind, or spirits or feelings, by mythic or imaginative means. The apparent separation they made, between engaging with these realities most deeply, and then presenting them in poetry of decoration or dress, was not a separation at all. For language was conceived of as itself emanating from the 'Word', from the very expressibility of reality's mysteries.

Now my argument is that a modern attempt to describe in what way poetry is cognitive need not be diverted by a feeling that there has been a radical change; that we now see cognition and delight as one whereas traditionally they were separate. On the contrary, that split has occurred precisely in our formal and positive modes of cognition *aside* from poetry. Our aim in science or history is not to delight. If delight is achieved that is well, but the fundamental distinction the post-Enlightenment world has made between fact and value means, not that value is not important, but that valuing occurs after fact has been established. The single important criterion for judging fact is accuracy, not movement or delight, and this division now proves important in our argument. For as a result of this division any *poesis* in the language that presents man's knowledge formally in the modern world has disappeared. Certainly there is a lucidity and clarity in the formal prose of the outstanding philosopher or historian; indeed they are intrinsic to advance in knowledge. But the pleasure there lies in the appropriation of unknown and obdurate material into a form that can fit in with, even if reversing, our existing epistemological system. The relation between language and knowledge is thus present and inextricable, but it is not itself the object of attention, less still of celebration. It too is 'taken for granted'.

As a result the stating of knowledge can come always to subserve direct communication first and foremost, as our sociality insists.

Poetic cognition and poetic delight, by contrast, are close, even synonymous. Since poetry does not attempt to build knowledge by a systematic, cumulative probe into an area of reality, the modern mind regards it as merely a Cinderella among the adults of the search for knowledge, and for that fullest possible account of reality our efforts can attain. Poetry may be cognitive, we may think, but that is somewhat incidental next to the larger and mature cognitive disciplines such as history, philosophy and science. We may feel that in some vague way it 'expands our perceptions'. But the larger epics of earlier ages seem obsolete for our cognitive needs; the millions of small lyrics of our century seem too occasional to catch more than the briefest passing interest; and the few longer modern poems to attract attention become 'culture-objects' and esoteric oddities. But I suggest that this very absence of disciplinary system in poetic cognition implies the key to the value of that cognition. Poetry, alone, does not state the end of its enquiry; it creates within language a tension between our familiar (already known) language use and the very possibility of newly knowing anything at all. Poetry does not merely rearrange familiar language in order to express some actual new thing; it radically and delightfully rearranges familiar language in order to de-familiarize that language itself, that very means by which anything may be expressedly known at all. It is 'radical' in the strict sense that it goes to the root; but it is delightful because it seems unboundedly to affirm and sustain; it is not merely 'revolutionary' in what might now be a deadened sense of that term.

For this reason poetry may be a matter of knowledge as the apologists argued, despite its differences from the systematic disciplines. Our other modes of knowledge are additive; in orderly and organic fashion, certainly, but it is a matter of increase and of the gradual domination of reality by cognitive imperialism. Our other arts furthermore, including the literary, have been the same. The serious novel and film are both ambitious. Their deepest driving forces have made them— the novel for a hundred and fifty years — larger and larger in size and scope. The wonderful tensions that exist within the major novels and films are, beyond question, superb in their artistry, but they are tensions always between two or more parts of a reality, society, community or social order whose parts are taken as in principle already mapped out. (The film cannot lie, and must record whatever passes across the camera, and the realistic novel was based on the premise that a known scene must first be established within which explorations can be made.)

But poetry goes further than that, for poetry meddles with language itself. Not the things named, however accurately or expansively, but the actual naming itself, the only intermediary between sensuous experience and self-consciousness that we have, is broken, reshaped, nudged, played with and wooed. Certainly the things named, the roses and mistresses, the emotions and indeed the technological gadgets of our world, are obdurately separate, cheerfully present, in each different poem; we are not saying simply that any subject-matter will do so long as the delightful tension is achieved. On the contrary, the greater poetry will want everything to be named, to touch everything as it were with its fingertips, so that everything will be brought into play in the celebration of how the object of cognition is perpetually engaged with cognition itself. For this very reason poetry is the one cognitive mode intolerable to the sociological idea, because that idea leases out language to its members on the strict understanding that all uses of language, however (and however fruitfully) elaborated, must answer to the quite different overriding demand that language be 'communication'; so that whatever is communicated is done so under the imposed laws of social communication itself. Poetry, challenging the permanent validity of those laws, is a reminder that they cannot be fully known to us, that they are not of our making, and that even if they were they might not remotely exhaust the cognitive possibilities the universe holds, or could hold, for man. For this reason the poet has been called (in varying terms by Gosson, Locke and A.J. Ayer)[9] a liar, because, when purporting to talk of sexual love, the suburb, sheepfarming or the waves breaking against the stone harbour, he is not referring to those things. He is referring to the naming of them. Poetry thus aspires to the pure distillation of meaning itself, and of meaning's delighting possibility.

The experience we get from poetry that seems to be of value is to do with the inherent tension at the heart of, not this or that meaning or naming, but meaning itself and naming itself. This leads to the most significant defence or apologia of all. By an inversion of emphasis made by the scientific attitude of the modern world, our experiences are thought to be products of causes seen as deeper. When we experience something, we are likely to regard as more fundamental still the causes, components, motives, social background and material conditions that seem to contribute to that experience. Our non-teleological mentality cannot regard the experience itself as the true reality, the contributing parts unfinished until the full experience emerges. However, all art removes, if temporarily, this emphasis by creating a tension between forces (between two characters in a drama, or between a tree painted and the paint itself) such that the resulting equilibrium is itself authentic experience, its causes ceasing to matter. But poetry's particular use of language gives that tension within the very idea of cognition itself. That is to say, it makes possible a general belief that cognized experience, not its prior components, actually is the central locus of reality, and is not a temporary illusion as suggested by the plastic arts. This is because poetry's medium is language itself, expressing in itself, naming in itself. Since expressing or naming in themselves are the things held in tension and suspense, we are necessarily brought to consider this teleological possibility for any experience, not just poetic experience. If I may attempt a final formula: poetry makes most delightful the possibility of authentic experience; it *is* the delight of that named experience and the pleasure in naming it; and it shows that very delight itself as an authentic guarantor of the teleological position.

In this light it could be thought curious that poetry is not the central art of our time. For the central philosophical question of the century has been that of knowledge itself, what we know, and how we know that we know it. Perhaps the wearinesses in Hardy, Eliot, Berryman and others came from impossible struggles in a new phase of cognition itself. If poetry were to matter in human consciousness once more, it might be through one poet's achievement of a new cognitive poem that overcame the dilemma of knowledge and innocence. The era of self-consciousness brought on by the Enlightenment, Hegel and Marx, and the liberal alternative, ended the mythic innocence, the non-separation between cognition and delight, which had previously held, and there would seem to be no going back. At the same time a truly new cognition, right out of our era and forward into something perhaps perversely recognizable, in hindsight, as very old, would be as Kierkegaard put it 'a leap in the dark', and the poetic leap Bloom suggests is the origin of every important poem. The leap covers in one event what conventional disciplines would cover through the orderly stages they already possess. It might, surprisingly, be in the mode of Yvor Winters' 'poetry of statement', re-assuming the intimate connection between word and reality (one denied by the sociological idea of language;) and comprehending the huge advances in official knowledge that self-consciousness and positivism have attained. This new *De Rerum Natura* would, to put it perhaps extravagantly, make the metalanguage of natural science seem subservient and our own daily interactions and formal sociality answerable to *poesis* itself.

If it appeared it might confirm what the scientist Jacob Bronowski has said in his survey of the traditional poetic defences: 'There is a truth which is free of the society in which it is found. . . . This truth is poetry. . . . Social living is not the whole life of man. The mind of man has a knowledge of truth beyond the near-truths of science and society. Poetry tells this truth'.[10] Sidney put the same thing in the only language available to him: 'Onlie the poet, disdayning to be tied to any such subjection, lifted up with the vigor of his owne invention, doth grow in effect another nature . . . so as hee goeth hand in hand with Nature, not inclosed within the warrant of her gifts, but freely ranging onely within the Zodiac of her owne wit'.

Notes

Abbreviations

ICA — Institute of Contemporary Arts, London
THES — Times Higher Educational Supplement
TLS — Times Literary Supplement

Part I

Chapter 1. INTRODUCTION

1. *The Sociology of Literature; Applied Studies* (Sociological Review Monograph, Keele 1978), edited by Diana Laurenson. I refer to this point and a number of other themes in the present book in 'The Poem's Defiance Of Sociology', *Sociology*, January. 1979.
2. *Sociology of Literature and Drama* (Penguin 1973), edited by Tom and Elizabeth Burns.
3. Elizabeth Burns, *Theatricality* (Longman 1972).
4. Particularly in his selections in the Burns' anthology (see above, Note 1) and in *The Sociology of Art* (Paladin 1972). Sociological studies of the novel have come from Goldmann, Lukacs, Eagleton, and others.
5. Raymond Williams has written of poets a little: there is the Romantic section in *Culture and Society*, and some parts of *The Country and the City*. His interest, however, is hardly in the poetry as poetry, and I take his real absorption in words' nature to be exemplified by *Keywords* (Fontana, 1976).
6. A fact known to Sam Weller, of all people: 'Poetry's unnatural: no man ever spoke poetry'.
7. F.R. Leavis, *New Bearings in English Poetry* (Chatto & Windus 1932), p. 1.
8. Anthony Giddens, *New Rules of Sociological Method* (Hutchinson 1976), p. 13.
9. Dennis Wrong, 'Convergence and Critique', *TLS*, 11 February 1977, p. 155.
10. R.D. Laing, *Knots* (Tavistock 1970).
11. A likely reason for this is suggested by Alan F. Blum, *Theorizing* (Heineman 1974), chapter 9. Blum says that modern speech has ceased to hear itself and is therefore not an end in itself either.
12. Raymond Williams, *Marxism and Literature* (Oxford University Press 1977), a theme *passim*. The social is 'categorically reduced' (p. 133).

13. Ernest Gellner, 'The Crisis in Humanities and the Mainstream of Philosophy', in *Crisis In The Humanities* (Penguin 1964) edited by J.H. Plumb; p. 81.
14. John Hick, *God and the Universe of Faiths* (Collins 1973), p. 92.
15. Donald Davie, *Thomas Hardy and British Poetry* (Routledge & Kegan Paul 1973), p. 1. The other remark referred to is in a review by him, *PN Review* No 9 (Vol. 6 No. 1), p. 57. He is discussing 'home' as that is characterized in *Solent Shore*, a book of poems by Jeremy Hooker.
16. John Weightman, 'Literature', in 'Modernism: A Symposium', in *The New Review*, Vol. 1 No. 10, January 1975, p. 24.
17. For example, from the *THES*: John Holloway, 'Wanted — A Survival Kit for English Studies', 20 February 1976, p. 11: Frances Gibb, 'Great Tradition's end is near', 5 March 1976, p. 6: Patrick Parrinder, 'The Case of the Missing Avant-Garde', 15 July 1977, p. 15. From the TLS: George Watson, 'Literary Research: Thoughts for an Agenda', 25 February 1977, p. 213.
18. I derive the distinction, though not the precise wording, from Jonathan Culler, *Structuralist Poetics* (Routledge & Kegan Paul 1975), pp. vii-viii.
19. A frequent refrain in his Cambridge lectures, elaborated in print in his *Education and the University* (Chatto & Windus 1943), chapter 3.
20. Northrop Frye, *An Anatomy of Criticism* (Princeton University Press, 1976), third essay, especially pp. 163-239.
21. See note 18 above. This has also been the conclusion of another recent study: Stein Haugom Olsen, *The Structure of Literary Understanding* (Cambridge University Press 1978).
22. Jurgen Habermas, 'Toward a Theory of Communicative Competence', in *Recent Sociology No 2* (Collier-Macmillan 1970), edited by Hans Peter Dreitzel, pp. 115-48.
23. R.H. Robins, 'The Structure of Language', in *Linguistics at Large* (Paladin 1973): ICA Lectures edited by Noel Nimms: especially pp. 17-18.
24. Bob Hodge, 'The Sorry State of British Linguistics', *THES*, 16 July 1976.
25. For example, Roland Barthes, *Elements of Semiology* (Jonathan Cape 1967), translated by Annette Lavers and Colin Smith, p. 23: 'The sociological scope of the language/speech concept is obvious. The manifest affinity of the language according to Saussure and of Durkheim's conception of a collective consciousness independent of its individual manifestations has been emphasized very early on. A direct influence of Durkheim on Saussure has even been postulated'. Also Jonathan Culler, *Saussure* (Fontana Modern Masters 1976), especially chapter 3, pp. 70-8; and Raymond Williams, *Marxism and Literature* (op. cit.) pp. 27-8.
26. Jacques Lacan, *Ecrits* (Tavistock 1977), translated by Alan Sheridan, p. 68.
27. Fredric Jameson, *Marxism and Form* (Princeton University Press 1971).
28. Terry Eagleton, *Criticism and Ideology* (New Left Books 1976), p. 43.

Chapter 2. THE FIVE TYPES OF SOCIOLOGY

1. This summary comes broadly from a discussion of the facticity of the social in Durkheim, and especially the subjection of our wills to the social, in Paul Q. Hirst, *Durkheim, Bernard and Epistemology* (Routledge & Kegan Paul 1975), pp. 90 ff. Hirst believes that Durkheim's view is of necessity an ideology.
2. These remarks come from Emile Durkheim, *Suicide*, (Routledge & Kegan Paul 1952), Preface, p. 39. They are however characteristic of the whole argument of Durkheim's *Rules of Sociological Method* (Free Press, N.Y. 1938).
3. This and the other central features of Weber's theories of sociology's nature and method are found in Max Weber, *The Theory of Social and Economic Organization* (Free Press, N.Y. 1964) translated by A.M. Henderson and Talcott Parsons, especially Part I, 'The Fundamental Concepts of Sociology'.
4. Talcott Parsons, *The Structure of Social Action* (Free Press, N.Y. 1949); *The Social System* (Routledge & Kegan Paul 1951).
5. Robert Nisbet, *The Sociological Tradition* (Heineman 1967), p. 8.
6. The source is George Herbert Mead, *On Social Psychology*, selected papers edited by Anselm Strauss (University of Chicago Press, Phoenix Books 1964).
7. Howard Blumer, *Symbolic Interactionism* (Prentice-Hall, New Jersey 1969).
8. Some references are: Ralph Linton, *The Study of Man* (Appleton-Century-Crofts, USA 1936) especially pp. 113–19; Robert K. Merton, 'The Role-Set', in *Social Theory and Social Structure* (Free Press, N.Y. 1949). In Britain, M. Banton, *Roles* (Tavistock 1965). Finally *Role Theory: Concepts and Research* (John Wiley, N.Y. 1966), edited by B.J. Biddle and E.J. Thomas is a copious source of readings in the field.
9. Erving Goffman's several books have provided a unique, vivid set of insights into interaction behaviour. Important are *The Presentation of Self in Everyday Life* (Allen Lane 1969), *Encounters* (Bobbs-Merrill, USA 1961), and *Interaction Ritual* (Penguin 1967).
10. Cf. Ronald Frankenberg, *Communities in Britain* (Penguin 1966), and Bell and Newby, *The Sociology of Community: Selected Readings* (Cass 1974). Frankenberg summarizes and Bell and Newby give selections from the large corpus of empirical studies done in Britain since the war and up to the publication of their books.
11. Margaret Stacey, 'The Myth of Community Studies', in *British Journal of Sociology*, Vol. 20, 1969.
12. As originally practised for example at the Centre for Contemporary Cultural Studies, University of Birmingham.
13. Edmund Husserl, *The Idea of Phenomenology* (Nijhoff, The Hague 1964) translated by Alston and Nakhnikan: M. Merleau-Ponty, *The Primacy of Perception*, edited and translated by Edie (Northwestern, USA 1964).

14. Alfred Schutz, *Collected Papers* (2 Vols.) (Nijhoff, The Hague 1973).
15. Harold Garfinkel, *Studies in Ethnomethodology* (Prentice-Hall, New Jersey 1967).
16. R.H. Brown, *A Poetic for Sociology* (Cambridge University Press 1977); Robert Nisbet, *Sociology as an Art Form* (Heineman 1976); John O'Neill, *Making Sense Together* (Heineman 1978).
17. Louis Althusser, *For Marx* (Penguin 1969), translated by Ben Brewster, p. 13.
18. A theme in George Lichtheim, *Marxism* (Routledge & Kegan Paul 1964): David McLellan, *Marx* (Fontana Modern Masters 1975); Octavio Paz, 'The End in the Beginning', in *Alternative Current* (Wildwood House 1974), pp. 178–86.
19. Octavio Paz, op. cit., p. 179.
20. A phrase from George Lichtheim (op. cit.) to whose last two chapters I am particularly indebted for much of what I think on this subject.

PART II

Chapter 3. SPENSER AND SOCIAL PHENOMENOLOGY

1. C.S. Lewis, *The Allegory of Love* (Oxford University Press 1958) especially chapters 1, 2, 6 and 7.
2. 'Astonishment' is of course etymologically connected to 'thunder', what happens in a storm or tempest. But the themes of amazement, illusion, isolation from society (the island setting) are all present in that play, which is a gold-mine for phenomenological themes. There are even fruitful cinematic comparisons, for example cf. Jan Kott, *Shakespeare Our Contemporary* (Methuen 1967), p. 252.
3. Graham Hough, *Preface to the Faerie Queene* (Duckworth 1962), p. 46. Hough is actually discussing Ariosto, and indeed emphasizing that, despite the great influence of Ariosto on Spenser, Ariosto leans toward pure romance, Spenser toward allegory. It is exactly my point that, because of his phenomenological stance, Spenser's moral concerns and aesthetic performance can both stand in the poem, but at different levels.
4. Anthony Giddens, op. cit. p. 40.
5. 'By ensample of which excellente poets, I labour to portraict in Arthure, before he was king, the image of a brave knight, perfected in the twelve private morall vertues, as Aristotle hath devised'. (A Letter of the Authors to the Right Noble and Valorous Sir Walter Raleigh).
6. Aristotle, *Nichomachean Ethics* (Everyman, Dent 1911) translated by D.P. Chase, p. 12.
7. Peter Bayley, *Edmund Spenser, Prince of Poets* (Hutchinson 1971), p. 110.
8. John O'Neill, op. cit. (his sub-title is 'An introduction to Wild Sociology'.) The quotation is from a publicity leaflet for a new magazine,

'Writing Sociology', circulated by Paul Filmer and Mike Phillipson, University of London Goldsmiths' College.
9. As a sample of the rhetoric: 'Modern sociology affects nothing and celebrates nothing. It suppresses the great commonplaces of love and hate, joy and grief, time and place, care and concern. . . . It is to the suffering and celebration that this book addresses its care. . . . But is it *Sociology*? If you will go on asking that question in that way, what more can I say to you but who cares? It is the conversation of humanity: just listen'. (Alan Dawe, on the back cover of John O'Neill, op. cit.)

Chapter 4. DONNE AND SOCIAL INTERACTIONISM

1. Started by Pierre Legouis, *Donne the Craftsman*, (Didier, Paris 1928), pp. 61–8. In *The Monarch of Wit* (Hutchinson 1951) J.B. Leishman wrote that The Extasie was 'the most analytical, conceptual and, in a sense, philosophical of Donne's love-poems; his most elaborate attempt to describe what was neither merely invisible beauty nor merely "virtue of the minde" which he had declared in "Negative Love" that he was searching for and which he had now found'. In a footnote on the same page Leishman goes on: 'From which the reader may rightly conclude that I do not agree with Prof. Pierre Legouis in regarding *The Extasie* as a kind of solemn and elaborate joke, a dramatic lyric in which Donne has chosen to represent himself as a hypocritically philosophical Don Juan'. Murray Roston (in *The Soul of Wit*, Oxford 1974 p. 136) cites Legouis and agrees with him, but concedes that most critics now take the poem as a genuine expression of love. Critics as diverse as C.S. Lewis (in *John Donne*, edited by Helen Gardner, Prentice-Hall 1962 p. 92) and J.F. Kermode (in *Renaissance Essays*, Collins 1973, p. 122) would appear not to agree, although Helen Gardner herself seems to take the poem seriously.
2. Roston, op. cit., chapter 4.
3. Angel: suppose there's a place we know nothing about, and there,
on some indescribable carpet, lovers showed all that here
they're for ever unable to manage — their daring
lofty figures of heart-flight,
their towers of pleasure, their ladders,
long since, where ground never was, just quiveringly
propped by each other — suppose they could manage it there,
before the spectators ringed round, the countless murmuring dead:
would not the dead then fly their last, their for ever reserved,
ever-concealed, unknown to us, ever-valid
coins of happiness down before the at last
truthfully smiling pair on the quietened
carpet?
Rilke's *Duino Elegies*, (Hogarth Press 1948) translated by Leishman and Spender.

4. Louis L. Martz, *The Poem of the Mind* (Oxford University Press 1966) p. 3.
5. Roston, op. cit., chapter 4.
6. William Empson, *Seven Types of Ambiguity* (Chatto & Windus 1956) pp. 139 ff.

Chapter 5. MILTON AND MARXIST SOCIOLOGY

1. Most elaborated by A.J.A. Waldock, *Paradise Lost and its Critics* (Cambridge University Press 1947), chapters 2 and 3. This book however works in a context largely dealing with the earlier arguments (of Tillyard and Lewis particularly) dealing with Milton's moral and theological legitimacy.
2. Bernard Bergonzi, 'Criticism and the Milton Controversy', in *The Living Milton: Essays by Various Hands*, edited by Frank Kermode, p. 180. This book moves Milton criticism forward from those earlier arguments (as well as the Leavis-Eliot position on Milton's stature) to the emphasis Bergonzi makes; which I share, but the logical conclusion I am suggesting is not, I think, reached. In fact, the lines I quote from Bergonzi are the last lines of his paper.
3. Discussed in H.P. Adams, *Karl Marx in his Earlier Writings* (Allen & Unwin 1940), and David McLellan, *Marx Before Marxism* (Pelican 1970). Our information on this aspect of early Marx is admittedly sparse.
4. Christopher Hill, *Milton and the English Revolution* (Faber 1977).

Chapter 6. POPE AND SOCIAL FUNCTIONALISM

1. Ferdinand Tonnies, *Community and Association* (Routledge & Kegan Paul 1955), translated by Charles P. Loomis.
2. Tillotson identified eleven permutations of the antithetical couplet as used by Pope. Geoffrey Tillotson, *On The Poetry of Pope* (Oxford 1950), pp. 124–8. Since Tillotson, other analytical approaches include two essays by W.K. Wimsatt in *The Verbal Icon* (Methuen 1970), an interesting 'binary' analysis by Winifred Nowottny of the first four lines of 'Where'er you walk', in *The Language Poets Use* (University of London, Athlone Press 1962) pp. 11–12, and Donald Davie, *Articulate Energy: An Enquiry Into the Syntax of English Poetry* (Routledge & Kegan Paul 1975), chapters 6 and 7.
3. Wimsatt, op. cit., p. 177.
4. Hugh Kenner, in *Alexander Pope, A Critical Anthology* (Penguin 1971), edited by F.W. Bateson & N.A. Joukovsky, pp. 426–32.
5. Pope's friend Warburton, on reading a draft of the Moral Essays, remarked on their being 'a number of fine observations, without order, connection or dependence', the point being that, when Pope acted on this by rearranging the poems' parts, he did so with ease, so much was

their nature accretive rather than organic. [This comes from Ian Jack, *Augustan Satire*, (Oxford 1952).] 'Saturation' also conveys the accretive idea, and is a word etymologically descended from the Latin 'satura', or satire.
6. Marshall McLuhan, *The Gutenberg Galaxy* (Routledge & Kegan Paul 1962), pp. 255–63.

Chapter 7. WORDSWORTH AND SOCIAL ANTHROPOLOGY

1. I have elaborated this elsewhere. J.P. Ward, 'Wordsworth and the Sociological Idea', in *Critical Quarterly*, Winter 1974, pp. 331–56. (especially pp. 345–8).
2. A recurring theme, highlighted in the influential *Family and Kinship in East London* by Peter Willmott and Michael Young (Pelican 1962), p. 116: 'Either length of residence or localised kinship does something to create a network of local attachment. . . . When they are combined, as they are in Bethnal Green, they constitute a much more powerful force than when one exists without the other'.
3. 'It seems to be the case that any human community relies on ignorance of itself for its smooth working; that there are all sorts of things that go on in a community which everybody knows about but nobody likes to see in cold print. . . . [There is a] problem of whether a society which is fully self-conscious can operate. . . . It may be that a certain degree of ignorance and concealment and reluctance to face the facts is a necessary condition of ordinary human life as we know it'. John Barnes, interviewed by Renford Bamborough, *The Listener*, 5 August 1971, p. 175.
4. Roman Jakobson & M. Halle, *Fundamentals of Language* (The Hague, Mouton 1956), and other works. Lacan (op. cit.) p. 175, says 'the symptom *is* a metaphor whether one likes it or not, as desire *is* a metonymy, however funny people may find the idea'.
5. J.P. Ward op. cit., pp. 336–7.

PART III

Chapter 8. INTRODUCTION AND BAUDELAIRE

1. This is a complex matter. Michael Hamburger's question, 'What makes modern poetry modern?' is the first sentence of his book *The Truth of Poetry: Tensions in Modern Poetry from Baudelaire to the 1960s* (Pelican 1972). But he disclaims the ability to answer it, and the very serious and knowledgeable text that follows is certainly rather inconclusive, for he prefers 'to do justice to the diversity after Baudelaire' rather than 'confining my enquiry to a single development'. On the other hand, a variety of solutions is precisely the point, it seems, in *Modernism (1890—1930)* (Penguin 1976), edited by Malcolm Bradbury and James McFarlane.

Richard Sheppard sees the modern lyric as responding to a crisis of language, G.M. Hyde as a result of the pressure of urbanism, while Graham Hough suggests that poetry is so unimportant to the forces that control the modern world that that very fact can free poetry to keep alive other vital manifestations of the human spirit in this difficult period. Interestingly, the diversity suggested in both these books is explicitly made the defining feature of Modernism itself, in what to me at least has been a very convincing definition of Modernism, by Daniel Bell the social economist, in his *The Cultural Contradictions of Capitalism* (Heinemann 1976). Bell argues that Modernism is precisely its rapid turnover of modes, as though in the twentieth-century world it must always keep ahead of the public in offering always different and new qualities of stimulation. This certainly squares with the view the present book tries to put forward, that poetry too in our time is continually looking for a new way to counter the sociological idea — not that it is as explicit as that.

2. Mario Praz, *The Romantic Agony* (Oxford University Press 1970) p. 145.
3. Marcel Raymond, *From Baudelaire to Surrealism* (Methuen 1970) p. 9.
4. Walter Benjamin, *Illuminations* (Collins/Fontana Books 1970) translated by Harry Zohn, pp. 157–202.
5. Emile Durkheim, *The Division of Labour in Society* (Free Press, New York 1964), chapter 2 and *passim*.

Chapter 9. THE POEM ITSELF – MALLARMÉ, STEVENS, WILLIAM CARLOS WILLIAMS, YEATS

1. Quoted and discussed in Raymond, op. cit., p. 19.
2. Paz, op. cit., p. 5.
3. Louis L. Martz, op. cit., p. 207.
4. Cf. the quotation at the start of this book, from *The Necessary Angel*.
5. *William Carlos Williams: A Collection of Critical Essays,* (Prentice-Hall, New Jersey 1966), edited by J. Hillis Miller, especially Introduction. Also Hillis Miller's contribution to *William Carlos Williams: A Critical Anthology* (Penguin 1972), edited by Charles Tomlinson, pp. 373–81.
6. 'The red wheelbarrow, the locust tree in flower, stand fixed in the span of an instant', J. Hillis Miller, op. cit. (1966). p. 8.
7. Eric Homberger, *The Art of the Real* (Dent 1976), p. 130.
8. Yeats' Diary, 1930, quoted in *Explorations*, selected by Mrs W.B. Yeats (Macmillan 1962), p. 325.
9. 'Major Robert Gregory is as much a fictive creation as any of Spenser's knights. Professor D.J. Gordon once told me that Gregory was a very indifferent horseman, no artist at all, and the 'scholar' got a very undistinguished Third in the schools'. I am grateful to Brian Morris for this personal communication.

Chapter 10. THE POEM AND SOCIETY – ELIOT, POUND, THE COMMUNIST POETS

1. Hugh MacDiarmid, 'The Kind of Poetry I Want', in *Collected Poems* (Macmillan 1962).
2. Like Pound's 'consult the originals' and David Jones, introducing *The Anathemata*, 'I have made a heap of all I could find'. The method in *The Waste Land* is illustrated very strongly by the water imagery. There is a central balanced pair of themes concerning water and rock, as is clear enough, and in the central (Eliot-Tiresias) voice these are generalized: 'If there were water/And no rock', and so on. But at all other points the water is historical, its actual occasions; the water written of by Spenser, 'a damp gust bringing rain', the 'dull canal' by which the writer fished, the girl from the Hyacinth garden 'arms full and hair wet', and the crowd going over London Bridge under which flows the Thames. Water is found all over and under this poem, and it is thereby more poignant and the symbol more powerful.
3. i) the opening section of tight blank-verse conveying speculation in imagery, ii) the short lyric followed by a much looser conversational piece of speculation, iii) a blank-verse section where those meditations are elaborated and grow more foreboding, iv) a formal lyric which is effectively a prayer, v) a section of meditation in which the matter of language and writing is raised.
4. Cleanth Brooks, 'The Waste Land: Critique of the Myth', in *The Waste Land* (Macmillan 1968) edited by C.B. Cox and Arnold Hinchcliffe, p. 145.
5. Certainly a theme of *The Use of Poetry and the Use of Criticism*, (Faber 1933), made explicit in the last chapter.
6. Hugh Kenner, *The Invisible Poet* (Methuen 1965), p. 137.
7. George Dekker, *Sailing After Knowledge* (Routledge 1963).
8. Ezra Pound, *Make It New* (Faber 1934), p. 389.
9. Michael Hamburger (op. cit., p. 248) quotes the poem 'Nada Mas' (Nothing More) and comments: 'What this poem implies is that the social and political functions of poetry cannot engage the whole of Neruda's imagination, that a "conversation about trees", or only a contemplation of trees in silence and in solitude, is a human need as real, if not quite as general, as the need for bread. . . .'

Chapter 11. THE POET IN THE SOCIOLOGICAL WORLD: HARDY, BERRYMAN

1. Gabriel Pearson, 'Robert Lowell', in *The Review* No. 20, March 1969, p. 4.
2. For a sociological discussion cf. David Sudnow, *Passing On: The Social Organization of Dying* (Prentice Hall, New Jersey 1967).

3. Valéry expressed his disappointment with the poem by saying that at the death of his friend, Tennyson indulged in reminiscence when he should have been broken-hearted. In fact I would have thought that the obsessive, almost incredibly extended disturbance Tennyson feels is measured precisely by the extent to which it reverberates in every part of society and the world of which Tennyson is thinking, and renders those things secondary to the sobering fact of death itself.
4. 'There are so many poems [of Hardy] in which dead men speak that it must be defined as a normal occurrence in his poetic universe'. J. Hillis Miller, *Thomas Hardy: Distance and Desire* (Oxford University Press 1970), p. 226.
5. Tom Paulin, *Thomas Hardy: The Poetry of Perception* (Macmillan 1975).
6. Donald Davie, *Thomas Hardy and British Poetry* (op. cit.), chapter 1, 'Hardy as Technician'.
7. Brought out recently in Robert Pinsky, *The Situation of Poetry* (Princeton University Press, New Jersey 1976), especially Part II.
8. Emile Durkheim, *Suicide* (op. cit.).
9. Ibid., Part I.
10. A. Alvarez, *The Savage God: A Study of Suicide* (Penguin 1974).
11. John Berryman, *The Freedom of the Poet* (Farrar, Strauss & Giroux 1976), p. 328.
12. Op. cit., also Part II.
13. Jonathan Raban, *The Society of the Poem* (Harrap 1971). The title of chapter 7 is 'Talking Heads'. Sisson's remark was in a recent magazine article which I cannot trace.
14. Songs 147, 155, 173.

Chapter 12. CONCLUSION

1. J.P Ward, 'The Poem's Defiance of Sociology', in *Sociology*, January 1979, p. 91.
2. Laura Riding Jackson, 'Some Notes on Poetry and Poets in this Century, and my Influence', in *Poetry Nation Review*, Vol. 6 No. 1, p. 21.
3. Culler, op. cit. (see chapter 1, note 18).
4. Especially Harold Bloom, *The Anxiety of Influence* (Oxford University Press 1973). His later *A Map of Misreadings* gives more expanded and detailed examples.
5. I mean mainly his view of poetry's diminishment since the post-Enlightenment period. This has strong parallels with our argument, in Part III, about the poet's anxiety in the face of the sociological idea itself. The introduction to *The Anxiety of Influence* makes this explicit.
6. Tony Bennett, *Formalism and Marxism* (Methuen/New Accents 1979), p. 168.
7. Terry Eagleton, op. cit., pp. 63, 73 and elsewhere.
8. This starts with Max Black's 'interaction' theory of metaphor, in his

Models and Metaphors (Cornell University Press, USA 1962) especially chapter 3, and is more sharply encapsulated by Winifred Nowottny, who concludes that 'A metaphor is thus a set of linguistic directions for supplying the sense of an unwritten term'. (*The Language Poets Use*' Athlone Press, University of London 1962) p. 59. This theme is strongly elaborated in certain papers in a recent special number, devoted to metaphor, of *Critical Inquiry*, University of Chicago, Autumn 1978, particularly Paul Ricoeur, 'The Metaphoric Process as Cognition, Imagination and Feeling', pp. 143–59.

9. Gosson was made famous by Sidney's answer, and there is a renowned passage in Locke's *Essay Concerning Human Understanding*. Ayer characteristically writes, 'If the author writes nonsense, it is because he considers it most suitable for bringing about the effects for which his writing is designed'. A.J. Ayer, *Language, Truth and Logic* (Pelican Books 1971), p. 60. That Ayer was, admittedly, favourably comparing the poet to the metaphysician in this passage does not, I think, alter the deeper import.

10. Jacob Bronowski, *The Poet's Defence* (Cambridge University Press 1939), pp. 10–11.

Acknowledgements

I am grateful to the following for permission to use their copyright material: to Faber and Faber Ltd, for extracts from *The Waste Land* and *Four Quartets* by T.S. Eliot, for an extract from *The Cantos* by Ezra Pound, for an extract from *77 Dream Songs* and extracts from *His Toy, His Dream, His Rest* by John Berryman, and to Faber and Wallace Stevens for extracts from *The Collected Poems of Wallace Stevens*; to Macmillan & Co. and A.P. Watt Ltd for extracts from *Collected Poems* by W.B. Yeats; to the translators and The Hogarth Press Ltd for an extract from Rilke's *Duino Elegies* translated by Spender and Leishman; to New Directions Publishing Corporation, New York, for an extract from *Collected Later Poems* of William Carlos Williams, copyright 1950 by William Carlos Williams; to C.H. Sisson and Carcanet Press for an extract from *Exactions* by C.H. Sisson.

I am also grateful to copyright holders in the USA in the following cases:

'Excerpts from Sunday Morning', 'Le Monocle de Mon Oncle', 'Sea Surface Full Of Clouds', 'The Man With The Blue Guitar' and 'Notes Toward a Supreme Fiction' from *The Collected Poems of Wallace Stevens*. Reprinted by permission of the author and Alfred A. Knopf, Inc. Copyright by Wallace Stevens, 1954.

'The Girl' by William Carlos Williams in *Collected Later Poems* of William Carlos Williams. Copyright 1950 by William Carlos Williams. Reprinted by permission of New Directions Publishing Corporation, New York.

Excerpts from 'Ego Dominus Tuus' by W.B. Yeats. Copyright 1918 by Macmillan Publishing Co., Inc., renewed

1946 by Bertha Georgie Yeats. Excerpt from 'The Phases of the Moon' by W.B. Yeats. Copyright 1919 by Macmillan Publishing Co., Inc., renewed 1947 by Bertha Georgie Yeats. Excerpt from 'The Tower' by W.B. Yeats. Copyright 1928 by Macmillan Publishing Co., Inc., renewed 1956 by Georgie Yeats. All these excerpts reprinted from *Collected Poems* of W.B. Yeats by permission of Macmillan Publishing Co., Inc.

Excerpts from 'The Waste Land', 'East Coker' and 'Little Gidding' by T.S. Eliot are reprinted from his volume COLLECTED POEMS 1909–1962 by permission of Harcourt Brace Jovanovitch, Inc.; copyright © 1943, 1963, 1964 by T.S. Eliot; copyright 1971 by Esme Valerie Eliot.

Excerpt from 'Canto LXXX' of *The Cantos* of Ezra Pound. Copyright 1948 by Ezra Pound. Reprinted by permission of New Directions, New York.

Selections from 77 *Dream Songs* by John Berryman. Copyright © 1959, 1962, 1963, 1964 by John Berryman. Selections from *His Toy, His Dream, His Rest* by John Berryman. Copyright © 1965, 1966, 1967, 1968, 1969 by John Berryman.

Index

(Bold type is used where writers or topics receive fullest attention relative to this book.

The great majority of entries in this index are writers, sociologists and critics. A few major topics such as 'criticism', 'sociology', 'language' are given, and a few historical events or cultural traditions, such as 'French Revolution' or 'positivist science'. Titles of literary works are given only when they are not the subject of extended treatment as some point in the book. For others, entry on author should be consulted.)

Aeneid, the, 101
Althusser, L., 54, 57
Alvarez, A., 190–1
Animal Farm, 106
apology for poetry, 23–4, 217–20
Arendt, H., 140
Aristotle, 17, 24, 27–8, 70–2
Arnold, M., 26, 33, 88
Auden, W.H., 134, 138
Ayer, A.J., 222, 235

Barnes, J., 231
Barthes, R., 19, 226
Baudelaire, C., 33, **137–43**, 144–6
Bayley, P., 71
Bell, C., 227
Bell, D., 232
Benjamin, W., 140–2
Benn, Gottfried, 139
Bergonzi, B., 98, 230
Bergson, H., 48, 74, 136
Bernstein, B., 19
Berryman, J., 32, 135, 182, **191–7**, 223
Betjeman, J., 134, 213
Bible, the, 92 (Genesis)
binary thought, 37–8, 104, 109–11
Black, M., 234
Blake, W., 123–5
Bloom, H., 214, 220, 234
Bloomfield, L., 121
Blum, A., 225
Blumer, H., 40–1

Booth, C., 42
Brecht, B., 4, 134, **177–80**
Bronowski, J., 224
Brontes, the, 4
Brown, R.H., 51
Bunting, B., 134
Bunyan, J., 25
Burns, E., 3, 5
Burns, T., 3, 5
Byron, G.G., 113

Calvin, J., 25
Chomsky, N., 18, 90, 121, 156, 218
Civil War (English), 25, 102
cognition, 220–4
cognitive disciplines, 14
Coleridge, S.T., 123
Communist poets, 177–80
community (in sociology), 42–5, 115–18
Comte, A., 30, 53–4, 176
Cooley, C., 4
criticism, 15–21, **210–17**
Culler, J., 17–18, **212–15,** 226
cummings, e.e., 133

Dante, 3, 115, 159
Davie, D., 15, 189
Dawe, A., 229
Day, J., 170
death (as twentieth century response to society), **182–9**
defence of poetry, 217–20

240 Index

Descartes, R., 158
Dickens, C., 117
Donne, J., 24–5, 42, 75, **76–89,** 141, 184, 193
drama, 3, 22–3
Durkheim, E., 4, 19, 25, 30, **31–3,** 34–7, 39, 41, 44, 53–6, 103–4, 109, 142–3, 167, **189–91,** 210
Duvignaud, J., 3

Eagleton, T., 20–1, 215–17
elegiac mode, 183–4
Eliot, G., 117
Eliot, T.S., 7, 16–17, 28, 34–5, 40, 86, 90, 134–6, **164–73,** 176, 180–1, 188, 195, 197, 214, 223, 233
Empson, W., 85
epic, 101–2
ethnomethodology (in sociology), 49–52

film, 3–4, 65, 221–2
Frankenberg, R., 43–4
French Revolution, the, 31
Freud, S., 25, 76, 98, 185
Frye, N., 3, 16–17, 188, 214
functionalism (in sociology), 103–14

Gardner, H., 229
Garfinkel, H., 4, **49–52,** 73, 150
Gellner, E., 14
Giddens, A., 8, 69, 73
Godwinism, 119
Goffman, E., 4, 42, 227
Gosson, S., 222
grand theory (in sociology), 31–9
Greenlaw, E., 64
Gregory, Robert, 163–232

Habermas, J., 18, 52
Hamburger, M., 231, 233
Hardy, T., 32, 135–6, 182, **184–9,** 223, 234
Harvard University, 36
Hawthorn, G., 8
Hazlitt, W., 64
Hegel, G., 46, 216, 224
Hemingway, E., 191
Herbert, G., 26, 130
Herrick, R., 88
Hirst, P.Q., 227
history (in sociology), 33–5, (as basis of poetry), 134–5, 164–7
Hobhouse, L.T., 42
Hodge, B., 18
Homberger, E., 159
Homer, 101, 130

Horace, 26
Hough, G., 68, 228, 232
Hulme, T.E., 5, 133, 176
Husserl, E., **47–9,** 69, 74, 136
Hyde, G.M., 232

Iliad, The, 26, 101
In Memoriam, 184
institutions, 16–18, 212–15

Jackson, Laura Riding, 209
Jakobson, R., 6, 122, 212
Jameson, F., 20, 216
Johnson, Dr S., 5, 92, 214
Jonson, Ben, 88
Jones, David, 134, 172–3, 176, 180
Juvenal, 26
Junkers landowners, the, 33

Keats, J., 25, 123, 130, 212
Kenner, H., 106, 173
Kierkegaard, S., 224
Kuhn, T.S., 14

Labour Party, the, 13
Lacan, J., 10, 19–20, 122, 218, 231
Laing, R.D., 11
language, *passim* and 10–12, 29, 52, (freedom in Spenser) 71–3, (natural in Milton) 90–4, (of mind in Wordsworth) 119–23, vernacular in Berryman) 193–7, (influence of sociological idea on) **207–10,** 222–3
Larkin, P., 7, 133, 136
Laurenson, D., 3
Leavis, F.R., 8, 16–17
Legouis, P., 229
Leishman, J.B., 229
Levi, P., 7
Levinson, D.J., 41
Lévi-Strauss, 152
Lewis, C.S., 63
Lichtheim, G., 228
linguistics, 18–19, 211–12
Linton, R., 4
literature as institution or canon, 16–18, 212–15
Locke, J., 158, 222, 235
Lowell, R., 135, 142, 182–3, 192, 213

MacDiarmid, H., 23, 134, 164, **177–80**
Macherey, P., 20, 28
Magritte, R., 63
Mallarmé, S., 133–4, 139, **144–8,** 158, 160
Marshall, A., 14, 36
Martz, L., 84, 151

Index

Marvell, A., 88, 170
Marx, K., **53–7**, 101, 224, 230
Marxism, 20–21, **53–7**, 90, 99–102, (approaches to literature) 215–17
materialism, 93–4
Mcluhan, M., 114
Mead, G.H., 4, 25, **39–42**, 76
Merleau-Ponty, M., 47–9, 69, 151
Merton, R.M., 4, 41, 109
metaphor, 219
Mill, James, 14
Miller, J. Hillis, 155, 232, 234
Milton, J., 24–5, 57, **90–101**, 115–16, 168, 177, 213, 216, 220
mind (in Wordsworth), 120–2
Modernism, 130, 137
Morris, B., 232
Muse, music, 152–4

Neruda, P., 134, **177–81**, 233
Newby, H., 227
Newman, J.H., 219
Newton, I., 119, 158
Nisbet, R.A., 37, 51
novel, 22–3, 221–2
Nowottny, W., 230, 235

Odyssey, The, 98
Oedipus, 76, 172
O'Neill, J., 51
Owen, W., 26

Pareto, V., 36, 176
Parsons, T., 4, 25, **35–9**, 41, 43, 103, 109, 112, 176–7
Paz, O., 56, 145
Peacock, T., 219
Pearl, 184
Pearson, G., 183
phenomenology (in philosophy) 47, (in Spenser) 69–70
Pinsky, R., 193–5
Plath, S., 32, 182, 191–2, 195
Plato, 24
poem itself, (as response to sociological idea) 133–4, **144–63,** (as icon) 154–6, (as image in Yeats), 161–3
poet, (as response to sociological idea) 135–6, 181–2
poetry, *passim* and 5–7, (incompatible with sociological idea) 25–6, (response to contemporary sociology) 133–6, (what is poetry?) **201–2,** (self-referring) 5, 23, **202–3,** (as silence) 205, (as music) 152–4, **203–4,** (as object) 204, (as knowledge and cognition) **220–4,** (as delight) **220–4** (in tension with sociological idea of language) *passim* and 7, 25, 129, 218–19
Pope, A., 24–5, 37, 39, 101, **103–13**, 116, 138
Popper, K., 55
positivistic science, 30, 130–1
Pound, E., 5, 34–5, 134–5, 157–8, 164, 172, **173–7,** 180–1, 193, 205, 212
practical criticism, 4
Praz, M., 138
Private Eye, 105
Protestantism, 25, 35, 166

Raban, J., 193
Raymond, M., 138
regular form, 5, 205–6
Ricoeur, P., 235
Rilke, R.M., 79, 135, 229
Rimbaud, A., 145
Roethke, T., 133, 204
Romantics, the, 123–5
Rossetti, D.G., 133
Roston, M., 84, 229
Rowntree, B.S., 42
Ryle, G., 121

Sarbin, T.R., 41
satire, 106–11
Saussure, F., 19, 211
Schutz, A., 4, **48–50**
Schwartz, D., 192
Sexton, A., 192
Shakespeare, W., 73, 90, 130
Shelley, P.B., 24, 123–5, 130, 184, 218–19
Sheppard, R., 232
Sidney, Sir P., 24, 71, 219, 224, 228, 235
Sisson, C.H., 134, 173, 193
social anthropology, **42–6**, 115–18
social interactionism, **39–42, 76–89**
social phenomenology, **46–9,** 62–3, **69–75**
sociological idea, *passim* and 8, 12–13, 29, 31–2, **129–33,** (influence on language) 207–10
sociology, *passim* and 4, (origin of) 9–14, **123–5,** (grand theory) **31–9, 103–14,** (ethnomethodology) 49–52, (Marxism) **53–7,** 90, 99–102, (reflexive sociology) 42, **46–52**
sociology of literature, 3–4
sociology of poetry, 3–4
Sophocles, 172
Spenser, Ed., 24–8, 51, **61–75,** 115, 150, 170, 220

Index

Stevens, W., 6, 51, 74, 133–4, 136, **148–54,** 158, 197, 204
structuralism, 39–42, **76–89**
suicide, (as response to society) 189–91

Tate, A., 134
Tempest, The, 25, 67, 73
Tennyson, A., 26, 188, 234
Thomas, Dylan, 133, 193
Thomas, E., 135, 182
thought and sound (in Wordsworth), 119–23
Tillotson, G., 230
Teiresias, 165
Tolkien, J.R.R., 63
Tolstoy, L., 117
Tonnies, F., 103, 109
Troilus and Criseyde, 68, 98

Valery, P., 133, 234
Vaughan, H., 116, 204
Vergil, 101
Verlaine, P., 170

vers libre, 5, 205–6

Waldock, A.J.A., 230
Waller, E., 89, 193
Wang Wei, 26
Warburton, W., 230
Weber, M., 4, 25, **33–5,** 36–7, 39, 48, 103, **166–8,** 171–2, 176
Weightman, J., 15
Welsted, L., 113
Whitman, W., 151, 157
Whorf, B., 10
Williams, R., 3, 14, 225
Williams, W.C., 133, **154–7,** 192–3
Willmott, P., 231
Wimsatt, W., 104
Winters, Y., 224
Wittgenstein, L., 14
Wordsworth, W., 24–5, 42, 87, **115–25,** 141, 218–19

Yeats, W.B., 133, **157–63,** 193, 203
Young, M., 231

OHIO UNIVERSITY LIBRARY

Please return this book as soon as have finished